Don't Tell Me Words Don't Matter

Also by Joel B. Pollak

The Kasrils Affair: Jews and Minority Politics in South Africa
(Published by University of Cape Town Press, 2008)

ii

Don't Tell Me Words Don't Matter

How Rhetoric Won the 2008 Presidential Election

Joel B. Pollak

Publisher:
HC Press
4240 Dempster Street, Suite F
Skokie, Illinois 60076

Website:
Creator: David A. Cramer
www.donttellmewordsdontmatter.net

Editor: Raymond Pollak

Cover Art: Liz Seibert, Graphic Design www.lizseibert.com

Front Cover Photographs: used with permission, courtesy of:
i) William White-blue photograph originally published at
http://www.flickr.com/photos/diggersf/2227207264/
and
ii) Rachael Dickson-red photograph originally published at
http://masonvotes.gmu.edu.

Printer:
Imagicom Media Graphics, Inc.
8700 W. Bryn Mawr Ave., Suite 800 South
Chicago, Illinois 60631
www.imagicommedia.com

Table of Contents

Acknowledgements.. vii

Chapter 1 - The Power of Words 1

Chapter 2 - The Illegitimate President............................. 31

Chapter 3 - The Ambivalent Hero 67

Chapter 4 - The Obama Insurgency................................... 109

Chapter 5 - The Fall.. 151

Chapter 6 - Obama's America 199

Endnotes... 241

Index 269

For

Julia Inge Bertelsmann

Acknowledgements

This book was made possible by the boundless love, support, and inspiration of my wife-to-be, Julia Bertelsmann. Rhoda Kadalie was generous with her time and insights as she edited the first draft of the manuscript. My colleagues from the McCain campaign—Owen Paun, Becki Donatelli, and Mark MacKinnon—were a great source of support, both during the campaign and afterwards. Quinn Le Dang and Morgan Kelly Radford were kind hosts in Cambridge, and Professor Alan M. Dershowitz offered much-appreciated encouragement. Finally, I wish to thank my father, Dr. Raymond Pollak, for his thorough editing and for his investment in this project, as well as my mother, Naomi, for her enduring patience.

1

The Power of Words

Do Words Matter?

"Don't tell me words don't matter."

So said Senator Barack Hussein Obama on the campaign trail in Wisconsin in February 2008, defending himself against Democratic rival Hillary Rodham Clinton, who had claimed her opponent had little to offer other than high-sounding, empty rhetoric.

" 'I have a dream'—just words?" Obama asked sarcastically, warming to his theme. " 'We hold these truths to be self-evident, that all men are created equal'—just words? 'We have nothing to fear but fear itself'—just words? Just speeches?"[1]

The audience applauded politely. Few realized at the time that Obama's speech had been given before—by Massachusetts governor Deval Patrick, in October 2006, from whom Obama had borrowed the remarks without attribution.[2] It was, the Clinton campaign later charged, "plagiarism"[3]—a transgression that had once ended the 1988 presidential campaign of Obama's former presidential rival, and future running mate, Senator Joseph R. Biden, Jr.

But Obama managed to escape unscathed, telling journalists who asked about the borrowed lines that it was what his campaign was "doing and generating" that was important, "based on the core belief in me that we need change in America." It was actions, not words, that mattered, he seemed to say.

In December, addressing reporters as America's new president-elect, Obama declined to respond to questions about his rhetoric just a few months before.

"I think this is fun for the press, to try to stir up whatever quotes were generated during the course of the campaign," he said dismissively.

So perhaps words really didn't matter after all.

Or did they?

Early in John McCain's presidential campaign, he delivered a speech on video to a packed crowd in Greenville, South Carolina that was also watched on television by five million professional wrestling fans.

McCain looked into the camera and growled:

> How are ya, South Carolina? Finally the Mac has come back to Greenville. Looks like Hillary Clinton and Barack Obama wanna settle their differences in the ring. Well, 'at's fine with me. But lemme tell ya: If you wanna *be* the man, you have to *beat* the man.[4] Come November, it'll be game over. And whatchu gonna do when John McCain an' all his McCainiacs run wild on ya?

> You wanna pull out of Iraq? Well, I say: "No surrender." America can win the war against terror. I'm gonna introduce Osama bin Laden to the Undertaker. You wanna raise taxes? Well, I want a smaller government, and bigger individuals.

> You see, my friends, I believe that America is the greatest nation in the world. And Americans don't watch wrestling because we're "bitter." We watch WWE because wrestling is about celebrating our freedom. It's about fighting to be the very best. So, can you smell what the Mac is cookin'?

> Lemme give ya a little straight talk, WWE fans. You might need a ticket to the Fatal Four next weekend. But you don't need a ticket to the cage match in November. All you have to do is get out there and vote. *You* decide the champion. *You* make the difference. And that's the bottom line, because John McCain said so.[5]

In eighty-seven short seconds, McCain managed to squeeze in references to every major professional wrestling icon of the preceding twenty years. But he also managed to describe everything he stood for: lower taxes, a tough foreign policy, and an embrace of individual liberty. The crowd roared, and even the color commentators were impressed:

2

"How about that? You heard it—cage match in November. Get out there and vote."[6]

Clinton and Obama also appeared on the program, seeking to reach the same audience. But Clinton looked thoroughly wooden, while Obama read awkwardly from his prompt and grinned clownishly at the camera. Former wrestling champion John Bradshaw Layfield recalled the next day, "A lot of wrestlers were really disappointed that Obama didn't come across better." McCain, by contrast, "tore the place down."[7]

That same candid energy, that same bravado and zany sense of humor, eluded McCain through the rest of the campaign. Instead, he had to overcome countless rhetorical disasters, including the one in September that sent his poll numbers plunging, never to recover:

"The fundamentals of our economy are strong."[8]

Those words mattered.

In fact, words were crucial to the 2008 presidential election. Words were Obama's main claim to power. He had few legislative achievements to point to, nor had he fought for any great causes. He also had an ideological background on the far, marginal left of the American political spectrum. But he did have a way with words. He had risen to national prominence on the strength of a single speech at the 2004 Democratic National Convention, a call to unity that resounded with voters across the land. And in 2008 he used his speeches to offer Americans a utopian vision of a future of greater harmony—with each other, with the world, with the planet. Words were the alpha and omega of what he offered to the American electorate.

His rival, Senator John Sidney McCain III, had also become famous for his words—or rather, for the self-proclaimed truth of his words, a style of speech that he dubbed "straight talk." McCain, unlike Obama, had a long record of advocacy for causes that were unpopular with his party—and even, on occasion, with the American people. He was a hero of the Vietnam War—one of the few celebrated

3

figures of that widely-regretted conflict, a man who had withstood torture and years of solitary confinement rather than allow his release to be used as a propaganda weapon by the enemy. Aside from his command assignments in the U.S. Navy, he had never held any executive office. But in his "straight talk," he offered Americans not just words but the truth as he saw it, and the pledge that he would always do and say the right thing, even if it was unpopular. Whether he lived up to that pledge was a matter he left to the voters themselves to decide.

To say that the 2008 election was about words is not to assert, cynically, that it was not about substantive issues, or the personal attributes of the candidates. On the contrary, there were real differences at stake: stark divisions over the role of government in the economy and society, different views on the importance of American military strength in foreign affairs, plus the contrast between a leadership style that valued the appearance of consensus and one that was more combative in its posture, if not necessarily its execution. But beneath these differences, expressed in words and political rhetoric, lay a deeper contest about the meaning of words in a democracy: whether words ought to inspire the people to undertake great tasks through their collective will, or whether words were also a restraint on that will, the last guarantors of the most basic freedoms.

It is always a risk, of course, to place too much emphasis on political speech as a way of understanding political events. You know a politician is lying, the old joke goes, when his lips are moving. Yet the 2008 election stands out as a case in which many voters seemed willing to suspend their ordinary disbelief for the sake of a single candidate, choosing the great promise of Obama's words over the hard and humble guarantees of McCain's.

"Don't tell me words don't matter," Obama proclaimed—using words that were not only borrowed, but tautological. To *tell* someone to disregard words would be to ask the listener to accept a logical contradiction, to rely on the

4

truth of a particular set of words to deny the truth of words in general, to make a unique exception. It was the sort of exception that Obama asked the American public to make for him—to abandon politics as usual for politics without skepticism or even scrutiny. He promised words that "mattered"— though he offered no guarantee that he would live up to his end of the bargain.

And when the election finally ended, it began to appear that he wouldn't honor his words. These words, for example, certainly didn't seem to mean much, in retrospect:

"I am running to tell the lobbyists in Washington that their days of setting the agenda are over. They have not funded my campaign. They won't work in my White House."[9]

That was Obama's pledge in the early days of his run for the presidency, one he would reiterate throughout the weeks and months that followed. But it was a promise he bent throughout his campaign and finally broke when, as president-elect, he appointed numerous lobbyists to his administration. One was William Lynn, a well-known defense industry lobbyist, whom Obama chose as his Deputy Secretary of Defense.[10] Another was former congressman and Freddie Mac director Rahm Emanuel—who had been with the troubled sub-prime mortgage lender when it misreported billions of dollars in profits[11]—as his White House chief of staff. And the president-elect's transition team was stacked with lobbyists for a colorful variety of interest groups and causes.[12] More than a dozen lobbyists would eventually find their way into his senior staff.[13]

To borrow a turn of phrase he had employed many times on the campaign trail, when throwing former allies and supporters "under the bus": This was not the Barack Obama we thought we knew.

The Great Exception

Some appearances, of course, are important, just as some words are acts on their own, and some images create new re-

5

alities. It would be folly to deny the significance of Obama's achievement in becoming the first person of African descent to be elected President of the United States. It is a feat that is all the more striking when viewed in the light of recent history. Obama is a very young man—not the youngest president, but close to it—yet when he was born in 1961, black Americans were still struggling to exercise their right to vote. He had broken racial barriers at Harvard—his tenure as the *Harvard Law Review*'s president was the first by a black student—and in becoming the first black American to hold the nation's the highest office, he offered the country a chance to move beyond its troubled past.

There is an aspect to Obama's racial identity that makes his triumph more extraordinary—though it also may have helped his chances: the fact that his mother was white, his father black. He was not only a minority, but a minority within a minority. His mixed heritage was a source of great consternation for much of his life; he struggled with it mightily, as he reveals in *Dreams from My Father*, the first of his two memoirs (thus far). He rejected labels like "biracial" and constantly strove to identify himself with black role models from the left wing of American politics—the more radical, the better. On the campaign trail, he seemed to struggle to retell the stories about his mother's family, as if the narratives were new and unfamiliar to him after a lifetime chasing his father's roots. Yet very early in the campaign, Obama was seen by many African-American voters—who favored Hillary Clinton by wide margins[14]—as "not black enough," not just because he was a first-generation African-American, but also because of his mixed parentage. Cornel West, criticizing Obama for not attending a gathering of black leaders on the day he launched his campaign, said: "He's got folk who are talking to him who warrant our distrust."[15] The Reverend Jesse Jackson, in an unguarded moment, said, "See, Barack's been talking down to black people ... I want to cut his nuts off."[16] Paradoxically, that may have made some white voters more open to him, as Barack Obama—known to peers in school as

"Barry"—spoke to them in a language they recognized as essentially their own, though they still recognized its self-consciously African-American cadences.

Regardless, Obama's success was an inspiration across the world. In South Africa, which I visited a few days after the election, black South Africans seized on Obama as a role model. In their own country, the idea of a black president had been a dream less than a generation before; now America, too, had shown that it could accept racial equality in deed as well as in word. To many, he was also an example of a black man who had succeeded purely by appealing to the American people—and to a majority-white electorate, no less—not by being appointed by someone of higher power but through his own efforts. Even white South Africans were inspired by Obama. They were excited by the idea that a member of a minority group could win a democratic election. South Africa's political opposition had, after all, been mostly headed by white politicians since 1994; with the ruling African National Congress losing supporters every day, perhaps Obama's victory would encourage voters to consider an opposition candidate, regardless of color.

In South Africa and elsewhere in the world, America's most cynical critics were silenced by Obama's win—at least for a time. The Russian media absorbed the victory quietly, dropping for the moment its theme of American democracy as a sham controlled by two feuding family factions.[17] Iran, too, offered its congratulations, the first time it had done so since the 1979 revolution.[18] These countries would return to their skepticism and hostility soon enough, with the Chinese media censoring footage of Obama's inauguration and the Russian media describing Obama's election as a deliberate manipulation by shadowy forces determined to see him fail.[19] Iran's president would soon demand an apology from Obama for American "crimes" over the previous sixty years; Iranian state-sponsored mobs had already begun burning Obama's effigy before he had even taken his oath of office.[20] But in the moment of his victory, at least, Europe celebrated, and Asia

7

took notice: America, the supposedly fading superpower, had once again proven its ability to renew itself.

Yet there were other black Americans who might have also claimed the honor of being the first to reach the Oval Office, had it not been for the startling success of Obama's long-shot campaign. Some had years of public service behind them—records far longer, and more impressive, than Obama's. There was Corey Booker, the former college football star and Rhodes scholar who fought the city of Newark's corrupt political insiders all the way to the mayor's office. There was Colin Powell, appointed as the first black Secretary of State in Bush's first term, who served as the Chairman of the Joint Chiefs of Staff under Clinton and may even have defeated Clinton, according to poll numbers, had he run on the Republican ticket in 1996.[21] There was also Powell's successor, Condoleeza Rice, who had been touted as a possible running mate for McCain and had earned respect in both the academic and foreign policy worlds.

Perhaps, too, America could have proven its ability to look beyond race more convincingly by giving Obama a fair chance, and then rejecting him on the merits, rather than allowing him the benefit of the doubt because of the symbolic significance of his candidacy. On paper, after all, he looked less impressive than many of his rivals. Few of even his most ardent supporters knew what he stood for; fewer still could name anything he had done. He had promised, in fact, not to run for president once he had been elected to the Senate—not yet, anyway. There was more to do, more experience to be earned—and as his wife, the future First Lady, Michelle Obama, said just after her husband won his Senate seat: "He hasn't done anything yet."[22] He himself had once dismissed the idea of running for president: "I am a believer in knowing what you're doing when you apply for a job," he told journalists in Illinois in 2004.[23] True colorblindness would require examining a black candidate and a white candidate against the same standards of experience, demonstrated competence, and policy prescriptions, while refusing to give the black candi-

8

date any preference on the basis of prior handicap, real or imagined. Some of Obama's supporters might have seen any loss as evidence of racism. But America was certainly capable of rejecting Obama for the right reasons.

For despite persistent and inflated fears about the hidden racism of the white American electorate—the so-called "Bradley effect,"[24] repeatedly cited by liberal columnists and the foreign press—race was more of an advantage to Obama than an obstacle. He is no token, of course—he has extraordinary political abilities, at least as an orator and campaigner, and had to fight every step of the way to the White House in an unusually long, brutal and costly race. But Obama was always treated as an exception—partly because he held himself out as one, as a black candidate who could, and did, transcend race.

Whatever the reason, it was clear that no other candidate enjoyed the same glowing media attention as Obama—not even McCain, who had once been a media favorite. No other politician could have run on so thin a résumé and been taken as seriously. No other politician could have excited such breathless praise from journalists and news broadcasters as Obama did. No other candidate could have had an army of volunteers organized through the Internet—spontaneously—long before he had declared his candidacy or begun raising money. No other candidate would enjoy the same hagiographic treatment by otherwise skeptical reporters, or iconographic portraiture by news photographers.

And no one else could have survived the potentially campaign-ending revelations and blunders that Obama did. His connections to the Reverend Jeremiah Wright and the Trinity United Church of Christ, with sermons crying "God Damn America" and teachings exhorting black Americans to separate from the values and society of "white" America, very nearly did destroy Obama's presidential ambitions. But Obama evaded criticism—at least among the largely sympathetic media—by giving one of his celebrated speeches. And even when he borrowed words without attribution—

"plagiarized," in common parlance and in the view of the Clinton campaign—his campaign survived, with nary a scratch. The same rules did not apply to him. The same criticism was never launched by a press corps inclined to leave its poison arrows in their quivers, hypnotized as they were by the power of his words.

The Technological Breakthrough

Obama did run a bold and unprecedented campaign. He defeated the vaunted Clinton political machine, which not only had thousands of high-octane donors in tow but also had connections to churches, unions, community groups and a variety of grass-roots organizations across the country that were capable of getting out the vote on Election Day. He even overcame the historic nature of Hillary Clinton's bid for the presidency: hers would be the first female candidacy with a serious chance at success, and she had recruited thousands of energetic, loyal volunteers—including many women inspired by her example—ready to take her cause forward. In order to defeat Clinton, Obama had to build his own, new political organization almost entirely from scratch. He had to rely on volunteers who had never campaigned before, canvassers who had never gone door to door before, donors who had never given to a politician before. And he had to do so in competition with the simultaneous efforts of the Clinton machine, fighting for the same votes on the same turf.[25] On the positive side, Obama's new political juggernaut would be totally loyal to him, since so much of his operation was free from prior political entanglements. On the negative side, many of his volunteers and strategies were untested and inexperienced, and would run into opposition from established political interests backing the reliable Clinton ticket. The fact that a first-time presidential candidate was able to build a political machine that worked in these circumstances, with little more than name recognition, was simply remarkable.

Obama also used technology the way few other campaigns had. He was by no means the first or the only candidate to make use of the Internet; others, both Democrat and Republican, had done so before. But Obama used the new tools more successfully—partly because he enjoyed the full-time assistance of Chris Hughes, one of the co-founders of the popular Facebook website.[26] He used technology not only to advertise his policies and his events, or to contact donors and voters, but also to give millions of volunteers the technical tools they needed to give life to their own ideas. The Obama campaign turned any laptop computer into a portable campaign office, able to contact voters, print canvassing maps and coordinate fundraising drives. He also took advantage of the new "social networking" technologies, such as YouTube, Facebook and other systems that had been developed in the few short years since 2004. These not only enabled the campaign to contact millions of voters but to tailor its message to specific interests and groups—again, largely by leaving the tools in the hands of enthusiastic online volunteers. In making use of these new media, Obama captured the support of a new generation of online left-wing activists—the "netroots," who had built a strong foundation for political dissent during the Bush years. These activists would prove critical in driving the campaign's message, and countering that of its opponents, day in and day out.

Moreover, Obama also excited a passion for politics among groups of voters that had historically been disengaged from, and disenchanted with, the entire political process: African-Americans and young people. Black voters rapidly switched their support from Clinton to Obama when it became clear, after Obama's primary victory in stark-white Iowa, that it was actually possible that a black candidate could win. And young people, divided as they initially were among several candidates, were partly attracted to Obama for his growing celebrity, as well as his demonstrated ability to relate to them—a magnetism even more powerful than Bill Clinton had exerted among members of the MTV generation in the

11

1990s. These two groups of voters, together, would put Obama ahead in the delegate race with Hillary Clinton in the Democratic primary; they would ultimately prove the decisive margin in several "swing states" in the general election; and they were Obama's most loyal constituency throughout the campaign.

Not all of Obama's tactics were new. Former Vermont governor Howard Dean, running in the 2004 Democratic primary, had pioneered the use of the Internet to reach voters. The "netroots" had also pushed anti-war challenger Ned Lamont ahead of incumbent Democrat Joseph Lieberman in the 2006 primary for the U.S. Senate seat in Connecticut. Even Republican Ron Paul had built a hugely successful online fundraising effort and grassroots election drive in the 2008 primaries, running as an anti-war candidate within the party that had followed its president to the front lines in Iraq. As for the use of the media, John McCain similarly had made himself the favorite candidate of journalists—he referred to them as "my base"[27]—in 2000, before the media latched onto Obama in 2004 as the future salvation of the Democratic Party.

Yet there was something special about Obama, a special attribute—beyond race—that put him in a unique position to make the most of these new political tools and technologies. Obama's gift was to appear to represent everyone in general, while fighting for—or against—no one in particular. As he wrote in his book *The Audacity of Hope*, his second memoir: "I serve as a blank screen on which people of vastly different political stripes project their own views."[28] Obama was able to cast himself as a symbol of a vast range of backgrounds and experiences, though his actual political past remained largely hidden from view.

That allowed millions of people from different walks of life to identify with Obama, while offering little fodder for disagreement with him. People idealized him as a leader, and subsequently, they seemed able to imagine that he understood them intimately and spoke to them directly. In fact, Obama's roots on the far left made him one of the most politically extreme candidates ever to contest the presidency, let alone win it. But with his unique charisma, Obama was able to present himself—convincingly enough—not only as a moderate, but also as a universal symbol of hope. And with his use of new social networking technology to connect his far-flung supporters to one another, the medium soon became the message. Words mattered for Obama—not in a concrete or precise manner, but in a general sense, in which rhetoric was the engine of myth-making, the basis of a new American legend.

The Ambivalent Hero

In McCain, Obama met an opponent who had earned his place as one of America's great heroes—a man who syndicated columnist Charles Krauthammer would later describe as "the most worthy nominee ever to be denied the prize."[29] A fighter pilot who had commanded the U.S. Navy's largest air squadron, he was the heir to a military dynasty dating back generations. After being shot down over Hanoi in October 1967, McCain not only survived five-and-a-half years' imprisonment in a North Vietnamese prisoner-of-war camp, but actually turned down his captors' offer of an early release because it would have violated the U.S. military's rules that the first POW to arrive must be the first to leave. In so doing, he also denied his captors a propaganda victory. Unbeknown to him at the time, his father, John S. McCain, Jr., had been promoted to commander-in-chief of the U.S. Pacific Command and was responsible for all American fighting forces in Vietnam. The younger McCain's stand for principle in the most extreme conditions cost him years of further confinement and torture, but prevented his country from suffering a deep blow to its morale. There were few more selfless and principled acts in the vast annals of American military history.

In the Senate, McCain earned the nickname "Maverick" as a leader who would do what he thought was right for the country, even if it meant defying his party or his president.

13

He had led bipartisan legislation efforts on a host of issues, from campaign finance reform to immigration to climate change. And he had often battled fellow Republicans—not just in fighting for his own initiatives, but in opposing those of his party that he disagreed with on principle. A self-described "foot soldier in the Reagan revolution," McCain nonetheless opposed President Ronald Reagan when he felt it necessary, most notably over his decision to send the U.S. Marines to Beirut in 1982, which McCain saw as a doomed mission with no clear objective and no exit strategy. He identified himself as a conservative, but was capable of opposing fellow conservatives with a frequency and ferocity that made him few friends among the party's base. He exposed corruption wherever it lay, and reached out to Democrats to work together on matters of principle and the most pressing challenges of the day. Not since Henry Clay had a Senator so exemplified compromise for the sake of the national interest.

McCain also pioneered a candid style of politics, one that Obama would later emulate in many ways. With the assistance of his long-serving speechwriter and chief of staff, Mark Salter, he wrote several revealing memoirs in which he bared his colorful past and revealed his own personal and political flaws. The best and most widely read of these, *Faith of My Fathers*, recalled his early life and his experiences in Vietnam; *Worth the Fighting For* chronicled his Senate career; and *Hard Call*, released just before the 2008 election, focused on political leaders who had been forced to make tough decisions under pressure. In his 2000 presidential campaign, he toured the country in his bus, the "Straight Talk Express," dispensing off-the-cuff opinions to journalists, aides and anyone who would listen. It was an honest, somewhat ironic, post-partisan approach—the antidote to the political gridlock and impeachment hysterics of the late 1990s.

Yet there was also a certain ambivalence to McCain's maverick approach. At times—at its best—his stance reflected a firm commitment to sound principles. Campaign finance reform, for example, was an issue that few politicians

14

on either side wanted to touch, even though the American public wanted the influence of big corporate and labor interests sidelined. After several failed attempts—all of which occurred during the Clinton administration, which gave lip service but little actual support to the idea—McCain finally succeeded in pushing his bill through Congress, together with Democratic Senator Russell Feingold of Wisconsin. Likewise, during the war on terror, McCain stood up against the Bush administration's policies on torture, championing a legislative reform that became known as the McCain Amendment and which restricted interrogators to the limited techniques described in the U.S. Army Field Manual. Military attorneys later related that the day McCain's bill passed was one of their proudest days in the armed forces. During the Iraq War, McCain's criticism of the administration continued. He supported the effort to topple Saddam Hussein but bitterly criticized American mismanagement of the country in the aftermath of victory. And he backed a plan to send a "surge" of 20,000 additional U.S. troops to provide much-needed security to the fledgling democracy, staggering after a spate of terror attacks and on the brink of ethnic civil war. The surge was far more ambitious than what many senior military officials were willing to commit to at the time, as the Iraq War became more and more unpopular in the country and in Congress. Yet in time, the surge—and McCain—were vindicated.

On other occasions, McCain's maverick stance seemed merely contrarian—opposition to his party for opposition's sake. That made him something of a foil, in the view of many Americans, to President Bush, his rival from the 2000 Republican primary. It also endeared him to Democrats and to the media while enraging Republicans, creating a delicate "moderate" position that McCain occupied almost uniquely in the intense battles of the Bush years. Yet such gestures also left McCain holding together fragile compromise positions that had narrow policy foundations or miniscule constituencies among the broader public, particularly on domestic issues such as financial regulation and immigration reform.

15

McCain was, therefore, an unlikely standard-bearer for the Republican Party and for conservatives more generally in 2008. However, it soon became clear that he was the only Republican with a real chance at winning against the background of Bush's extreme unpopularity, public unease about the war in Iraq, and an increasingly shaky economy. But beyond foreign policy and security—McCain's strongest issues—it was not clear that McCain understood what was really at stake in the ideological contest with Democrats in general and Obama in particular. Still less was it clear that McCain, for all his physical and political courage, had the will to do whatever it took to defend the fundamental ideas and policies that Obama and the Democrats were eager to topple in their haste to turn back the political clock—not merely on the Bush administration but on the Reagan revolution, and on the consensus that had governed American politics for a whole generation. Against Obama's dramatic words and promises of "Change We Can Believe In," the prospects of McCain's "Straight Talk" seemed uncertain.

Radical in Disguise

If anyone had once underestimated the political potential of Barack Obama, by the time the general election was under way in June, the McCain campaign was certainly taking him seriously. Obama had burst onto the scene in 2004 at the Democratic National Convention as a man who could cross all boundaries. He was introduced by Dick Durbin, the senior senator from Illinois, as "a candidate for the Senate whose life celebrates the opportunity of America; a candidate for the Senate whose family reflects the hope of an embracing nation; a candidate for the Senate whose values rekindle our faith in a new generation; and a candidate who has the extraordinary gift to bring people together of all different backgrounds...a man who can help heal the divisions of our nation."[30]

Obama's keynote address took America by surprise—and by storm—as he spoke of unifying the country:

> Now even as we speak, there are those who are preparing to divide us—the spin masters, the negative ad peddlers who embrace the politics of "anything goes." Well, I say to them tonight, there is not a liberal America and a conservative America—there is the United States of America. There is not a Black America and a White America and Latino America and Asian America—there's the United States of America.
>
> The pundits . . . like to slice-and-dice our country into Red States and Blue States; Red States for Republicans, Blue States for Democrats. But I've got news for them, too. We worship an "awesome God" in the Blue States, and we don't like federal agents poking around in our libraries in the Red States. We coach Little League in the Blue States and yes, we've got some gay friends in the Red States. There are patriots who opposed the war in Iraq and there are patriots who supported the war in Iraq. We are one people, all of us pledging allegiance to the stars and stripes, all of us defending the United States of America.[31]

For all the rhetoric about unity, there was a sharpness in Obama's remarks, a hostility towards unnamed enemies, "spin masters," "negative ad peddlers," and "pundits"—that was more than mere boilerplate. Indeed, it suggested a skepticism about ordinary democratic politics—a subtle hypocrisy, perhaps, for a man who made ample use of "spin" in his race for the Senate and whose electoral prospects were boosted when his own strategist leaked scandalous details of his opponent's divorce to the press. In addition, Obama used a portion of his speech to attack companies that were moving jobs to Mexico and overseas—a stance that one otherwise admiring critic regretted: "How can Democrats be the party of diversity at home but xenophobia abroad, the party that loves Mexican-Americans but hates Maytag plants in Mexico, the party that thinks Obama's [American] mom deserves a job more than Obama's [Kenyan] dad does?"[32] Nevertheless, in his speeches, his mannerisms, and his very person, Obama seemed to be able to bring together liberal and conservative, black and white, red state and blue.

17

And yet his core beliefs remained radical. He framed his 2008 tax plan—unveiled especially for the general election— as a "middle-tax cut" that would benefit "95 percent of Americans," though only 60 percent of Americans actually paid income taxes to begin with.[33] He also favored the broad redistribution of wealth, lamenting in a 2001 interview with a local National Public Radio affiliate:

> ...the Supreme Court never ventured into the issues of redistri-
> bution of wealth and sort of basic issues of political and eco-
> nomic justice in this society....I think one of the tragedies of the
> civil rights movement was that the civil rights movement became
> so court focused. I think there was a tendency to lose track of
> the political and organizing activities on the ground that are able
> to bring about the coalitions of power through which you bring
> about redistributive change, and in some ways we still suffer
> from that.[34]

Obama repeated these beliefs—perhaps inadvertently— on the campaign trail, when in his first door-to-door cam-paigning of the general election he was confronted by one Samuel J. Wurzelbacher—soon known nationwide as "Joe the Plumber"—and asked about the effect his tax plan would have on small businesses. Obama's response—"I think when you spread the wealth around it's good for everybody"[35]— caused an uproar, but it was true to his core belief about the role of the state in the economy.

Obama believed in large, activist government. He pep-pered his speeches with disclaimers that seemed to indicate he had learned the lessons of the failed interventions of the past—at least the political lessons, if not the economic ones. But he remained committed to the left-wing, liberal Democ-rat ideal of a strong, ambitious government, able to engineer positive social outcomes by fiat. In his first major address as president-elect, just two weeks before taking the oath of of-fice, Obama repeated these themes in what came to be known as the "only government" speech. Attacking the "worn-out dogmas of the past"—by which Obama meant the free market philosophies of Reagan and the conservative Republicans, not the old Keynesian stimulus spending he planned to introduce—Obama declared: "It is true that we cannot depend on government alone to create jobs or long-term growth, but at this particular moment, only government can provide the short-term boost necessary to lift us from a recession this deep and severe."[36] The Bush administration had vastly expanded the size and expense of government, too—particularly in its final months in office, when it pledged hundreds of billions of dollars in "bailout" funds to rescue ailing banks and provide liquidity to a frozen market. But while Republicans saw such spending as a temporary measure, Obama seemed to see it as a permanent fixture, warning Americans to expect "trillion-dollar deficits for years to come."[37]

Obama, aware that the American public had not completely forgotten the events of September 11, 2001, and that Democrats had lost the previous presidential election partly through appearing weak on national security, pledged to protect Americans from terrorism. Yet the means he prescribed to achieve that end involved unilateral concessions to America's enemies: withdrawing from Iraq regardless of military conditions on the ground; abandoning America's plans for missile defense emplacements in Europe; and talking, without preconditions, to dictatorial regimes in Iran, North Korea, Cuba and the like. Once he came under fire for these positions—most notably from Hillary Clinton, who mocked his pledge to hold talks with America's enemies—Obama scrambled to cast a tougher image, promising to kill Osama bin Laden and even pledging to invade Pakistan were it necessary to do so. This earned further criticism from none other than Joe Biden, Obama's future vice president: "The last thing you want to do is telegraph to the folks in Pakistan plans that threaten their sovereignty."[38] Later, Obama promised that his negotiations with foreign leaders would be "tough diplomacy," but never defined the term, which seemed little more than bluster.

19

In common with the trend among many Democrats seeking to close the gap with Republicans among socially conservative voters, Obama emphasized his church-going habits. But his church was a radical and avowedly Afrocentric congregation that mocked "bourgeois" values and called down hellfire on the American government and its policies. Obama spoke enthusiastically about preventing unwanted pregnancies, hoping the conservative tones of his message would reach evangelical voters. However, his voting record revealed that he was more starkly pro-choice on certain issues than even the most pro-choice groups.[39] He was the lone Illinois legislator, for example, to speak out in opposition to the Born Alive bill, designed to save the lives of children who survived botched abortions.[40] Even pro-choice groups had been prepared to let the legislation pass.[41]

In *The Audacity of Hope*, Obama revealed a supple ability to understand and articulate all sides of an issue. But when action had to be taken, he came down almost unfailingly on the side of left-wing orthodoxy, on the safe side of the entrenched interests of the Democratic Party. At times he adopted positions merely to signal a general protest against the Bush administration, not because it was actually wrong on particular issues, or because the Democrats had proposed better alternatives, but because he simply wanted to oppose the White House. He understood and even displayed an ability to empathize with opposing views, as well as critiques of his own positions. Yet his votes in the U.S. Senate earned him a rating from the non-partisan *National Journal* as the most left-wing senator, even more extreme than "democratic socialist" Bernie Sanders of Vermont.[42] He could speak the language of unity, but between Barack Obama and the rest of America lay a vast chasm of values.

The Conservative Abdication

Still, some conservatives were charmed by Obama and his rhetoric. Some, like former Federal Reserve chairman Paul

Volcker—long derided by the far-left for his hawkish approach to inflation—even advised Obama's campaign. Others defected in the campaign's closing weeks, when McCain fell definitively behind Obama. They included an astonishing range of intellectual and political leaders—from dyed-in-the-wool conservative thinkers to moderate, from liberal northeastern Republicans to rugged western libertarians. They abandoned their party and its chosen candidate for the promise of Obama's words.

McCain suffered the final defeat, but Hillary Clinton was the first to feel the sting of betrayal. She lost the support of moderate "New Democrats" whom her husband had led to power in the 1990s, and suffered the scorn of party officials whose careers had once depended on her ambitions. She even lost the black community, where her husband had long been an icon. The departure was best symbolized in the decision by congressman John Lewis, a civil rights leader and Clinton supporter, to switch his support to Obama. Lewis claimed that he was merely reflecting the will of his Georgia constituents, but also admitted he was afraid of falling on "the wrong side" of history.[43] Many other black politicians followed his lead. Later, McCain had hoped to pull many of Clinton's former supporters into his camp. There were many, especially among female voters, who seemed ripe for the poaching; some even formed an organization called PUMA: "Party Unity My Ass." But instead, McCain watched in sadness and frustration as old friends and advisers crossed over to the Obama camp, one by one.

These defections and abdications, whether from mainstream Democrats or old-time conservatives, all had a common theme: the absence of any compelling reason, other than the abstract yet fervent hope that Obama could fulfill all that was expected of him. As conservative radio host Mark R. Levin noted in the dying days of the campaign:

> I can't help but observe that even some conservatives are caught in the moment as their attempts at explaining their support for Barack Obama are unpersuasive and even illogical. And the pull

21

appears to be rather strong...[they] reach for the usual platitudes in explaining themselves but are utterly incoherent. Even non-conservatives with significant public policy and real world experiences, such as Colin Powell and Charles Fried, find Obama alluring but can't explain themselves in an intelligent way.[44]

Among many Clinton Democrats who had opposed Obama in the primaries, former McCain allies who had drifted from the campaign, and disgruntled members of the media and policy elite in general, there was a common purpose. They had backed Obama in the hope that he would adopt sensible policies, latching onto his quiet nods of acknowledgement towards conservative critiques of the left, or swayed by his appeal to the most conservative of impulses—nostalgia—in speeches that touched on themes from American history. They trusted him to do the right thing, even though there was no evidence in his record that he would, and plenty of evidence to the contrary. For these converts, Obama's promise of "hope and change" meant hope that *Obama* would change. It was pure wishful thinking, which could yet have real and potentially dangerous consequences.

The Challenges Ahead

For the Democratic Party, at least, the immediate consequences of Obama's victory seemed clear. After the euphoria of Obama's win, and the high-flown promises of his speeches, Democrats would have to face the real task of governing, which they had dodged for two years despite controlling both houses of Congress. And their greatest opponent would not be the Republicans—now in disarray, perhaps for years to come, with only 41 seats in the Senate and nearly eighty fewer seats than the Democrats in the House of Representatives—but the high expectations of the American public. After all, Obama had promised, at a speech to mark his victory in the Democratic primaries, that he was "absolutely certain that generations from now, we will be able to look back and tell our children that this was the moment when we

22

began to provide care for the sick and good jobs to the jobless; this was the moment when the rise of the oceans began to slow and our planet began to heal."[45] As George Orwell noted once—it was, in fact, one of the last things he wrote in his diary before he died: "For a left-wing party in power, its most serious antagonist is always its own past propaganda."[46]

But the Democrats' success masked deeper weaknesses. They had not won in 2008—or in the midterm elections of 2006, in which they had wrested control of Capitol Hill from the Republicans—on their strength of their ideas. Instead, they had run on a single issue, both times: public dissatisfaction with the Bush administration. Whatever the constituency, whatever the issue—Iraq, corruption, economic disarray—the Democrats could link the problem to Bush and the solution to voting against the Republican Party. With Bush gone, however, this approach would slowly lose its potency. Furthermore, the increasingly leftward drift of the party seemed to have sidelined many of the conservative Democrats that had made the 2006 victory possible, as well as many of the centrist ideas that had made the Clinton era one remembered fondly by most Americans. Speaker of the House Nancy Pelosi—a representative from a San Francisco district that is among the most liberal in America—looked on as left-wing Democrats wrested committee chairmanships away from their centrist colleagues.[47] And Barney Frank of true-blue Massachusetts attacked Obama's economic stimulus plan for offering "too much tax-cutting,"[48] signaling that left-wing Democrats might hold Obama back from delivering on the compromises he had promised and which Republicans had half-heartedly expected.

More damaging still was the elitist drift of the party. Obama had been labeled, not entirely fairly, as an elitist who attempted to empathize with ordinary Americans by sniffing at the price of arugula,[49] and who had told wealthy donors in San Francisco that small-town Midwestern voters "get bitter, they cling to guns or religion or antipathy to people who aren't like them or anti-immigrant sentiment or anti-trade sentiment as a way to explain their frustrations."[50] While he claimed to be fighting for the "middle class," and his vice president styled himself as a man with "working class" roots (though his father had been an oil company executive), the Obama campaign often found itself at odds with real, live middle class Americans. From Republican vice presidential candidate Sarah Palin, whom Democrats mocked as stupid and incompetent; to "Joe the Plumber," whom Democrats set out to smear the moment he became a threat to Obama's ambitions, the Democrats no longer identified easily with the average American. Wendy Button, a former Democratic speechwriter, left the Obama campaign before the election because of its treatment of working Americans:

> ...I found the initial mocking of Joe [the Plumber] so offensive and I realized an old line applied: "I didn't leave the Democratic Party; the Democratic Party left me." The party I believed in wouldn't look down on working people under any circumstance... I can no longer justify what this party has done and can't dismiss the treatment of women and working people as just part of the new kind of politics. It's wrong and someone has to say that.[51]

Conservative columnist David Brooks of the *New York Times* crowed approvingly that Obama had employed so many Ivy Leaguers: "If a foreign enemy attacks the United States during the Harvard-Yale game any time over the next four years, we're screwed."[52] Yet that same elite focus marked a distance from the lives and perspectives of ordinary Americans—one that Democrats had foolishly expanded in years of mocking President Bush and his constituency.

Republicans faced far more acute challenges. Obama's victory exposed a huge technological gap between the parties. Democrats had pioneered the use of the Internet to contact voters, raise funds and maintain the interest of new activists far beyond Election Day. McCain and the Grand Old Party (GOP) made up much of the difference by November 4th— using "crowdsourcing" to attract ideas for the party platform, for example, and sending voter call sheets directly to supporters' email inboxes—but the party desperately needed new talent and new tools to protect its shrinking share of the American electorate. The "Voter Vault," the behemoth database that had enabled the party to reach specific groups of voters through "microtargeting" in 2004, was now useless next to the massive database that the Obama campaign had developed through the Internet. Worse yet was the Republican philosophy towards technology. The party tended to use new tools solely as a means to get its message out, rather than as a way to help voters shape the message for themselves. It was clear to both supporters and opponents that Republicans needed new leaders and staff who could connect it to the new country that America had become during the complacent twilight of the Bush years.

Republicans had also lost touch with an entire generation of Americans, perhaps irretrievably. The youth vote, which had split evenly in the 2000 election, went two-to-one for Obama in 2008.[53] Among voters aged 18 to 29, the word "Republican" tended to conjure the most potent—if rather outdated—stereotypes of the Gingrich era: mean, selfish, cruel and provincial. The satirist Stephen Colbert, for one, kept that image alive with his nightly "Colbert Report" on cable television's Comedy Central channel, offering tongue-in-cheek triumphalism and paeans to plutocracy. Such relentless criticism had a lasting effect. The Republican Party had lost its dominant position in the western states, and even lost ground in the South, losing North Carolina, Virginia and Florida together for the first time in generations and very nearly losing Georgia as well. In the Northeast, the Republican Party had become so weak that it did not have a single member of the U.S. House of Representatives from any of the six states of New England. It seemed to have become a regional party—perhaps even less than a regional party—and stood to lose more ground in the future, as old GOP senators continued to announced their plans to retire.

Above all, Republicans seemed almost as short of ideas as Democrats. Many felt the need to re-examine their philosophies and principles, which had not changed much since the Reagan era. They faced pressure to resolve simmering debates about the role of social conservatives in the party, who seemed to have alienated significant numbers of moderate voters. And they also needed, some argued, to reconsider their approach to foreign policy, which seemed to have alienated the party's old guard and saddled it with a "cowboy" image. The old three-legged stool of the GOP—strong national security, tight fiscal discipline, and stern traditional values— was still the foundation of the party and its core promise to its voters. But these values also needed to be made relevant to a new age and a new generation of voters. And they needed to reckon with the failures of the recent past in the Republican-dominated government.

Yet the challenges facing the nation as a whole were even more pressing. In addition to the continuing war against terror on two fronts—the gains in Iraq were far from secure, while the conflict in Afghanistan seemed to be intensifying— Americans were reeling from the financial crisis that had struck in September with the economic force of a tsunami. Jobless figures continued to rise, and consumer confidence reached all-time lows, as the year 2008 came to a close.[54] Much had gone right during the Bush presidency, but much had also gone wrong on his watch, and Americans had blamed many of the failures on Bush himself. Even when external threats arose—the 9/11 hijackings, the sub-prime mortgage crisis (which Bush had attempted to prevent in many ways), even a natural disaster like Hurricane Katrina— many Americans, egged on by Democrats and left-wing opponents of the administration, seemed to regard Bush as culpable. Now, the public expected Obama to stand astride the world and change its course—not just to slow the rise of the oceans, but also to bring peace among nations and to restore prosperity to all—just as he had promised he would.

Words and the Millenarian Man

As America had come to understand its own failings as the failures of one single, detested individual, so now it began to see its salvation through the elevated and exaggerated virtues of another, who had offered little but his own words as proof of his intentions and abilities. Even in a country more used to a "presidential" style of politics than most other representative democracies, this focus on single, individual leaders was unusual. It was reminiscent, perhaps, of the mythology surrounding the Latin American *caudillo*, or the hagiography (and demonology) of the African "big man." Middle East scholar Fouad Ajami noted that the vast crowds at Obama's campaign rallies recalled the ecstatic masses under authoritarian regimes in the Middle East:

> Hitherto, crowds have not been a prominent feature of American politics. We associate them with the temper of Third World societies. We think of places like Argentina and Egypt and Iran, of multitudes brought together by their zeal for a Peron or a Nasser or a Khomeini. In these kinds of societies, the crowd comes forth to affirm its faith in a redeemer: a man who would set the world right... These crowds, in the tens of thousands, who have been turning out for the Democratic standard-bearer in St. Louis and Denver and Portland, are a measure of American distress.[55]

Though he did his best to dampen expectations as his swearing-in ceremony approached, Obama had launched the beginnings of a cult of personality. The fulfillment of America's democratic potential, he had told his supporters, required that the country unite—not just in general, but behind his presidential campaign in particular.

Obama's campaign's constant refrain—"Yes We Can"— was a plural verb whose direct object was a singular noun: Obama himself. And yet the phrase itself was essentially empty—so pliable and open to interpretation that it had in fact been the slogan of a right-wing party in New Zealand six years before.[56] When Winston Peters, the leader of the anti-

27

immigrant New Zealand Party, had used the phrase, he had been ridiculed for its resemblance to the opening jingle of a children's cartoon. Nonetheless, the same slogan, in Obama's hands, hypnotized the American electorate. It was a style of politics America had never encountered before—a style, as Mark Levin worried, which signaled "a recklessness and abandonment of rationality that has preceded the voluntary surrender of liberty and security in other places." Whether such concerns were overblown or not, it was a new form of personal politics, unknown—and perhaps threatening—to American democracy.

Thanks partly to his predecessor, who had vastly increased the administrative powers of the White House through the doctrine of the "unitary executive," Obama would inherit a presidency with powers far in excess of any enjoyed by any president before him. Through his party, he also controlled three branches of government—not only the Democrat-dominated legislature, but a judiciary with a number of anticipated vacancies at the highest levels, waiting to be filled. And after Bush's emergency interventions, the government held significant stakes in the country's major banks and the insurance industry, with a vast boom in government spending on the way. Investors began to warn of the nationalization of the banking system as a "destination [that] seemed just over the horizon," and telling their clients to "shake hands with the government; make them your partner by acknowledging that their checkbook represents the largest and most potent source of buying power in 2009 and beyond. Anticipate, then buy what they buy, only do it first."[57] And yet Obama himself had never managed any enterprise beyond his numerous campaigns for political power.

To millions of Americans, Obama represented hope. In many ways, he represented the best promise of America— that a child of immigrant parents could rise to the top, that an outsider with little experience could still be trusted by a nation that never quite seemed to shed its optimism even in the darkest times. But he also represented the danger of unparalleled, unchecked power in a man who had grasped the opportunity to contest the nation's highest office when his only contribution to American life thus far had been his oratory. And with the rise of faith in Obama's words came a decline of faith in ideas, on both sides of the political divide—a faith that had been almost unique to America, and which constituted the core of its greatness. In the elevation of one single, special individual, there was the danger of a decline of the fate of individuals in general. The looming shadow of greater government commanded by an Olympian in the Oval Office foretold the advent of a new age of civic lethargy. At best, Obama's ploy for greater power and immediate, sweeping and decisive action was a calculated gamble. At worst, it was a desperate rush into the void, the culminating act of a dangerous millenarian creed.

Perhaps more than any other concern aroused by the Obama presidency, Obama—great rhetorician that he is—challenged the truth of political speech. "Don't tell me words don't matter," he had declared—but those words were borrowed. He could state his beliefs one day and then deny them the next. In June 2008, for example, just after wrapping up the Democratic nomination, Obama told the annual policy conference of the American Israel Public Affairs Committee: "Jerusalem will remain the capital of Israel, and it must remain undivided."[58] The next day, following protests from Palestinian leaders, he retracted and recanted. "Jerusalem is a final status issue, which means it has to be negotiated between the two parties," his campaign said, adding that "it's not going to be divided by barbed wire and checkpoints as it was in 1948-1967" but implicitly allowing for its eventual division.[59] Obama could and did make promises in the abstract that would not and could not be honored in the particular.

Most politicians bend the truth, on occasion; few could so bend the public to believe them. But the power Obama wielded through his words was not simply the result of their eloquence. Of the many things, good and bad, that Obama had inherited from the Bush administration, the most useful

29

to his political ambitions was the profound frustration of the American public with a president who had lost their trust. By 2008, many Americans were yearning for more than promises of good government. They did not want a president who would merely succeed Bush; they wanted one who offered to transcend him. The infamous inarticulateness of the 43rd president set the stage for a 44th who held out not mere truths but great visions. Perhaps these were "just words," but for a brief and historic moment, they won the faith of millions of earnest Americans looking for an answer.

2

The Illegitimate President

The Worst President?

When George W. Bush left office on January 20, 2009, he was viewed by many Americans as one of the worst—if not *the* worst—presidents in the history of the United States. "Well, maybe besides one of the corrupt ones," said a leading American economist who viewed Bush's handling of the financial crisis with alarm. Even after Obama's election to succeed him, the criticism and demonization did not abate. The Democrats' majority leader in the Senate, Harry Reid, declared: "I really do believe President Bush is the worst president we've ever had."[1] Bush was certainly one of the least articulate presidents in recent memory. Reagan, too, had been derided as stupid by his critics, yet he was also admired as "The Great Communicator." Bush was not so lucky: he was a man of his word, perhaps, but not a man of words in general.

And yet he had not been impeached, as his immediate predecessor had; he had been re-elected, unlike his own father; he had led the country to war twice and likely to eventual victory, something Ronald Reagan himself had not done. And despite grumbling about closed bidding for contracts in Iraq, no one could accuse Bush of having stolen public money or unjustly enriching his cronies. His was a relatively "clean" administration, certainly compared with the one that had preceded it, in which high-dollar donors had been offered accommodation in the Lincoln Bedroom and inconvenient documents had disappeared and re-appeared at convenient moments. And, of course, there were no garish extramarital affairs to speak of, no seduction of interns or romps in the Oval Office. In his final weeks in office, Bush was even gracious towards Barack Obama, who had won the primary and the general elections largely on the back of his unrelenting attacks on the incumbent. Still, he returned to Crawford, Texas, as a man scorned by the country that he had served. If he was a "cowboy," as he was so often labeled, he was not the bandit of the silver screen but the complex Western archetype of the vigilante—a man who had been called upon to provide necessary protection and guidance, but who remained hated by the town he had tried to help, partly for his own faults.

An objective assessment of Bush's tenure would struggle to place him among America's best leaders, but it would probably fail to place him among the worst. Though such facts may have been hard to remember in the midst of a deep financial crisis, Bush had inherited a recession from Bill Clinton, and went on to preside over six years of economic growth. Those years also included fifty-two months of uninterrupted job growth—the longest such period in American history.[2] Bush's tax cuts in 2001 and 2003 may have been fiscally irresponsible, especially since they were never balanced by spending cuts. But they did help create millions of jobs. The economic achievements of the Bush presidency are even more remarkable when the terror attacks of September 11, 2001 are considered. It was thought at the time that the attacks would plunge New York, and the rest of America, into a deep economic trough. But the opposite happened: the economy soon recovered, and Americans enjoyed an age of prosperity that saw growth levels peak at 4.4% per annum in 2005—a remarkably fast rate of expansion for a developed economy. Sadly, perhaps, that prosperity would be forgotten before it had ever been properly celebrated.

In the wake of the 9/11 attacks, Bush had also performed his most basic and important duty as president: he kept the country safe. There was not a single terror attack on American home soil after that terrible bright morning when Al-Qaeda hijackers killed thousands of Americans at the World Trade Center in New York and the Pentagon in Washington

D.C. Dozens also died on United Flight 93, which crashed into a field in southwestern Pennsylvania after passengers struggled with the hijackers for control of the aircraft. Despite numerous scares, the government under Bush's administration managed to thwart the repeated efforts of Al-Qaeda to score another hit on the American homeland. True, some of the security policies Bush had employed to that end were highly controversial. The imprisonment of "unlawful combatants" at Guantánamo Bay and the use of wiretapping to monitor telephone conversations all created alarm about the state of civil liberties in America. Moreover, the foreign policies Bush had crafted to respond to terror—the pre-emptive war in Iraq in 2003, the hands-off approach to the Israeli-Palestinian conflict (at least initially), and the war against the Taliban in Afghanistan 2001 (though to a far lesser extent)— were also controversial. Still, the fact that American voters were far more worried in the 2008 election about the prospects of an economic downturn than they were about the threat of a terror attack was partly a reflection of Bush's success in fighting terrorism, even if it was also proof of his inadequate stewardship of domestic affairs.[3]

Left-wing Americans ought to have found reasons to cheer a few aspects of the Bush legacy. Bush vastly expanded access to health care for poor Americans by creating or expanding nearly 1,300 community health clinics across the country.[4] He also signed into law the Medicare Prescription Drug Modernization Act, which provided prescription drug coverage for Medicare patients. That was a very expensive bill, and one criticized heavily by policy experts, but one that fulfilled his promises to Americans concerned about their ability to afford ever-costlier medicines for chronic illnesses. In addition, Bush also employed a number of protectionist measures and subsidies favored by the left, such as steel tariffs and massive farm aid, that were costly to consumers and hostile to good economic sense, but which were supported by unions and the domestic agriculture industry.

Bush also presided over a period of accelerated immigration—despite the new restrictions after 9/11—that allowed millions of aspiring new Americans a chance at a better life. Some of that immigration was illegal, but Bush strongly favored providing a path to citizenship for those immigrants already living in the United States, and proposed a "guest worker" program to give some legal status to productive alien workers. Another area of progress was Bush's aid to Africa, which tripled the amounts provided by his predecessors.[5] Thanks to Bush's efforts with the President's Emergency Plan For AIDS Relief (PEPFAR), hundreds of thousands of Africans received life-saving anti-retroviral drugs directly from the American government. And Bush's firm support for the peace process in southern Sudan helped end a civil war there that had dragged on for generations. When Arab militias began slaughtering hundreds of thousands of innocent people in the western Sudanese province of Darfur, the Bush administration did not hesitate to call those actions "genocide," though the rest of the world wavered. And when Robert Mugabe terrorized his once-prosperous country into abject poverty, the Bush administration stood strong in its vocal opposition to the Zimbabwean regime and other "outposts of tyranny."[6] These were strong words, and notable achievements.

No other president or politician had ever made the case for democracy so boldly in the Middle East, and committed his best efforts to achieve in reality what he had promised in words. No other world leader, save perhaps Tony Blair of Great Britain and Ariel Sharon of Israel, had been prepared to recognize the radical evil of terror for what it was—not just a result of frustration but, like fascism, a self-created and self-sustaining phenomenon that could neither compromise nor be compromised with. In many ways, Bush was the right man at the right time for the unique challenges that America faced during his presidency. His words were clumsy, but in moments of danger his instincts were uniquely sound.

In the spring of 2001, some Americans chafed at the country's willingness to tolerate what the left saw as Bush's "electoral coup" in 2000. By 2004, however, this view had softened somewhat, as Bush prevailed against terror and earned respect for his refusal to temporize with extremists when American lives and values were at stake. The Democrats in the 2004 presidential election still felt some burden of proving they could confront terror as well as the Republican administration had. Despite the best efforts of the "netroots" to nominate an anti-war candidate, the party selected Senator John F. Kerry of Massachusetts, a man who boasted significant combat experience. The expected Kerry victory brought out the champagne at Democratic election-watching parties in November, but the bottles soon went back to the refrigerator. After a closely fought contest, the expected triumph did not materialize, and many at home and abroad were surprised that Americans were prepared to tolerate four more years of Bush in office.

Bush persevered through a second term, though he was a severely flawed president. Just as former Reagan speechwriter Peggy Noonan once wrote that Reagan would have been impossible without the failures of Jimmy Carter before him— "There was no Reagan without Carter. Only four years of steady decline and lack of clarity could have lurched the country over to this—this *actor*"[7]—so, too did Bush enable the far-left Obama to rise to the presidency. Bush's tax cuts, combined with runaway war spending that had been grossly underestimated, created hundreds of billions of dollars in deficits and trillions in new debt. He failed to restrain even his own party from loading important congressional bills with "pork" for their contributors and constituents. Though his fault in the Hurricane Katrina disaster was vastly overstated, he made matters worse by having hired an inexperienced crony, Michael Brown, to run the Federal Emergency Management Agency (FEMA), though Brown had no prior emergency management experience. Bush also attempted to appoint his White House counsel, Harriet Miers—a lawyer with no judicial experience—to the Supreme Court. His first two appointees to the office of Attorney General, John Ashcroft and Alberto Gonzales, were controversial figures in their own right. The latter resigned in 2007 after a scandal involving the firing of several U.S. Attorneys across the country. Bush's first defense secretary, Donald Rumsfeld, likewise left office after the Republicans lost control of both houses of Congress in the 2006 mid-term elections. Bush also frittered away whatever trust the public may have had in Republicans to manage the country's finances more conservatively, or to handle sudden crises more competently, than their Democratic opponents.

Under Bush, the powers of the executive branch also increased substantially, with Bush exercising new authority to make decisions on the grounds of national security with little review and few checks and balances. Together with Vice President Dick Cheney, he sought to assert the prerogatives of the White House not just against the other branches of government but over the broader administration under the doctrine of the "unitary executive." And if Bill Clinton had famously declared that "the era of big government is over," Bush seemed eager to bring it back, presiding over the largest expansion of government spending since Lyndon Johnson's ambitious yet ineffective Great Society, during a time when Republicans still had the votes in Congress to force spending cuts.[8]

As Bush departed Washington, America was no longer the confident nation, the "shining city on a hill," that Reagan had fashioned. It doubted its values of free ideas and free markets; it doubted its place in the world and its ability to defend itself; and it even doubted its future as a world power. Bush's 2000 promise of "compassionate conservatism" had produced an administration that seemed, to many Americans, neither conservative nor compassionate. A sense of despair set in—one that bred a political climate ripe for millenarianism of the type Obama would offer.

The Shroud of Illegitimacy

In fairness, Bush had faced immense obstacles from the beginning of his presidency. Even as he took the oath of office, Bush was considered an illegitimate president by a sizeable, vocal minority of the country. The left claimed that he had "stolen" the 2000 presidential election after winning the majority of electoral college votes while losing the popular vote. His win had been sealed by his victory in Florida, which itself had only been secured when the U.S. Supreme Court's decision in *Bush v. Gore* overturned the Florida Supreme Court and stopped an ongoing recount of the vote in four hotly disputed counties. Bush won a narrow victory in the state on Election Day, but had benefited from a confusing ballot format—known as the "butterfly ballot"—that had been used in heavily Democratic and Jewish Palm Beach County. The ballot confused many elderly voters and resulted in thousands of votes going to Reform Party candidate Pat Buchanan instead of Democrat Al Gore. The idea that Jewish voters would back a man known for defending alleged Nazi war criminals over a Democratic ticket featuring the first Jewish vice-presidential candidate was preposterous. Even Buchanan acknowledged that most of his votes in the county ought to have gone to Gore.[9] There was also the problem of "undervotes"—ballots on which a voter had intended to make a mark but failed, usually because of failure to fully separate a cardboard "chad" from its housing in the punch card ballots used in many Florida countries. After Bush took office, a comprehensive recount of all the ballots in the state—one that also considered overvotes, where a voter chose more than one presidential candidate, as well as undervotes—revealed that he had indeed won the state and would not have needed the Supreme Court's intervention to prevail in the Electoral College.[10] Still, a large number of Democrats refused to acknowledge the result, or did so only grudgingly, claiming that Republicans had used other methods—purging otherwise eligible voters from the rolls without properly in-

37

forming them, for example—to ensure victory in Florida and the nation.

Later, it became axiomatic on the left to believe that Bush had lied to the nation and to the world in making the case for the Iraq War in 2002 and 2003. "Bush lied; people died!" was the cry at anti-war rallies around the country. After the invasion of Iraq and the toppling of Saddam Hussein's regime, it became clear that Iraq did not have weapons of mass destruction. Saddam himself had apparently believed he still had such weapons (he had possessed them until shortly after the Gulf War in 1991), and the common assessment of intelligence agencies around the world was that he very likely did. Only the war convinced Saddam, belatedly and incompletely, to permit access to United Nations (UN) weapons inspectors, and only victory in that war allowed the world to know the truth. But Bush was still cast as a liar—and a war-mongering one at that.

Bush's entire presidency was, therefore, shrouded in a cloud of illegitimacy, one that not even his 2004 re-election—the first time since 1992 that any U.S. president had won an outright popular majority—could dispel. It was that sense of illegitimacy that invited contempt for Bush from his opponents far beyond that which could be considered normal or healthy in a democracy. It was that sense of illegitimacy that encouraged Bush's opponents to voice wild outrage against him instead of polite disagreement; it was that sense of illegitimacy that encouraged Barack Obama to attack his predecessor in his inaugural address, even as Bush looked on; it was that sense of illegitimacy that encouraged Speaker of the House Nancy Pelosi to describe Bush's departure from Washington by helicopter as "like having a 10-ton anvil lifted from my shoulders"[11]; and it was that illegitimacy, cultivated and fanned by his domestic rivals, that damaged Bush's standing in the world and doomed his legacy as president.

So bitter were Bush's many critics that they inspired columnist and former psychiatrist Charles Krauthammer to invent the term "Bush Derangement Syndrome," or BDS, to describe the common phenomenon of ordinary critics abandoning reason and restraint when criticizing Bush. There were many exemplars. One was sportscaster-turned-pundit Keith Olbermann, who fancied himself something of a latter-day Edward Murrow squaring off against a reincarnated Joe McCarthy, and featured nightly rants against his own ideological bugbears in a commentary segment entitled "Worst Person in the World." Another was Dan Rather of CBS News, who lost his job after decades in the anchor's seat when he ran a story about Bush's absenteeism from the Texas National Guard that turned out to have been based on forged documents.

Some of the opposition to Bush was well-founded, or grounded in genuine differences of principle and policy. Some of it, however, was simply mindless and reflexive, slavishly following the political fashion of the day. As left-wing columnist-turned-Iraq War-supporter Christopher Hitchens observed, calling Bush "stupid" had become the favorite political joke of stupid people.[12] And even serious, well-considered policies offered by the Bush administration—such as immigration reform—were often ridiculed in the press and savaged by Democrats without much thought as to their merits. Far from overcoming the partisan savagery of the Clinton years, America entered a period of political division that was even more intense. Eight years later, it was clear that Bush had failed to deliver on his election promise of being a "uniter, not a divider" in Washington. And it was also clear that it was not entirely his fault.

But Bush himself had been partly to blame. After so close an election in 2000, he could have governed from the center, especially given his promises to do so and the close and contingent nature of his victory. Yet egged on by his most conservative advisers and constituents, Bush governed as if he had been given a mandate to govern from the right. One of his first executive acts was to cut off U.S. funding to aid organizations overseas that provided abortions to poor women in the third world, a move that created alarm among pro-choice advocates.[13] He also nominated several controversial conservatives to his cabinet, most famously John Ashcroft, who had recently lost his seat in the U.S. Senate in an election in which his Democratic opponent had died a few weeks before the vote.[14] In addition, he pushed a massive tax cut through Congress that was deeply controversial (because the bulk of its benefits fell to wealthy households that paid the most taxes), and whose fiscal sustainability had not yet been proven. This was not a good way to make friends or influence people, especially among an electorate whose confidence in the entire electoral system had been shaken by the Florida recount controversy. Bush also brought several personal weaknesses to the Oval Office. He had little travel experience; his military experience during the Vietnam War had been confined to the Texas National Guard; he had led several businesses into failure, only to be rescued by other investors, especially those connected with his father. He was also a master of malapropisms—"Bushisms," as they became known—in his speeches, and he was a very poor debater. These flaws would haunt him constantly throughout his two terms. To much of the country and the world, his words were neither to be taken seriously nor trusted.

The Left Goes Wrong

Despite the many political challenges he faced, as well as his own administrative inadequacies, Bush did remarkably well in standing up for America's fundamental interests and values when they were most at risk. And when old policies did not work, he showed a remarkable willingness to adapt. The terror attacks of 9/11, for example, changed his presidency entirely. He came into office having promised a more reserved, even isolationist, foreign policy, one that would avoid the humanitarian interventions and complex diplomatic entanglements that had dominated the agenda of the Clinton administration. There were to be no more Somalia invasions, no more rushed handshakes on the White House lawn whose promise could be so easily overturned by war just a few years later. In debates with his opponent in the 2000 election, Bush criticized Vice President Al Gore for supporting "nation building" overseas.[15] The Bush administration even hinted, in its early days, that it would revisit the policy of sanctions against Iraq.[16] The sanctions had merely punished Iraqi civilians while enriching the regime and its overseas enablers, without improving Saddam's cooperation with international weapons inspectors.

Yet on September 14, 2001, as Bush surveyed the smoking rubble at Ground Zero in Manhattan, he immediately realized not only the wrong that had been perpetrated, but the vile principle at its very core: it was not merely an attack on America, still less against anything America had done, but rather against America's democratic values and openness to the world. Bush saw the attacks not as a legitimate response to a political grievance, but as an assault on the ideals of freedom, democracy and the open society. And so he radically changed his foreign policy. Before, he believed America could best tend to its interests by looking inward; now he realized America had to fight for its ideals or risk losing them entirely.

Much of the international media condemned America's military response before it had even begun. Some voices in the Middle East warned America not to attack a Muslim state during the upcoming holy month of Ramadan, though many Muslim and Arab states had previously launched and fought wars against Israel and each other during Ramadan.[17] Caricatured as a "cowboy"—an image Bush contributed to, he later admitted, by using old Texan lingo such as "smoke 'em out" and "dead or alive"—Bush actually considered his response to the attacks carefully. He and British prime minister Tony Blair, working closely together, offered the Taliban in Afghanistan the chance to save their regime by giving up Al-Qaeda leader Osama bin Laden. Only then did the coalition forces attack—strengthened by the North Atlantic Treaty Organization (NATO), whose Article V self-defense provision was invoked for the first and only time in the organization's history. Bush did not manage to capture or kill bin Laden then, and had not done so (though there were speculations that bin Laden had died) by the time he left office, either. Yet in a few short weeks the American-led coalition forces had deposed the Taliban and freed the people of Afghanistan —and especially the women—from the most brutal religious tyranny in contemporary times.

The left mocked the crudeness of Bush's words and decried the forceful nature of his actions. However, its own reaction to the 9/11 attacks was alarmingly ambivalent. While issuing perfunctory disclaimers against terror, left-wing organizations and politicians called on the world to consider its "root causes," refusing to see terrorism as a self-generated evil or one for which the perpetrators themselves might be held fully responsible. They suggested—overtly, in some cases—that America was somehow to blame. Some even seemed delighted that the U.S. had received its comeuppance, and hoped the attacks would force America to listen to its critics. It was not long before the radical western left joined the radical Islamic right, which expressed sympathy (and, at times, overt support) for the 9/11 hijackers. Few of those at the vanguard of anti-war marches cared what terrorist groups said in their own words about why they hated America and threatened Americans.

Barack Obama, then an obscure state senator with few achievements to his name, blamed the attacks on an "absence of empathy."[18] Even as late as 2008, he continued to urge Americans to consider the "root causes" behind terror groups such as Hamas and Hizbollah,[19] ascribing Islamic extremism to "the failures of governments and the failures of the West to work with many of these countries."[20]—just as he would call for American forces to begin leaving Iraq in 2005,[21] declaring in 2006 that "there is no military solution to this war."[22] But Bush's instincts on terror—and how to defeat it—were more definite, and determined. And his decisive action and air of moral certainty only enraged his critics all the more.

42

As the left found it difficult to mourn the events of 9/11 sincerely, without using it for some form of political mobilization—"another world is possible," beseeched a consortium of anti-globalization activists[23]—so, too, it found little to celebrate in the American victory over the Taliban. The very political constituency that claimed the exclusive mantle of human rights and moral righteousness was clearly less worried about ending tyranny and restoring liberty to Afghanistan, or ensuring the basic security necessary for enlightened civilization to exist and thrive, than it was about symbolic confrontations with power. It wanted to see Bush humbled far more earnestly than it yearned to see Afghanistan's women set free from the *burqa* and the religious police. Though Bush would soon be ridiculed for using the term "axis of evil" to describe totalitarian states and was criticized for applying simplistic moral oppositions to the complex world of foreign affairs, it was in fact his critics who had adopted a simplistic, either-or world view. They identified everything he did as axiomatically wrong and embraced the opposite with varying degrees of enthusiasm.

The left behaved similarly in reacting to the Iraq War, which was launched in March 2003 by the U.S and its allies. Anti-war activists accused Bush of acting beyond the authority of the UN—and hence in violation of international law—by launching an attack, together with Britain and others in the "coalition of the willing," that had not been specifically authorized by the UN Security Council. That claim was widely repeated in the media—even in pop songs—and by international legal scholars as well. But it was a completely unfounded assertion. Recent wars that had been widely considered legitimate—such as the NATO-led bombing of Yugoslavia to stop ethnic cleansing in Kosovo—had been fought without UN approval. And many interventions that ought to have happened—even steps far short of military action, such as sanctions against regimes like Sudan, Myanmar (Burma) and Zimbabwe—had been blocked by the Security Council. The reality as it stood in 2003 was that Saddam Hussein had violated seventeen binding Security Council resolutions, which the UN had been unable and unwilling to enforce. Although the Council voted unanimously in favor of a new resolution on weapons inspections in November 2002,[24] there seemed to be no political will to enforce it. France and Germany seemed unwilling to consider military action. Russia and China were allowing Iraq to play for time, and Syria and Pakistan opposed war outright. No one except Britain and a few other states seemed willing to support international law in deed as well as word. It was clear that if international law meant anything beyond mere words on a page, a military response to Saddam's violations on this most serious of issues would eventually be necessary.

That had been true before Bush brought the issue to the UN. After he had done so, the case for war was strengthened—not merely by apparent evidence of weapons of mass destruction, but by the risk of backing down in the face of intimidation by a brutal dictator, and hand-wringing by European powers more interested in protecting their commercial ties to Iraq than in standing up for substantive principles of international law. After the war, when the full extent of the corruption involved in the UN's "Oil-For-Food" program in Iraq was revealed, it was clear that many of the governments and political parties that had been the most vociferous opponents of the Iraq War had also been receiving millions of dollars in illegal oil vouchers from Saddam's regime. Contrary to the claims of anti-war protestors, who charged that the U.S. was acting solely out of its thirst for Iraqi oil, it was in fact opponents of the war whose stance had been dictated by illicit oil interests. If America had caved to the pressure being applied by such opponents of a tough approach to Iraq, the blow to American power and prestige would have been devastating. And contrary to the paranoid fantasies of the extreme left, that would not have meant a better world, but a worse one—one exposed to ever-more ambitious forms of tyranny and ever-more brutal violations of human rights by dictators in defiance of the democratic values that were once thought to have triumphed in the post-Cold War era.

Again, in the confrontation over the Iraq War, the left revealed itself to be more interested in adolescent protest against the symbols of power than in the substance of human rights, democracy and international law. The anti-war movement portrayed Bush as a worse evil and greater threat to global security than Saddam, a dictator who had killed millions of Muslims, invaded his neighbors and used chemical weapons against citizens of his own country. Aside from the scale of Saddam's brutality, there was also the fact that Americans could get rid of Bush in the next election, whereas Iraqis could never democratically unseat Saddam. Iraqis had, in fact, lost hundreds of thousands of lives in attempting to depose him after the Gulf War in 1991. In creating what was, at best, a moral equivalence—or rather, *immoral* equivalence—between a dictator and a leader subject to democratic accountability, the left revealed its astonishing contempt for democracy.

Worse, the left seemed prepared to ignore or excuse the human rights abuses perpetrated by Saddam against the Iraqi people. It did so under cover of many different excuses, the most egregious of which was that America was ultimately responsible for the abuses anyway, since it had backed Saddam in the Iran-Iraq war and failed to protest loudly against his tyranny until he invaded oil-rich Kuwait and threatened Saudi Arabia. Another excuse was that other countries had the sovereign right to be left to their own devices, or that invasion would cause more pain to Iraqis than their restored human rights would be worth. Thus it was that in a debate about a genuinely debatable war—for though war might have been eventually necessary, there were also strong arguments against launching it before other alternatives had been exhausted—the left chose to trash human rights, democracy, and international law simply to attack Bush.

A Failure of Values

In these critical debates, and others that followed, Bush failed—in word and deed—to defend the core values of American democracy and western civilization as he ought to have done. One of the most important failures was the creation of the detention facility at Guantánamo Bay, Cuba. There, the U.S. held those it captured on the battlefield as "unlawful combatants"—a somewhat contrived legal category that appeared to circumvent the provisions of international law dealing with prisoners of war. Often, these prisoners were also spirited away from—or to—foreign countries in "extraordinary renditions"—another legal innovation tailored for the war on terror. Inmates at the initial facility, "Camp X-Ray," and the prison that replaced it were denied many of the core procedural rights that Americans—indeed, most citizens of any democracy—take for granted. They were also initially denied the protections of the Geneva Convention, and denied access to the American courts—including, at first, even military courts.

The Bush administration argued that such detainment was necessary for American security. And, to be sure, many of the inmates were hardened terrorists; many who were later released returned to terror operations in the field. It was also true that interrogations at Guantánamo yielded information about terror attacks, both past and present, that helped the U.S. prevent future attacks and round up more Al-Qaeda operatives. But the prison also became a focus of anti-American protest around the world. A grim mythology also gripped the facility, which featured in false news stories about desecrated Qur'ans and whispered accounts of torture. Though conditions at the prison improved substantially over time, and the Supreme Court imposed a military tribunal system with minimal due process rights, the image of America suffered at precisely the moment when its fight to protect its values needed the most international support. Bush attempted to rally the world to America's side by speaking about the importance of human rights, but seemed at the same time to strip his own words of their credibility.

Aside from questions of public relations and substantive justice, Guantánamo suggested that Bush had a lack of faith in the American military justice system—and its principles— to try terror suspects. Instead, he proposed a process of secret tribunals, citing Franklin Delano Roosevelt's trials of Nazi infiltrators during World War II. Even some conservatives, such as *New York Times* columnist William Safire, objected to the suspension of habeas corpus rights for detainees and the refusal of the Bush administration to turn to the ordinary justice system:

> The [Uniform Code of Military Justice] demands a public trial, proof beyond reasonable doubt, an accused's voice in the selection of juries and right to choose counsel, unanimity in death sentencing and above all appellate review by civilians confirmed by the Senate. Not one of those fundamental rights can be found in Bush's military order setting up kangaroo courts for people he designates before "trial" to be terrorists. Bush's fiat turns back the clock on all advances in military justice, through three wars, in the past half-century.
>
> His advisers assured him that a fearful majority would cheer his assumption of dictatorial power to ignore our courts. They failed to warn him, however, that his denial of traditional American human rights to non-citizens would backfire and in practice actually weaken the war on terror.[25]

The administration took an uncompromising, and in many respects self-defeating, position, accusing its critics of negativity and implying they did not share a strong commitment to fighting terror. It could afford to speak so boldly and conclusively in the weeks after 9/11, with the wind of public opinion at its back; but the strident talk of early days would soon come back to haunt Bush—and America—as the customary American unity behind a president in wartime began to dissolve.

Another glaring failure was the mistreatment of Iraqi prisoners at Abu Ghraib. The notorious Baghdad prison once

47

used by Saddam Hussein to torture dissidents had been a symbol of tyranny under the old regime. But it soon became a symbol of American misrule in Iraq when photographs emerged of American soldiers at the prison abusing Iraqi detainees. Mock executions, sexual humiliations, and attacks on naked prisoners with fearsome dogs were exposed and caused outrage throughout the world—not just in the Middle East, or among opponents of the war, but everywhere.

It was true that Abu Ghraib represented an aberration. Conditions for detainees under American occupation in Iraq were vastly improved over what they had been under Saddam, and what they continued to be elsewhere in the Arab world. It also emerged later that defense secretary Donald Rumsfeld had offered to resign over the scandal, realizing both the immense damage the Abu Ghraib incident would cause to America's mission in the Middle East, and acknowledging his own indirect responsibility via the chain of command.[26] That, at least, was a sign that the American leadership did not intend to evade responsibility—and, indeed, the soldiers involved were tried and convicted.

But the Abu Ghraib incident undermined the most important justifications for the Iraq War: namely, the promotion of human rights and democracy as a path to peace in the Middle East. These were perhaps the only solid reasons that remained after weapons of mass destruction were not found in Iraq, and one that Bush took far too long to articulate. In a speech to the National Endowment for Democracy in November 2003—sadly, more than seven months after the start of the Iraq War, when such aims might best have been spelled out—Bush declared:

> Our commitment to democracy is also tested in the Middle East, which is my focus today, and must be a focus of American policy for decades to come. In many nations of the Middle East—countries of great strategic importance—democracy has not yet taken root. And the questions arise: Are the peoples of the Middle East somehow beyond the reach of liberty? Are millions of men and women and children condemned by history or culture to live in despotism? Are they alone never to know freedom, and

48

never even to have a choice in the matter? I, for one, do not believe it. I believe every person has the ability and the right to be free.[27]

But within months, Abu Ghraib would join Guantánamo Bay as a symbol of American hypocrisy and as tools for propaganda and recruitment efforts among terror groups in Iraq and beyond. These examples rendered Bush's fine words moot. They suggested, fairly or unfairly, that Americans did not fully understand, or care about, human rights—certainly not for Arabs or Muslims—and reinforced the worst fears that had been bred about both America and democracy in a region where freedom faced an uphill struggle.

The decline of America's image—and its self-confidence in the righteousness of its own struggle—was deeply unfortunate, because the Bush administration did in fact care about human rights. It struggled, however—and perhaps understandably so—to implement them in the face of the profound terror threat it now faced. The view Bush eventually came around to was that of Natan Sharansky—the former Soviet dissident turned Israeli minister—that peace in the Middle East would be impossible without democracy. It was a view Sharansky had articulated in his book *The Case for Democracy*, which Bush had read and publicly endorsed as a guide to his own foreign policy thinking.[28] The idea was, in a way, a substantially revised version of *New York Times* columnist Thomas Friedman's "Big Mac" thesis—that no two countries with McDonald's restaurants (and the open societies and market economies necessary for them to succeed in the first place) had ever gone to war. Sharansky, instead, put a premium on the political question of whether a country was a "free society" or a "fear society," a distinction measured by whether one could enter the town square and speak one's mind without fear of repression.[29] Peace was always possible with the former, but never—at least not in a comprehensive way—with the latter, because rulers of fear societies needed to maintain external enemies to excuse their abuses against their own populations.

49

Words of Peace, Words of War

Bush's commitment to human rights and democracy in the context of the war against terror found a new focus in the administration's steadfast support of Israel. At first, following 9/11, the administration seemed inclined to concede certain demands to the Palestinians in the hope of softening Arab and Muslim anti-American sentiment, both in general and relating to the war against terror, which many feared would provoke further hostility towards the United States. It was on October 2, 2001—only three weeks after 9/11—that Bush became the first American president to support explicitly the goal of creating a Palestinian state alongside Israel.[30] The Bush administration's approach prompted an unusually harsh and controversial rebuke from Israeli prime minister Ariel Sharon: "Don't repeat the terrible mistakes of 1938, when the enlightened democracies in Europe decided to sacrifice Czechoslovakia for a comfortable, temporary solution."[31] Bush continued, for a time, to seek a more active role in mediating between the Israelis and Palestinians. But in January 2002, Israel intercepted an Iranian ship bound for Gaza—the *Karine A*—carrying weapons that had been paid for in disbursements authorized by Palestinian Authority Chairman Yasser Arafat. That sent a clear signal that Arafat was not cooperating with the new foreign policy of the United States, which had made the war on terror its top priority, and blunted America's enthusiasm to court the Palestinian leadership.

What followed was a period in which the Bush administration began resolutely supporting Israel in a way it had never quite done before, and in a way that few other democracies had the courage to do. In the propaganda war that had ensued against Israel, American support would prove crucial in defending the values of freedom and democracy that the two countries shared, as well as confronting the attacks on truth committed by extremist groups and their apologists. The most profound example was the so-called "massacre" in

50

the West Bank town of Jenin. In April 2002, Palestinian suicide bombers killed thirty Israelis who had gathered at a
Passover *seder* in the city of Netanya.[32] In response, Sharon
launched Operation Defensive Shield, aimed at shattering the
terrorism infrastructure in Palestinian towns in the West
Bank. Fighting was most intense in the Jenin refugee camp,
where Hamas fighters battled Israeli soldiers in house-to-
house skirmishes. There were dozens of casualties on both
sides, just over fifty in all, most of them combatants. But Palestinian spokesman Saeb Erekat claimed that Israel had
committed a massacre of five hundred Palestinians. The accusation was picked up by the international media, and sensa-
tionalized with stories of whole families killed and buried beneath the rubble. But the Palestinian claims were proved
false—as even the UN had to admit—and the Israeli narrative proven correct.[33] The entire "massacre" myth was a
fraud, though few news outlets bothered to issue corrections
or retractions of their earlier reports, much less apologies for
misleading the public. Palestinian propagandists had been
prepared not only to excuse violence to Israel but to do violence to words whose meaning conjured the most serious
atrocities in human memory. Bush stood with Israel in the
face of these lies and against extreme international pressure,
whose basis was not concrete fact but fabricated blood libel.

Though Bush would later regret some of his colorful,
cowboy language in defending America's war on terror—as
well as his pose in front of a "Mission Accomplished" banner
on the deck of the U.S.S. *Abraham Lincoln* during the Iraq
War, when the worst fighting still lay ahead[34]—he generally
said what he meant. There was a fundamental commitment, if
not always a fundamental wisdom, in his words. And soon it
was Bush himself who was warning western democracies
about "appeasement," as he did in a speech to the Israeli
Knesset in June 2008:

> Some seem to believe that we should negotiate with the terror-
> ists and radicals, as if some ingenious argument will persuade
> them they have been wrong all along. We have heard this foolish

51

delusion before. As Nazi tanks crossed into Poland in 1939, an American senator declared: "Lord, if I could only have talked to Hitler, all this might have been avoided." We have an obligation to call this what it is—the false comfort of appeasement, which has been repeatedly discredited by history.[35]

Barack Obama and future running mate Joe Biden reacted angrily to the speech—Biden even termed it "bullshit"[36]—and evidently assumed it had been aimed at them, proving more by their protest than perhaps Bush had intended.

But Bush also made many errors in his approach to the Israeli-Palestinian conflict—mistakes that undermined the process, as well as American values and goals. His initial policy of non-involvement, for example, was largely unsuccessful. He then moved on to the "Road Map" towards peace in the Middle East in 2003, whose deadlines were endlessly deferred because of repeated Palestinian terror attacks. Later, Bush's repeated concessions to Palestinians, often made without consideration in return, and often simply for the sake of idealism and in the hope of calming outrage in the Arab world, gave unintended encouragement to extremist groups and helped undermine the struggle against terror. For example, Bush pressed for Palestinian elections to proceed in 2006 before Hamas had suspended violence—a move guranteed to turn the election into a sham, and which the Israeli government opposed, to little effect. When Hamas won control of the Palestinian legislature, the U.S. responded by providing weapons to its rival, Fatah, which still controlled the presidency—even though Fatah's own armed wing had been involved in terror attacks against Israel. It was a policy that was not only ineffective, but contrary to the very essence of Bush's commitments to fight terror and the states that supported it.

In the summer of 2006, the U.S. stood by Israel as it responded to the kidnapping of one of its soldiers by Hamas in Gaza, and to Hizbollah infiltration and rocket attacks against the north of the country. But as the Second Lebanon War (as it was later called) ground on, American diplomats leaned on Israel to accept the terms of a UN-brokered cease-fire, partly to save a fragile Lebanese government that had once mustered the courage to confront Syrian occupation. The end result was quiet on Israel's northern border, but a huge propaganda victory for Hizbollah and its sponsor, Iran. Emboldened, perhaps, by Hizbollah's success, Hamas staged a coup in Gaza less than a year later, exiling Fatah and seizing the weapons the U.S. had recently provided it—another failure of American involvement.

In the last year of his presidency, Bush became committed to an intense round of negotiations—the "Annapolis process"—aimed at securing a final peace agreement before he left office in January 2009. He had come full circle, picking up where Bill Clinton had left off, though Bush had initially been determined to do the opposite: offering Palestinians concessions in return for promises of peace whose terms were constantly shifting and whose guarantees were essentially empty. Amidst a flurry of negotiations, led by Secretary of State Condoleezza Rice—who reportedly saw the conflict in the moralistic terms of the American civil rights struggle[37]—Hamas and other terror groups continued to launch rockets into sovereign Israeli territory in an attempt to kill as many civilians as possible. Following a six-month cease-fire, which Hamas declared it would not renew when it expired in December 2008—making good on its word by launching a new barrage of rockets when the "period of calm" ended—Israel finally responded. It launched "Operation Cast Lead," targeting Hamas institutions, fighters and weapons caches in the Gaza Strip with pinpoint aerial strikes and a ground invasion. The operation was successful in damaging Hamas's military capacity substantially. And while Bush supported Israel's actions wholeheartedly, the U.S. failed to veto the manifestly lopsided UN Security Council Resolution 1860, which made an end to Hamas rocket fire conditional on Israel pulling back its forces.[38] Throughout his term, Bush had offered Israel strong rhetorical support, but in practice had ended up exactly where Clinton had—and worse, since Bush's interventions had actually weakened the principles of the war against terror on which Bush had staked his presidency since 9/11. Contrary to the common belief on the left, he had not "disengaged" from the Israeli-Palestinian conflict. He had, belatedly, become involved—and like his predecessors, he prevented the worst from happening but failed to bring about the outcome he sought.

Big Government and Its Abuses

Bush's most significant departure from the principles he had promised to uphold was his massive expansion of the size and cost of government. Having cut taxes, consolidated several agencies into the mammoth Department of Homeland Security, and committed the United States to two overseas wars, Bush also increased expenditures on prescription drug benefits, education spending, and a variety of other policies as part of his package of "compassionate" conservative policies. Some of the new spending was arguably made necessary by the new circumstances that emerged after 9/11, but much of it was discretionary—and most of it was unrestrained. Bush also passed massive farm bills and energy subsidies that sent billions of federal dollars to America's most bloated industries. He also backed away from conservative free-trade principles in supporting protective tariffs on steel—an action that was later struck down by the World Trade Organization, but one that foretold his response to the 2008 financial crisis and which bespoke a lack of commitment to the fundamental values of the movement he represented. This was "big-government conservatism" of a kind Reagan and Goldwater would not have recognized, much less endorsed. It began to eat away at the Republican Party at its core.

One of the more significant departures from conservative small-government philosophy was the federal government's intervention in state affairs on social issues. For example, Attorney General Ashcroft tried, unsuccessfully, to block Oregon from passing legislation that would allow doctors to prescribe drugs to assist suicide, which had been made legal by a state referendum in the 1990s.[39] For years, conservatives had been arguing that contentious issues of conscience such as abortion ought to be left to the states to decide. Liberals had charged that this was simply a way of trying to force through pro-life legislation wherever possible, in the hope of reintroducing it on the national level, something conservatives vehemently denied. But Ashcroft's actions turned the conservative states' rights insideout. It would be tough for American voters to trust future Republican guarantees that they would respect the decisions of state government that they did not agree with.

Bush also failed to keep pork-barrel spending under control. Though he did veto a few bills on the grounds that they were saddled with too many discretionary spending measures, he failed to take a hard line against such earmark spending, which neared $20 billion per year and which was indulged in by both Democrats and Republicans.[40] Theoretically, of course, not every dollar of pork was "wasted"; some money did sustain productive jobs and social agencies. However, there was no reason such spending needed to take place outside of the normal process of appropriations, which at least provided for rudimentary oversight to ensure that monies allocated were being spent, and spent efficiently. The secretive process of approving earmarks meant that many of them could be—and were—delivered to individuals and organizations as political favors or in return for campaign contributions, not because of their ability to serve the public interest. The entire phenomenon was essentially a legalized form of corruption, and one that undermined public faith in the government's ability to spend money fairly and wisely at the very moment that it was spending so freely—like a drunken sailor on shore leave, in John McCain's favored characterization.[41] Earmarks made a small contribution to the government's budget deficit, but a major impact on the erosion of public trust.

Citizens are generally prepared to tolerate some amount of waste and corruption, as long as the government provides basic services. It can be especially difficult in local government, where politicians interact daily and directly with their constituents, to separate self-dealing from honest public service. Mayor Richard Daley of Chicago, for one, has continued to be popular despite a string of high-level investigations, indictments and convictions of members of the city administration, and in spite of the fact that Chicago is essentially a Democratic one-party system in which corruption has been allowed to flourish. That's not just because city employees are used as campaign fodder, canvassing during work hours for preferred candidates,[42] but also because services have improved and jobs have grown during Daley's long tenure. Services would likely be even better, and the economy even more robust, were Chicago governed in a clean fashion. But—for better or for worse—city voters have low expectations, and Daley has tended to meet them, for the most part, until recently.

The most basic government service of all is protecting the lives and property of a nation's citizens. But when government fails to do so, even if the proximate cause of that failure is a natural disaster, citizens quickly lose patience. Bush's inadequate response to Hurricane Katrina was a case in point. Though Democratic state and local officials had botched the evacuation of New Orleans, and the federal response to the disaster was the largest rescue operation in the nation's history, Bush's management of the aftermath of Katrina aroused fierce public anger. His appointee to run FEMA, Michael Brown, was clearly unqualified for the job—his previous employment had been supervising horses—and he resigned shortly after the disaster.[43] Though the armed forces performed admirably in stopping the widespread looting, and were able to rescue stranded residents from rooftops and submerged houses, Bush himself appeared distant from the crisis, flying over the destruction in an aircraft, not emerging on the sodden ground himself to inspect conditions and evaluate progress.

The images of pain, suffering and abandonment in the predominantly black city added to the outrage. Poverty in New Orleans had not been Bush's fault. If anything, Hurricane Katrina merely exposed it, and aroused a painful shame in the African-American community that had not managed to take care of its own. But a popular, if completely fallacious, explanation for the Katrina debacle soon emerged: Bush had failed because the government and the military had diverted too many resources to the war in Iraq. The idea was even the theme of a popular music video by U2 and Green Day, "The Saints Are Coming," which portrayed Army helicopters returning from Iraq to aid a beleaguered New Orleans.[44] This idea—which proved irrepressible, though untrue—added the weight of an increasingly unpopular war to the portrait of insensitivity and incompetence that was rapidly becoming the public image of the Bush administration.

Increased government power is almost always followed by increased corruption, and increased abuses of that power. And though the Bush White House managed to avoid any serious or substantive allegations of malfeasance, the Republican Party was rocked by a series of scandals during Bush's second term. Some were rather contrived, such as the revelation that evangelical leader Ted Haggard, who opposed gay rights, had carried on a relationship with a gay prostitute. Critics of social conservatism elevated and exaggerated Haggard's prior prestige among evangelicals, the better to use his very public fall from grace as a weapon against the broader evangelical movement and its political offshoots. But other scandals hit closer to home for conservatives. While the Haggard story embarrassed social conservatives in general, when Republican Senator Larry Craig of Idaho was convicted of the misdemeanor of soliciting sex in a men's public bathroom, it hurt the Republican Party in particular.

So, too, did a scandal involving Florida congressman Mark Foley, a Republican who was found to have sent sexually explicit messages over the Internet to young students employed as congressional pages. The story broke in September 2006, just before the critical midterm elections. Ironically, the Democrat who replaced Foley, Tim Mahoney, was himself implicated in a sexual harassment scandal two years later. But his party affiliation was rarely mentioned—a common imbalance in media coverage of scandals, which tended to overemphasize Republican corruption and to suggest that corruption in the Democratic Party consisted merely of individual departures from the transparent and righteous norm. Conservative commentators, noting the absence of any indication of Democratic Party affiliation in reports about fallen Democrats, invented a term for the phenomenon: "Name That Party."

Far more important than these sex scandals, however, was the conviction of lobbyist Jack Abramoff, who had paid bribes to Republican lawmakers and defrauded some of his clients, including a Native American tribe. Another very serious and very public conviction was that of White House deputy chief of staff Lewis "Scooter" Libby. Though he was not the primary source of the leak, he was found guilty of perjury, obstruction of justice and making false statements to federal agents investigating the leak to the media of the name of CIA agent Valerie Plame. The leak had occurred as apparent retaliation after Plame's husband wrote an article in the *New York Times* critical of the administration's intelligence assessment in making the case for the Iraq War, including the assertion that the Iraqi regime had sought to obtain "yellowcake" uranium from the isolated African nation of Niger.[45] These scandals, taken together, suggested that there was a lack of principled leadership at the highest levels of the Republican Party, and that the rot was widespread.

The Plame affair, in particular, fit the growing public perception that Bush had not merely expanded executive power, but abused it. Already, from the first weeks of his term in office, there was a public outcry over the White House's refusal to list the participants in, or provide the agenda of, a meeting on energy policy from which environmental groups had been excluded. Legislation passed after 9/11, such as the USA PATRIOT (Uniting and Strengthening America by Providing Appropriate Tools Required to Intercept and Obstruct Terrorist) Act,[46] gave the government far greater powers to investigate and prosecute suspected terrorists, and broadened the legal definition of "terrorism" itself. As a result, concerns about potential abuses of executive power spread beyond left-wing groups to conservative civil libertarians as well. The posture of the White House towards criticism—denigrating it as unhelpful, and at times as unpatriotic—added to the image of an insular and perhaps paranoid administration. The outcry grew into outrage with each passing controversy, reaching heated levels when the *New York Times* revealed that the administration had authorized warrantless wiretaps on the telephones of suspected terrorists. There were calls to prosecute telecommunications companies that had cooperated with the wiretaps, though these died down in 2008 after Senator Obama and a Democratic Congress—going back on their pledge to hold the telecommunications companies accountable—agreed to grant the companies restrospective immunity.

But there were plenty of other allegations of executive overreaching for Democrats to continue to protest. One such was Bush's decision to dismiss several senior U.S. Attorneys, the officials entrusted with leading prosecutions in their federal jurisdictions in each state of the Union. Bill Clinton had dismissed every single U.S. Attorney when he took office—with the goal, some suspected, of stopping investigations into the Clintons' past business dealings.[47] But the Bush firings—aimed at prosecutors he himself had appointed—seemed targeted, critics charged, at specific prosecutors for political reasons: they had allegedly failed to investigate charges of Democratic malpractice in the 2004 elections, at least with the vigor and results demanded by the administration.

Another controversy concerned the infamous "torture memos," drawn up by attorneys in the White House counsel's office, who advised President Bush that certain forms of "enhanced interrogation techniques" might be legal and that the U.S. did not necessarily have to obey the Geneva Convention in dealing with terror detainees. Vice-President Dick Cheney also pushed for a strong approach toward suspected terrorists, which aroused a backlash across the globe. These controversies created the impression, at home and abroad, that the Bush administration was prepared to cross all moral and legal boundaries in its determination to exercise its will. And Bush's reluctance to admit substantive mistakes in these areas added to the public distrust, as did the steady stream of leaks that continued to paint a picture of executive abuse. Even in the administration's last days, new allegations that it had tortured or abused detainees in the war on terror continued to surface and to erode public trust in Bush's leadership.[48]

A Socialist President?

Having compromised on principles of small government, executive accountability, human rights, democracy—and even occasionally, with regard to Israel, the core goal of fighting terror itself—Bush completed his term of office by doing what no Democratic president might have dared until then: intervening, on a massive scale, in the nation's financial industry, bailing out lenders and obtaining large stakes in private American enterprises on a scale not seen since long before the Reagan Revolution.

Bush's last-gasp intervention brought to mind the massive expansion of federal powers, and the economic interventions, of Roosevelt's New Deal or of Bernard Baruch's World War I industrial policy. Administration officials, acting with a sense of desperate urgency, believed—possibly correctly—that such intervention had been necessary to save the world's financial system from collapse. They sadly noted the departure of such drastic actions from the playbook of conserva-

60

tive government, adding that they hoped the measures would be temporary. Instead, they stood to reverse the gains of an entire generation of conservative critique and policy, saddling future generations of Americans with a level of debt and government intervention few would have thought possible and only the most extreme left-wing activists had dared to dream about. Whatever the Bush administration's hopes about the temporary nature of its $700 billion Troubled Assets Relief Program (TARP), it was clear that the Obama administration would seize the opportunity to make permanent such changes in the size and reach of government. As Obama's chief of staff Rahm Emanuel was to say later: "Never let a serious crisis go to waste. What I mean by that is it's an opportunity to do things you couldn't do before."[49]

The financial crisis that hit in September 2008 had been brewing for months—or perhaps years. For decades, since the administration of Jimmy Carter, the federal government had been pressuring banks to give "sub-prime" loans to people who ordinarily would not have qualified for them. The Community Reinvestment Act, signed by Carter in 1977, sought to end the practice of "red-lining," through which banks limited or denied mortgages to would-be homeowners in certain neighborhoods, thereby—critics charged—discriminating against various minority groups. The act was strengthened by the Clinton administration, amidst a slew of lawsuits—including one in which a young Barack Obama had participated as co-counsel[50]—designed to ratchet up the pressure on private banks to comply. Many of the loans were carried by Fannie Mae and Freddie Mac, the formerly government-owned mortgage providers, which were regulated only loosely by the federal government.

The trend continued under Bush, who pledged to increase home ownership among Americans—especially among minorities and the poor, who still had low ownership rates despite the decades of attempted interventions.[51] He also presided over a large housing boom—and bubble—that had been partly triggered by a loose monetary policy under Fed-

61

eral Reserve chairman Alan Greenspan, and also by the unsteadiness in equity prices in 2000 and 2001. Uncertainty in the stock market after the "dot-com bust" in the last year of Clinton's administration, and after the 9/11 attacks in Bush's first year, made property an attractive asset. Millions of Americans became property owners and saw their wealth expand rapidly.

Despite being labeled—falsely—as a "de-regulation" president, Bush sought to increase regulation of Fannie Mae and Freddie Mac at the same time that he was overseeing the country's vast expansion in housing investment. The worry at the time—predicted by a few observers as early as the late 1990s—was that investment in "sub-prime" mortgages provided to those who could otherwise not afford them, and the creation of derivative securities that sold those sub-prime debts to investors on the open market, were both dependent on rising housing prices. Falling prices, it was predicted, could trigger massive financial losses and a swift contraction in available credit.[52] Yet Bush was rebuffed by Democrats in Congress, such as Barney Frank of Massachussetts, who not only favored Fannie Mae and Freddie Mac because of their policy interest in low-cost housing, but who also received vast campaign contributions from these lending institutions. Regulations came up again in 2006, but were defeated by left-wing Democrats that denied any problems existed at all.

When the bubble finally burst, it became common practice to blame financial deregulation for the ensuing financial crisis. And, to be sure, under both Clinton and Bush the financial markets had been liberalized to allow the sort of complex, leveraged transactions that regulators later often had trouble keeping track of. But under Bush, financial regulation had actually expanded rapidly, by almost one thousand pages of new regulations per year.[53] Following the Enron crisis in his first year in office—itself the result of over-optimistic investment, shoddy accounting and corporate malfeasance—Bush signed the Sarbanes-Oxley Act of 2002, and imposed strict new standards of accountability on the financial services industry. Many investors who were burned in 2008 were simply unlucky, or careless; some were duped by complex Ponzi schemes such as those of fraudster Bernie Madoff, who conned $65 billion out of investors. Madoff had been investigated by the Securities and Exchange Commission in 2006, but had been cleared of any wrongdoing. Whatever the reason investors abandoned ordinary caution, the problem had not been a lack of oversight, but the poor quality of that oversight, and the meager self-discipline of irresponsible investors who chose to ignore the growing risk. The crisis was also arguably precipitated by *excessive* government intervention. That included not just the "easy money" monetary policies of the Federal Reserve, but also the decades-long attempt by legislators to force banks into the subprime loan market, the guarantees of government backing that encouraged private speculators to take risks on leveraged securities, and the activist lawsuits that greatly expanded the reach of the courts into the financial system. Once homeowners began to struggle to pay back their loans, the securities that had been leveraged on them began to suffer as well, triggering the anticipated cascade effect in credit markets worldwide.

But investor anxiety had also been fanned by the antics of politicians on the campaign trail, particularly on the Democratic side. Candidates repeatedly spoke of an ongoing "recession" and of a looming economic crisis, even though gross domestic product grew at a rate of nearly 3% per annum in the second quarter of 2008.[54] That was a healthy rate by the standards of most industrialized countries, and was achieved just as the 2008 primary races were reaching their climax. Candidates who refused to join in the general prophesies of doom—in which blame was invariably laid at the feet of the Bush administration by Democrats and Republicans alike— were ridiculed as out of touch with the reality faced by the American public. When former senator Phil Gramm, an economic adviser to the McCain campaign, castigated his countrymen for succumbing to a "mental recession" and becoming a "nation of whiners,"[55] he had a point—but McCain was compelled to rebuke him immediately. And talk of crisis eventually proved self-fulfilling.

The Bush administration's responses to the financial crisis also fueled the panic. Initially, the government's interventions were incremental, careful and tentative. They began with the New York branch of the Federal Reserve, which helped engineer the rescue of investment banking giant Bear Stearns by former rival J.P. Morgan. The Federal Reserve's direct intervention in such a business transaction was unprecedented and in direct contradiction to the laissez-faire approach that had been prescribed by its chairman, Ben Bernanke, in his previous academic career. However, it certainly helped protect Bear Stearns and its investors from a likely collapse, and may have helped avert a broader financial meltdown. The economy continued to hum along, albeit somewhat nervously, while the most pressing concern among consumers was the rise of fuel prices as oil broke through $150 per barrel and gasoline reached $4 per gallon by July 2008.

But soon the ability of the Federal Reserve to assist came to an end. And when more financial institutions—Merrill Lynch, American Insurance Group (AIG), and Lehman Brothers—began to falter, the Bush administration stepped in. It helped Bank of America take over Merrill Lynch, intervened directly in AIG, and attempted to draw a line by denying Lehman relief when it could not find a private buyer. Lehman's subsequent collapse in mid-September 2008 triggered the long-awaited and long-feared financial panic. Days later, Treasury secretary Hank Paulson sought a staggering $700 billion grant from Congress to boost the financial markets with much-needed credit. The TARP—or "bailout," as it was soon called—was drastic enough, but the way Paulson sought the funds—telling senators that the global financial system could collapse if it was not passed by Congress[56]— undoubtedly made the panic worse.

In the midst of an election in which he had largely stayed beyond the public eye, Bush re-emerged to address the nation to explain and defend the bailout. But his efforts were a political failure. When first presented to the House of Representatives, the TARP bill was laden with pork-barrel riders, including grants to groups such as the Association of Community Organizations for Reform Now (ACORN), which was at the center of vote fraud investigations.[57] It failed—partly due to those provisions, partly due to partisan bickering, partly due to genuine misgivings and opposition among House Republicans, and partly—it must be said—despite (or in response to) John McCain's decision to suspend his campaign to muscle the bill through Congress (see chapter 5). When the bailout failed, the stock market tumbled by nearly 780 points on the Dow Jones Industrial Average, but recovered soon afterward. When a revised TARP bill was re-submitted to Congress a few days later, and passed, the stock market fell yet again, suggesting that investors were less sanguine than politicians about the ability of government to rescue the economy. Moreover, despite Paulson's claims of extreme urgency in September, the bailout money still had not been fully distributed by the end of Bush's first term, casting doubt on the question of whether it had really been necessary at all beyond its value as a confidence-boosting gesture.

Throughout the campaign, Obama told voters how grim their economy was—just as opposition parties traditionally do, and just as John Kerry and other Democrats had done in late 2003 before figures emerged showing the economy growing at the rapid rate of 7.2 percent,[58] whereupon the Democrats began claiming it was "jobless growth." Obama offered voters hope, but only by first selling them an image of despair that was, for a time, wildly inaccurate. Yet reality swiftly caught up to Obama's rhetoric. Suddenly, America resembled the grim world Obama had described, rather than the gruffly optimistic picture McCain had painted. It was a keenly-timed crisis—and, some suggested conspiratorially, a manufactured one, brought on by the irresponsible words of politicians.

Perhaps that was giving words too much weight. But what was most striking of all about the 2008 financial crisis and the bailout was the complete absence of any serious, sustained and articulate opposition to the Bush administration's response. McCain endorsed it; so, too, did many Republicans in Congress; and even conservative think tanks like the Heritage Foundation backed it.[59] Economists were also divided on the issue—and that, perhaps, was understandable, given the potential gravity of the crisis and the fact that nothing on the scale proposed by Bush and Paulson had ever been attempted before. Yet there was a crying need for political opposition to the bailout—even if only for the sake of simply standing up for the interests of the taxpayers. But there was none.

Everyone now owned the bailout—the most dramatic expansion of state economic power in decades. We were all, after a fashion, socialists now, and Bush—"compassionate conservative" that he was—had arguably become America's first socialist president. His earlier promises seemed utterly empty now; Bush had betrayed whatever meaning they once held. It seemed that for all Obama's radicalism, for all the misgivings about his extremist roots and his far-left ideas, nothing he would or could do in office could far surpass what Bush had done. As for McCain, he had suspended his campaign, even putting the first presidential debate in jeopardy, to help pass the bailout. He had hoped, in doing so, to display his leadership. But by the time he showed up for the debate—with the bailout not yet passed—he had already given up on the main political difference between him and his opponent. And that would make all the difference in November.

3

The Ambivalent Hero

Moderate or Maverick?

The year had been a bad one for Republicans from start to finish. President Bush's approval ratings hovered between twenty and thirty percent throughout 2008; on the eve of the election, only 11 percent of Americans would report that they believed the country was on the right track.[1] Remarkably, Congress—the "often absent and little loved 110th"—was even more unpopular,[2] but no one seemed—yet—to blame Speaker Nancy Pelosi or Majority Leader Harry Reid, who had led the legislative branch since the Democratic sweep in the 2006 midterm elections. Most predictions, in fact, forecast that Democrats would pick up additional seats in the House and Senate—perhaps enough in the latter chamber to undo the Republican filibuster for the first time since Jimmy Carter's presidency in the late 1970s. Though Democrats were deeply divided over which candidate—Hillary Clinton, Barack Obama or former Senator John Edwards—would win the nomination, they were signing up voters at a rapid, record pace. Republican registration, by contrast, was sluggish. The party's base was disillusioned and burnt out after eight years of power in the White House.

And John McCain's campaign was in trouble. An early favorite when the race to succeed Bush began to unfold in the early months of 2007, McCain suffered for his continued backing of the Iraq War, an adventure that had reached the nadir of its fortunes and its public support in 2006. Wracked by infighting and struggling to raise funds, McCain's campaign all but collapsed by the summer of 2007.[3] Political analysts on Capitol Hill declared his campaign "flat-out dead,"[4] as internal rivalries forced the departure of one key strategist after another.[5] The unpopularity of the Iraq War meant that McCain had painted himself into a political corner. "I'd rather lose an election than lose a war," McCain often said,[6] but in 2007 it seemed both might be possible, with Iraq still troubled and McCain's poll numbers slipping into oblivion.[7]

Still, the man who only four years before had been considered a possible choice to be John Kerry's running mate seemed to be the only Republican with a chance of winning in 2008. McCain was one of the few Republicans who remained popular among moderate Democrats. He was seen by many left-leaning analysts as the alternative to Bush—as the Republican who ought to have won in 2000, if the country had to be governed by a Republican at all. He was also popular among independent voters, that sought-after group whose fickle support was widely thought to be the key to winning elections. Other Republicans had failed to attract much attention or support from the mainstream or the middle. Even former Massachusetts governor Mitt Romney, a Republican who had won in one of the nation's most left-wing states and who had championed such traditionally Democratic issues as health care reform, seemed unable to reach across the divide. Only McCain, it seemed, could pull off a victory—if anyone could.

But while moderation is a widely admired virtue, as a platform it has a surprisingly narrow constituency. It is rarely easy to find the words to explain or defend moderate positions. Political rhetoric generally favors partisanship, and voters are often more inclined to turn out at the polls to oppose something they are against rather than to support something they are for. Thus McCain's appeal to moderates and Democrats was probably not the reason he was able to revive his campaign and capture the Republican nomination—in surprisingly swift fashion—in March 2008. The likely reason was his persistent commitment to the Iraq War, the very cause that had helped drag his campaign down in the first place, but which provided its only consistent thread of rhetorical coherence and demonstrated his willingness to take risks for his beliefs.

Among the Republican candidates for president, McCain was virtually unique in his determination that America should not abandon his mission, least of all under fire from Al-Qaeda. Only former New York major Rudy Giuliani, who had guided his city through the horrors of 9/11, expressed sentiments that were in any way similar. McCain stood mostly alone in supporting a continued American commitment to Iraqi security—and yet he alone was proved right. From the time the "surge" of 20,000 additional troops began in 2007, under the able command of General David Petraeus, both military and civilian casualties in Iraq began to drop precipitously.[8] And though McCain's motives for supporting the surge had been based on principle, not politics, he benefited from the victories of American troops with a slow but steady recovery in the polls. His position had been far more than a simple ideological stance in favor of the war and its aims. Rather, McCain offered a clear, winning alternative strategy, one based on an uncommon trust in the men and women of the U.S. armed forces. It was a stance that proved not only his fealty to the conservative principle of a strong military but also his superior judgment on military matters.

And so, early in 2008, McCain's electoral fortunes began to bounce back. He did not do well in the first contest, in Iowa—where he, singularly among the candidates of either party, had the courage to tell Iowan farmers that he opposed the ethanol subsidies that had enriched them at the expense of American consumers and third-world agriculture. But he did better than expected, finishing fourth, just behind late-comer Fred Thompson, and—critically—ahead of rivals who were thought to pose a threat further along in the primary season. In New Hampshire, where he had upset Bush in the 2000 primary, McCain once again pulled off a surprise victory, defeating Iowa victor Mike Huckabee as well as local favorite Mitt Romney. From that contest onward, McCain never looked back. By March 4th, the second "Super Tues-

69

day," he had wrapped up the nomination by passing the threshold of 1,191 delegates in the Republican Party's winner-takes-all contests. And as Clinton and Obama continued to fight, dragging each other lower and lower into the political muck, McCain surged into the lead in March and April 2008 in polls measuring support among *all* American voters. For a brief moment, McCain was the man to beat, a result that had been unthinkable only a few weeks before.

Even McCain seemed surprised. Months later, his campaign staffers who had been working since the early days in Iowa would simply shake their heads when questioned as to how he had come back from so far down in the polls. Some credited the success to extraordinary luck. Some said that McCain's rivals had defeated themselves. Former senator Fred Thompson, for example, had joined the race late and suffered a huge financial disadvantage as well as poor media coverage. Giuliani had made a gross strategic miscalculation, avoiding early contests where he was unlikely to do well in favor of a "firewall" stand in Florida, where he hoped to win and create enough momentum to carry the states that followed. Mike Huckabee struggled to reach out beyond his social conservative base, and his economic populism frightened the libertarian wing of the party, as did his veiled attacks on Mitt Romney's Mormon faith. Romney simply failed to excite the Republican base. He had flip-flopped on enough issues—abortion, for example—to leave voters unsure how to feel about him or whether to trust him. And aside from his enthusiastic Mormon constituency, he seemed to have trouble offering voters a way to identify with him. Ron Paul fizzled out, failing utterly to translate his fundraising success and Internet presence into votes.

So it was true that McCain's opponents had stumbled. Still, there were more than a few at the McCain campaign who believed that the reason for his success was not the strength of his organization, or the devotion of his volunteers, but the sheer will of the man himself. He had taken to driving his own campaign bus across the Iowa cornfields, meeting sparse groups of voters in unknown places, pressing forward relentlessly in spite of the seemingly insurmountable odds. He kept moving. And he kept rising.

The Failure of the Moderate Hypothesis

But McCain did not win, in the end. There were many reasons for his eventual failure, and one of them was certainly that he could not match the hypnotic rhetorical spells cast by his opponent. One of the more important and less noted explanations for his defeat was that his victory depended on a hypothesis about voters that was outdated—if indeed it had every been true at all: namely, that voters form a normal distribution (or "bell curve") on a spectrum of political opinion. According to this theory, taught to generations of high school freshmen in civics courses across the country, politics is a continuum from left to right, from "radical" to "reactionary," with liberals on the left, conservatives on the right, and the moderate majority clustered around the middle. A new innovation in political science has been to add extra dimensions to this simple picture. The Nolan Chart, for example, invented by American libertarian pioneer David Nolan, measures political views according to beliefs about both personal freedom and economic freedom. Similarly, the web site www.politicalcompass.org plots politicians and voters on a two-dimensional axis, with economic values on the horizontal and views about authority on the vertical. Yet the norm remains the middle.

These theories suggest that while candidates seeking the nominations of their parties—whose most active participants are likely to be those with the most committed and pronounced political views—might have to take more extreme positions in the primary phase of their campaigns, over time they have to move back to the center. That is, they have to "pivot" as the general phase of the election begins in order to appeal to moderate voters and win votes in the middle of the political spectrum. If that theory is true, then the trick to

71

winning is to choose the "pivot" issues carefully and execute the shift in a way that does not raise doubts about the candidate's credibility or commitment to his or her beliefs.

The case of John Kerry in 2004 is instructive, in that it illustrates quite vividly what *not* to do, according to the moderate hypothesis. Like many congressional Democrats, Kerry voted in 2002 to authorize military action in Iraq. Then, in 2003, he voted against funding the post-war rebuilding effort. With presidential ambitions in mind, he was afraid of appearing soft on national security, but also wanted to distance himself from the Bush administration in order not to alienate the "grass roots"—and "netroots"—of the Democratic Party. He knew he would need the support of both positions in a tough election campaign. The problem was that he could not adequately explain his posture to either side. His defense of his position on the rebuilding funds—"I actually did vote for the $87 billion before I voted against it"[9]—was easily and repeatedly used by the Bush re-election campaign in 2004 to discredit Kerry. What he ought to have done, at least according to the conventional assumptions about voters and the voting process, was to oppose the war and then support the funding—that is, to move from the left to the center, and not the other way around.

Kerry had also been up against the strategic calculations of Bush adviser Karl Rove, who was the first to challenge effectively the dominant theory of the massive, moderate middle. In 2000, Bush had followed the traditional pattern of pandering to conservatives before moving toward the center. But in 2004, Rove employed a tactic of "microtargeting" groups of voters who were ideologically committed to particular positions on particular issues and who, if brought to the polls in sufficient numbers, could outweigh the moderates.[10] The tactic helped Bush secure a majority of the popular vote in his re-election campaign, to the surprise and consternation of the media, whose exit polls had famously declared Kerry the winner on Election Day before those projections had to be dropped a few hours later.[11] Still, the old theory remained political orthodoxy—partly because Rove had been cast as "evil" and manipulative, rather than sensitive to a reality about voters that few others recognized.

Obama smashed the old theory completely. He defeated McCain soundly among moderates and independents, and poached moderate "New Democrat" voters from Clinton. Yet much of his key support—in both the primary and general phases of the 2008 campaign—came from the far left of the political spectrum: unions, African-American voters (who vote conservative on social issues but are the most reliable Democratic bloc), and students. On Election Day, the number of voters who turned out in 2008 was not substantially higher than the number who turned out in 2004. But Obama brought far larger numbers of core Democrats than McCain did core Republicans, and won.

The truly unusual feature of Obama's campaign was that he had run to the left in the primary, and then stayed left in the general election. It was true that he had modified more than a few of his more extreme positions—offering many examples of "flip-flops" to critics who were watching his shifts carefully on a variety of issues, from free trade to immunity for telecommunications companies for participating in warrantless wiretapping. And while he had spoken in the primary of raising taxes to pay for a new government health care system, by the time the general election began he had shifted his rhetoric to include a "middle-class tax cut." The tax "cut" was in reality little more than a shift of the tax burden to non-taxpayers. It did nothing to lower overall tax revenue, and in fact raised the effective marginal tax rates for most Americans. But his policies and philosophies remained firmly left wing, and they were not always dressed in moderate-sounding language. More often than not, Obama let them stand as they were.

What Obama showed in his victory—and McCain, too, in the resurrection of his campaign—was that after an era of broad ideological convergence between the political parties that had given an opening to third party candidates, American voters were attracted to candidates who took clear stances on issues. Not every stand would do: candidates still had to take positions that would appeal to *enough* mainstream and independent voters. But the days of offering voters a "third way," of the "New Democrats" and "compassionate conservatives," were long gone. Voters still wanted candidates to demonstrate their independence, and to offer promises of bipartisanship, but centrism was displaced from ideas and policies onto personalities—the "Maverick" McCain versus the dynamic Obama, a "Party of One," in the words of one admirer.[12] For Obama, the forumla worked. He even managed to poach votes from the conservative base despite his left wing views. His rhetoric transcended his actual beliefs and policies.

Distortion and Reality

Still, McCain's initial appeal among Americans in general was real. And Obama was determined to erode it. To do so, he had to connect McCain to everything negative that Americans perceived about the Republican Party, starting with President Bush himself. With help from the media—which covered Obama's attacks generously—as well as the left-wing "netroots," Obama portrayed McCain as a warmonger. He misquoted, for example, what McCain had told a town hall meeting in Derry, New Hampshire, after being asked whether he imagined American troops could remain in Iraq for another fifty years. Obama and his supporters claimed McCain had pledged one hundred years of war. Here is what McCain actually said:

> Q: President Bush has talked about our staying in Iraq for fifty years . . .
>
> McCain: Maybe a hundred [years] . . . We've been in Japan for sixty years, we've been in South Korea for fifty years or so, that would be fine with me as long as Americans are not being injured or harmed or wounded or killed. Then it's fine with me. I hope it would be fine with you if we **maintained a presence** in

a very volatile part of the world where Al Qaeda is training, re-
cruiting and equipping and motivating people every single day.[13]

McCain had not promised "war," but an American military presence in an unstable part of the world that had proven
its ability to threaten America directly. But Obama and anti-
war groups seized on the quote to portray McCain as dangerously out of control—just as Lyndon B. Johnson had done in
his 1964 campaign against Barry Goldwater. Yet Obama *himself* proposed that American troops remain in Iraq. Here is
what his campaign website reported at the very same moment
that he and his supporters were castigating McCain as a
bloodthirsty militarist:

> Obama will immediately begin to remove our troops from Iraq.
> He will remove one to two combat brigades each month, and
> have all of our combat brigades out of Iraq within 16 months.
> Obama will make it clear that we will not build any permanent
> bases in Iraq. **He will keep some troops in Iraq to protect
> our embassy and diplomats; if al Qaeda attempts to build a
> base within Iraq, he will keep troops in Iraq or elsewhere in
> the region to carry out targeted strikes on al Qaeda.**[14]

Obama's plan was smaller in scale than what McCain had
in mind. And it was certainly animated by a different foreign
policy philosophy—one that believed terror was only a spo-
radic threat rather than a dangerous and determined enemy
funded by rogue states. This approach defined the problem as
a matter for law enforcement rather than military contain-
ment and confrontation. But in its indefinite commitment of
American troops to the region, Obama was going as far as
McCain—perhaps even further, since McCain had at least
suggested some time horizon within which to end the mission. Another distortion, fueled by the Obama campaign, was
that McCain had confused Sunnis and Shiites in his analysis
of the Middle East. On a visit to the region, McCain had accused Shia Iran of supporting Sunni Al-Qaeda terrorists in
Iraq. Though McCain later retracted the statement, he had
made the same claim on other occasions.[15] The left ridiculed
McCain in terms suggesting he had gone dangerously senile.

In fact, there was ample evidence to suggest that Iran was backing both Sunni and Shia groups, Al-Qaeda included, in its efforts to destabilize its neighbor and thwart U.S. ambitions there.[16] Obama later made several egregious errors in statements about the Middle East—suggesting, for example, that the U.S. needed more Arabic translators in Afghanistan, a country with few native Arabic speakers[17]—but these went largely unnoticed and unpunished.

Obama often repeated the same tactics on other issues throughout the campaign, especially the economy. He distorted McCain's economic policies, casting him as a continuation of Bush, whom he in turn mischaracterized as a doctrinaire free marketer. To drive that argument, Obama pulled quotes selectively from McCain's interviews. For instance, in describing Bush's economic performance, McCain told Bloomberg TV in April 2008:

> I think if you look at the overall record and millions of jobs have been created, et cetera, et cetera, you could make an argument that there's been great progress economically over that period of time. But that's no comfort. That's no comfort to families now that are facing these tremendous economic challenges.[18]

Here is how Obama later described McCain's remarks to a crowd in Pennsylvania: "John McCain yesterday said that we are, that, that during George Bush's tenure, the economy actually made great progress. That's his quote."[19] Obama sneeringly distorted what McCain had said, and presented the economic reality that millions of jobs had been created as if it were an incredible, unbelievable lie or mistake. He also attacked McCain's wealth—though his own was considerable—and told voters that economic policies of "ownership" would leave them "on your own"[20]—a meaningless and negative rhetorical trick.

McCain also exploited some of Obama's more regrettable quotes, but this was not a symmetrical contest. McCain never distorted Obama's remarks to mean the exact opposite of what Obama had meant to say. Journalists also tended to allow Obama to escape criticism for the most absurd and intellectually dishonest statements about McCain's true beliefs. Contrariwise, McCain was sometimes called a "liar" for offering accounts of Obama's remarks and actions that were even slightly open to a more favorable interpretation. Obama boasted again and again that he had the toughness to stand up to Republican attacks—attacks that rarely materialized in 2008. "I will not be swift-boated," he often claimed,[21] referring to the criticisms of John Kerry's military record that had been made in 2004 by an independent group called Swift Boat Veterans for Truth. What Obama apparently meant was not that he would defend himself, but that he would go on the attack—that he, in effect, would be the swift-boater-in-chief.

The media eagerly took up many of Obama's effective, though wildly untrue, charges—and they would do so with even greater credulity and passion when the same treatment was meted out to McCain's running mate, Governor Sarah Palin of Alaska. Often, journalists took their cues directly from the Obama campaign or indirectly from left-wing blogs, such as DailyKos.com, which were working closely with Obama to sharpen and publicize his message. The accusation that McCain would bring about the "third term of George W. Bush," for example, began to ring true with many Americans, despite McCain's long history of battles with Bush the candidate and Bush the president, and despite McCain's frequent dissent from the Republican Party line and his own unique policies and beliefs.

The reality of McCain's past rivalry with Bush did, in fact, present something of an obstacle to Obama and the Democrats. Some Americans seemed to have forgotten the bitterness of the 2000 Republican primary, but many had not. Fresher still were the memories of the previous election, when many Democrats had been enthusiastic about the prospects of McCain as Kerry's running mate. As such, the Democrats had to invent a new theme for 2008: that McCain had "changed" over the past several years. He was no longer the brave maverick that had opposed Bush and the conservatives, the story went: he was now their eager servant.

It was certainly true that McCain had rebuilt some of the bridges to his party's conservative base. For example, after denouncing Christian conservative leaders like Reverend Jerry Falwell—who had opposed his candidacy in 2000—as "agents of intolerance,"[22] he began reaching out to them. He even delivered the commencement address at Falwell's Liberty University in 2006.[23] But that had been a change of strategy, not of principle. McCain had always been conservative on social issues, even in the days when Democrats loved him. He never wavered in his opposition to abortion and his belief that *Roe v. Wade* should be overturned. He also opposed gay marriage, though he favored recognition of the civil rights of gay partners and felt such issues should be handled at the state rather than federal level. He remained committed to the conservative viewpoint on judges, favoring the appointment of those who did not "legislate from the bench,"[24] as he often put it. He also dissented on certain issues, such as stem cell research, which he favored and the president did not. But rather than acknowledge that fact, Democrats claimed exactly the opposite—that McCain, like Bush, opposed stem cell research—in a series of attack ads.[25] Ironically, the ads stole a page right out of Bush's playbook. In 2000, the Bush campaign ran a radio ad in New York claiming that McCain opposed breast cancer research—a charge that was not only inaccurate but grossly insensitive, as McCain's own sister had recently battled the disease.[26] It would not be the first time Obama's tactics would seem to resemble those of his ideological and rhetorical foil.

It was also clear to anyone who had paid more than passing attention to McCain's political career in the eight years of Bush's presidency that McCain had continued to work with Democrats, both to oppose those Bush policies he disagreed with, and to push bold and idiosyncratic stances on a whole host of issues, from health care to climate change. The only reality that had changed from 2004 to 2008 was that McCain was now a viable candidate for president, instead of a lovable loser. He was also strongest on issues where the Democratic contenders, and particularly Obama, were weakest—from foreign policy to transparency in government. The new Democratic narrative about McCain's "regression" into Bush-style conservatism did significant damage among voters who might otherwise have been inclined to give McCain's candidacy serious attention. Yet the real McCain still shone through—and still managed to take everyone, including the Obama campaign, by surprise.

Everything Obama Was Not

What quietly worried Democrats more than anything else about McCain was that he represented everything Obama claimed to be, and aspired to be, but was not. After college, for example, Obama moved to Chicago and became a "community organizer" for radical political causes. His work involved not only voter registration but also left-wing "agitation" in poor urban neighborhoods in the style of radical activist Saul Alinsky.[27] His "organizing" was largely political, not actually providing impoverished communities with services but harnessing them to "causes" driven by external motivations and ideologies. From Chicago, Obama proceeded to Harvard Law School, and from there directly to a large corporate law firm—not the usual route for community-minded Harvard graduates, dozens of whom commit to work as public defenders, for legal aid organizations or other worthy causes. Other priorities, it seemed, trumped his supposedly intense desire to serve.

McCain, by contrast, had devoted half of his adult life to service in the country's military, placing his life at risk and surviving for five and a half years as a prisoner of war in North Vietnam. To emphasize McCain's service is not to denigrate *real* community service outside of the military, as the Obama campaign complained whenever his "community organizing" credentials were challenged. Rather, it is to contrast McCain's sustained sacrifice and commitment to clear ideals with Obama's murky and somewhat overly romanticized credentials.

Obama had dwelt extensively in his memoirs about the historical grievances of African-Americans—though it was not a history he himself shared directly—and identifying with the suffering of black people, almost to the complete exclusion of the other half of his heritage. It is telling that despite the fact that Obama was raised by his mother and maternal grandparents, he devoted his first autobiographical book to an extended reflection on a father who he barely knew and had met only a few times. There was real pain in Obama's past, as well as a colorful journey across oceans and continents, but it was not too different from what many Americans encounter in the ordinary course of their lives. Obama's rhetorical gifts enabled him to turn the various strands of his story into a persona that combined elements of Horatio Alger and Malcolm X. But it was exactly that: a persona, more alive as art than in reality.

McCain, however, had endured real personal and public ordeals—the pain of torture in Vietnam; the burden of enduring disabilities that prevented him from lifting his arms above his head; the scrutiny of public life in Congress for twenty-five years. Obama's autobiography—highly fictionalized by his own admission, with many details left deliberately vague—was remarkable for the articulate, introspective prose that animated it. But McCain's autobiographies were simply remarkable for the actual events of his life and career, all of which were clear, concrete, immediately knowable and known. Even his admitted flaws—his poor performance as a cadet at the U.S. Naval Academy, or the breakup of his first marriage, for instance—were described in clear terms. Obama was more vague about his flaws: "Pot had helped, and booze; maybe a little blow when you could afford it. Not smack, though," he said of his drug habit, for instance.[28] The admission was rather candid, but remained sparse in its detail and obscured any real introspection into the specific choices he had made in his personal life or political career.

Faith became an important theme in Obama's campaign—less so, perhaps, after the exposure of Obama's pastor, Jeremiah Wright, but important nonetheless. Obama borrowed the style and rhetoric of the black American pulpit; he even affected messianic tones of speech, telling students at one college: "My job this morning is to be so persuasive . . . that a light will shine through that window, a beam of light will come down upon you, you will experience an epiphany, and you will suddenly realize that you must go to the polls and vote for Barack."[29] He rarely quoted the Bible or offered any straightforward idea of what his own religious feelings were, beyond a loose connection to aspirations for social justice, and a sense that he had a mission to perfect himself—and through him, the world.

McCain was clearer, if quieter, about his faith. He was very private in his religious expressions, attending church on his own in the middle of the campaign, beyond the presence of campaign staff and cameras.[30] But he was candid about his specific beliefs—such as his conviction that life begins at conception, and that evil exists in the world and must be defeated. At the same time, he was equally open about the importance of the secular world in his public life. At one Republican debate in 1999, for example, he was one of the only candidates out of nine who did not name Jesus Christ when asked who his personal hero was: "Teddy Roosevelt," he said instead.[31] In short: McCain's faith was authentic, not just for show.

Obama spoke boldly about changing Washington, about freezing out special interest groups, cleaning up corruption and inaugurating a new era of post-partisanship in Washington. But he had never actually stood up to the leadership of his party, nor to its main contributors. His voting record put him on the far left, and he frequently stuck to party dogma even when—by his own admission—he knew better. Moreover, far from cleaning up Washington, he had enthusiastically joined in the frenzy of special appropriations for "pork," sending hundreds of millions of dollars in wasteful earmarks home to Illinois and even to contributors in other states. McCain, on the other hand, had never requested nor taken a single earmark in his entire career. He also spent prodigious energies in near-constant battles with his president and congressional leadership on key issues, exposing himself to the frequent criticism of the conservative wing of the Republican Party.

It was true that McCain had been implicated in the "Keating Five" scandal in the early 1990s. Charles Keating, a friend and contributor to McCain, had run one of the savings and loan businesses that collapsed during President George H.W. Bush's sole term. In an attempt to secure assistance from the government, Keating lobbied his numerous congressional contacts. Four Democrats had been involved intimately in Keating's lobbying efforts; McCain had merely agreed to meet with Keating, whereupon he refused him any support. But in the investigations that followed in the Democrat-controlled Congress, McCain was seen as an important Republican counterweight to the implicit charge that all of the alleged corruption fell on the left side of the aisle. Still, he was cleared of any wrongdoing beyond bad judgment, and he used the experience to launch an enthusiastic career of corruption-busting. In the years since, he had more than redeemed himself by standing up against pork-barrel spending, by exposing corruption in the military contracting process, and by leading a long, difficult and ultimately successful fight for campaign finance reform against his own and his party's political interests.

McCain also set the example for transparency in Washington. He was constantly accessible to reporters, and during his 2008 campaign he revealed the identity of every single one of his donors, even those giving less than $200, whom the campaign was not obliged by law to release data about. Contrariwise, Obama generally revealed only what he wanted to. His donor list was shrouded in secrecy, for example, with the campaign refusing to reveal the names of small contributors. His campaign also removed most of the anti-fraud protections from its website. The result was a string of illegal overseas contributions, as well as small contributions in odd amounts and contributions from people with false names or untraceable credit cards.[32] Moreover, when asked about his papers from his years in the Illinois Senate, Obama claimed to have lost them[33]—a difficult claim to believe from a man who had meticulously documented his life thus far. In short, Obama's ambitions were transparent and bold, but his achievements and his politics often fell short of the mark. That was why McCain posed a political threat: his authenticity highlighted Obama's essential emptiness as a candidate and leader.

In substance, McCain had achieved far more in his lifetime than Obama had in his short career. And in style, McCain had set an example of candor that Obama could not supersede. McCain was one of the first politicians to adopt a candid approach in his direct interactions with the media, speaking constantly about his controversial views, hiding nothing about his personal life. In 2000, he released 1,500 pages of records of his physical and psychological exams since returning home from Vietnam, partly in order to counter vicious rumors that his time in prison had made him emotionally unstable.[34] Obama was not as forthcoming with concrete information about himself. For example, in contrast to the 1,173 pages of medical records that McCain released for several hours to the media in 2008, Obama simply released a letter from his physician, the one-page equivalent of a high-school doctor's note. He also tended to avoid press conferences and unanticipated questions; as president-elect, he would even develop the habit of pre-selecting those journalists entitled to ask questions at each week's press conferences.[35] But he was more candid in his writing, and spoke openly about his struggles in the Senate in *The Audacity of Hope*, though his candor often tended to reveal more about his confusion than his convictions.

McCain also boasted an outstanding record of legislative accomplishments in the Senate. Unlike Obama, whose only bipartisan efforts had involved uncontroversial bills to track public spending and support efforts to stop nuclear proliferation,[36] McCain had done more than simply assume a bipartisan posture for the purposes of campaigning. He had joined Democrat Russell Feingold to push for campaign finance reform, persevering even after their bill had been defeated several times. He also joined arch-liberal Ted Kennedy in proposing sweeping immigration reforms that would have provided legal status to undocumented workers already in the United States, while at the same time ending America's family-reunification policy in favor of an approach aimed at attracting skilled professionals. These bills failed several times as well, and McCain eventually backed off, saying that he had heard the message loud and clear: voters wanted border security before immigration reform.[37] But he resolved to continue with his reform proposals, albeit in modified "borders-first" form, and was not afraid to pay the political price of failure. McCain also joined Democrat-turned-Independent Joe Lieberman, Al Gore's former running mate, in proposing legislation on climate change that would have created a cap-and-trade system for carbon dioxide emissions. McCain's health care proposals were also bold and innovative, using tax credits to allow families to choose their own insurance provider, thereby creating a mechanism for keeping runaway medical costs under control. Not all of these ideas succeeded, but they inspired applause from policy analysts and respect among politicians. There was a reality to the "Maverick" rhetoric, one that only the most hardened partisans could deny.

In 2005, in one of his toughest stands, McCain broke ranks with the Bush administration and opposed its policies on torture, which had become increasingly controversial. The result of McCain's push—the "McCain Amendment"—made torture illegal and confined American interrogators to the techniques used in the U.S. Army Field Manual. Controversially, the McCain Amendment did not outlaw "waterboarding," a technique that makes the prisoner feel as if he is drowning, which led critics to argue that McCain had not gone far enough. But McCain—as even Obama acknowledged in his second memoir[38]—had fought the president and won, as only a man with his credentials and credibility could have done.

A Different Kind of Campaign

The very idea of running for president as a post-partisan candidate had originated with McCain, who had cast himself as an independent in 2000. The roots of independent-style campaigns went much deeper in American history, of course; one early model was Theodore Roosevelt and his Bull Moose Party of Progressive Republicans, an example McCain surely kept in mind. More recently, Ross Perot and his Reform Party had made an impact on American politics in the 1990s among Americans dissatisfied with the gridlock of the two-party system. But McCain was the first major party candidate to offer an independent approach that remained within the political mainstream yet transcended party lines, even leaping ahead of partisan debates on certain issues where he offered unique proposals that would satisfy concerns on both sides of the political divide. Obama followed suit, adopting some of McCain's innovations in both his political rhetoric and his personal style on the campaign trail.

Most significant of all was the fact that McCain had pioneered the role of the insurgent candidate, the politician who builds an independent base outside the party and then brings those voters into the process, upending establishments and orthodoxies along the way. Others—such as Ted Kennedy in 1980—had mounted challenges to the party leadership by mobilizing the party base. But McCain attempted to bring new voters from beyond the party into the Republican fold. He had done it in the 2000 election, when running against Bush, and very nearly prevailed. Obama would use the same tactics in the 2008 Democratic primary—on a far larger scale, in an effort whose success was made possible in part by the Democrats' proportional representation system of assigning delegates in the primaries. In the general election, he would also use many of the same tactics and tools McCain had championed against McCain himself. Obama's ideals and voting behavior remained solidly partisan, but his rhetoric offered a new breakthrough, and the prospect of a "realignment" of American politics. Yet McCain had been the first, at least in the contemporary era of American politics, to break the mold of the two-party dialectic in challenging for power. Obama knew it—and his campaign would labor to undermine that reality, with some success.

In 2008, as in 2000, McCain promised voters a new kind of campaign—a nobler, more honest contest than the bruising partisan battles, something beyond the inflammatory accusations and attack ads that American voters had suffered through in elections past. He pledged that he would limit himself to the public financing available under the system he had helped reform—and he challenged other candidates to join him in limiting their campaigns to public financing. Critics charged that this stance was merely more convenient for McCain, since he had raised far less money than Obama and could not hope to match his fundraising totals. But McCain's performance as a fundraiser—before the public finance deadline kicked in—would go on to outstrip expectations. In his pledge, he was truly handicapping himself for the sake of political integrity—and he had no reason, at the time, to believe that Obama would renege on his commitment to join the public finance system as well.

McCain also announced that would not, as Republicans had in the past, make use of outside groups—the so-called 527s, named for the section of the federal tax code that governs them—to make charges against his opponent that were too risky or controversial for him to make directly. He also promised to re-shape the party itself in the course of the campaign, taking his "Straight Talk Express" beyond its traditional constituencies into "no-go" areas that Democrats had become used to taking for granted. His first major tour after securing the Republican nomination was through black communities across the South, including those that had been devastated by Hurricane Katrina. He criticized the federal government's response to the disaster, vowing that such failures would never happen again under his administration.[39] And he also offered a heartfelt apology in Memphis for his own failure to support a federal public holiday in honor of Martin Luther King, Jr.[40]—a decision he had tried to atone for when he supported his own state's (ultimately successful) attempts to do the same. It was a bold attempt to grapple with his party's failure to recruit black candidates, leaders and voters—an historical irony, given that the Republican Party had formed to oppose slavery, and that it had been Southern Democrats who had supported Jim Crow segregation laws into the 1960s. McCain was prepared to face that irony, to take responsibility for it—and confront it.

McCain also borrowed a page from one of his predecessors and role models, the late former senator Barry Goldwater. Goldwater had once proposed that he and John F. Kennedy tour the country together and debate each other's policies and principles. It was an idea Kennedy had apparently agreed to, and the debates likely would have taken place in the 1964 election if Kennedy had not been assassinated in November 1963. McCain offered a similar proposal to Obama, suggesting that they travel across the country together in the summer of 2008 to hold ten town hall meetings—not merely to debate, but to face unrehearsed and unscreened questions from the public together. The idea was to give the public access to both candidates in an unscripted forum, beyond the advertisements and speeches and official events, in which voters could challenge each of them and watch them challenge each other. The hope was that a real contest of ideas and values would emerge beyond the rhetoric of set-piece campaign speeches, one that preserved a civility of debate that often evaporated when the candidates merely attacked each other through the media and propaganda. It was a proposal that fit McCain's "Straight Talk" approach to rhetoric and politics perfectly. Partly for that reason, Obama rejected it.

Obama, too, promised a different kind of campaign. And he certainly delivered an inspiring run for the presidency. He surpassed all of his rivals, Republican and Democratic, in his use of technology to reach millions of supporters. He rolled out a massive and unprecedented effort to recruit and train activists, using new volunteers to recruit and train even more. He gave supporters the chance to take charge of the campaign in their own neighborhoods by making campaign tools available over the Internet, such as voter lists, canvassing maps, and printable promotional materials. And, of course, he inspired millions of new donors to give money to his campaign, many of them contributing for the first time in their lives. The percentage of small donors among Obama's funders was no different than the percentage that Bush had enjoyed during his re-election campaign in 2004.[41] But the sheer scale of donations was unprecedented, dwarfing all that had come before it.

Rhetoric aside, however, the contrast between Obama's approach and McCain's was striking. Obama had initially committed to public financing, and even agreed to sit down with McCain to prepare and sign a formal agreement. But he reneged and opted for a fully private campaign instead, weakly asserting that the current campaign system was "broken."[42] On the day of his announcement, his website produced a curious "declaration of independence" from the public financing system, as if Americans had been liberated from an onerous and corrupt scheme that was designed to use their tax dollars against their interests. In fact, the public finance system had been designed after the Watergate scandal of the early 1970s to prevent abuses of the democratic process by unscrupulous politicians and their even more unscrupulous backers. It had been amended by the McCain-Feingold legislation to close loopholes that had allowed millions of dollars in "soft money"—money contributed to the indirect expenses of a campaign—to flow to campaign coffers, a loophole that had favored Republicans. And Obama had endorsed the system before he realized just how great a financial advantage he could realize by avoiding it. But he abandoned it just as breezily as he had committed to it, cloaking his purely self-interested decision in the language of moral righteousness and patriotism.

Another of Obama's lapses was his commitment not to use lobbyists in his campaign. The Obama team constantly derided McCain for his reliance on former lobbyists, even though McCain's campaign was the first to require all lobbyists to resign as a condition of joining or remaining on his staff. MoveOn.org, one of the key "netroots" organizations, ran advertisements that complemented Obama's message, singling out specific McCain employees.[43] But Obama himself used the services of many former lobbyists, as well as advisers and staffers deeply involved in strategic advising for a host of politicians and political causes. (After winning the election, he would break his commitment to keep lobbyists out of the White House even more brazenly by hiring more than a dozen lobbyists and Washington insiders to key posts in his administration.) There was little public scrutiny, however, of Obama's campaign staff, and the McCain campaign decided not to press the issue, lest it amplify Obama's accusations.

Worst of all—and in sharp contrast to the transparency of the McCain effort—was the way in which Obama's campaign resisted any real public examination, either of the candidate himself or the machinery of his election effort. The fawning media showed little interest in challenging the problems with Obama's online campaign donations, for example, which the Obama campaign apparently hoped—correctly, as it transpired—it could defer until well after Election Day. There were also important pieces of Obama's biography that were missing or incomplete. A controversy about his birth certificate ended when the campaign produced a copy of his Hawaiian "Certificate of Live Birth" and published it on the DailyKos.com blog (which only fueled the suspicions of conspiracy theorists).[44] But there was much else that the public simply did not know about him, and which could not be gleaned from the partially fictionalized accounts in his first memoir, nor any of his murky disclosures since. His grades at Columbia University, for instance, were a mystery. He claimed that he had lost his senior thesis, which reportedly discussed Soviet nuclear disarmament.[45] McCain's faults were known—and exploited—by all and sundry; what was known about Obama was typically just what the campaign wanted the public to know, and what the media dared to ask—which generally was not very much at all. Perhaps Obama's real rhetorical gift lay not in what he said but in what he chose to reveal—and hide.

A Lonely Candidate

Nonetheless, McCain had a clear idea about the kind of campaign he wanted to run: strong and assertive, yet moderate and open. But after securing his party's nomination, he struggled to make headway among voters throughout almost the entire 2008 campaign. And the reason was simple: he knew and could describe *how* he wanted to run, but was less adept at explaining *why*. Not that Obama was all too clear on the subject, either. When he was asked by Pastor Rick Warren at the Saddleback Forum (see chapter 5) to explain his ambitions, Obama replied:

> You know, I remember what my mother used to tell me. I was talking to somebody a while back and I said the one time that she would get really angry with me is if she ever thought that I was being mean to somebody, or unfair to somebody. She said, imagine standing in their shoes. Imagine looking through their eyes. That basic idea of empathy, and that, I think, is what's made America special is that notion, that everybody has got a shot. If we see somebody down and out, if we see a kid who can't afford college, that we care for them, too.
>
> And I want to be president because that's the America I believe in and I feel like that American dream is slipping away. I think

we are at a critical juncture. Economically, I think we are at a critical juncture. Internationally, we've got to make some big decisions not just for us for the next generation and we keep on putting it off. And unfortunately, our politics is broken and Washington is so broken, that we can't bring together people of goodwill to solve these common problems. I think I have the ability to build bridges across partisan lines, racial, regional lines to get people to work on some common sense solutions to critical issues and I hope that I have the opportunity to do that.[46]

It was a rambling, unclear, self-referential answer. Summarized briefly, Obama had said: I want to be president because I want to give everyone the same opportunities I had, and I believe I can bring people together to do it. Not bad, perhaps, and appropriately sentimental—but not clear enough. McCain, at least, answered the question directly, but proceeded to unwind in several directions at once:

I want to inspire a generation of Americans to serve a cause greater than their self-interest. I believe that America's best days are ahead of us, but I also believe that we face enormous challenges, both national security and domestic, as we have found out in the last few days in the case of Georgia.

And I want to be - make sure that everybody understands that this is a time to come together. Throughout my life from the time I was 17 and raised my hand and was sworn in as a midshipman at the United States Naval Academy, I've always put my country first. I put my country first when I had the honor of serving in the military, and I had the honor of serving my - putting my country first as a member of the House of Representatives and then the United States Senate.

America wants hope. America wants optimism. America wants us to sit down together. I have a record of reaching across the aisle and working with the other party, and I want to do that, and I believe, as I said, that Americans feel it is time for us to put our country first.

And we may disagree on a specific issue—and I won't reveal them now...

(LAUGHTER)

… but I want every American to know that when I go to Gee's Bend, Alabama, and meet the African-American women there who are so wonderful and lovely, an experience I'll never forget, and when I go to places where I know they probably won't vote for me, I know that my job is to tell them that I'll be the president of every American and I'll always put my country first.[47]

It was one of the few weak moments during McCain's Saddleback appearance. McCain had essentially said: I want to inspire Americans to serve the country, because that's what I will do. But much of his accompanying commentary—his references to hope, his promise to reach out across partisan divides—was similar to what Obama had said. And neither man had given an explanation specific to the office of President; their answers could just as easily have described their reasons for being in the Senate.

Obama, at least, had the driving ambition to *be* president—an overt, rather premature ambition, one that a more critical press corps, not yet divorced from its ironic sensibilities or its obsession with race, might have mocked. But McCain lacked that focus, as well as the friendly reception of a media virtually *willing* their candidate to become the president. His very slogan in the general election—"Country First"—contrasted McCain's biography and his policies with Obama's, but it also abstracted from the candidate himself. (It was, at least, far better than his unwieldy slogan during the primaries: "Courageous Service. Experienced Leadership. Bold Solutions.") Neither McCain nor his staff could explain to voters why they should want *him* as their president. And the result was that even when Obama was losing policy debates or catching up to McCain's superior positions on a variety of issues, Obama still seemed to be setting the agenda of the election. Try though McCain might, his rhetoric remained largely "reactive," not "proactive"—always behind events, never creating them.

Part of the problem for McCain was also simply that Obama's message of "change" was so compelling. Democratic nominee Michael Dukakis, the former governor of Massachusetts, had used a similar refrain in 1988, to no good effect. But in 2008, voters were inclined to believe it, partly because Obama seemed to personify change in his very being. McCain's life story was one that voters had to know, or learn, in order to like; Obama's appeal was readily apparent. He would be the first African-American president, just as Hillary Clinton would have been the first female president; McCain offered none of those obvious "firsts," except that he would have been the first Vietnam combat veteran to be president (and Vietnam may be the one major American conflict never to be represented by a combat veteran in the Oval Office, a sign of Americans' continuing discomfort with it).

McCain's counter-offer of "reform" lacked the same punch as "change." He had a history, unlike his opponent, of pushing real change through Congress. But he soon found out that he could not "out-Obama" Obama himself. And to emphasize the themes of continuity and experience—the typical election-year response to offers of "change"—was unthinkable in a year when Clinton had just lost the Democratic primary on the same argument, and when both President Bush and Congress were suffering the lowest approval ratings in recent memory.

Even McCain's difficulty in describing exactly why he ought to be president could have been overcome if McCain had been able to articulate a coherent vision of the future. His attempt, in a speech in May 2008, to describe what life would look like after his first term was an effort at painting such a picture[48]—and, at least one critic suggested, hinting that he would only serve one term (a claim McCain denied).[49] But it was not a coherent, cohesive vision of America: it was merely a list of "what I would hope to have achieved at the end of my first term as President." It lacked the visionary element that ran through Obama's promises of change, vacuous though they were. What *kind* of America did John McCain want to live in? He seemed not to have an answer—at least not one that saw the forest instead of just the trees.

McCain seemed unable to capture or counter the spirit of a "movement" that Obama had excited. Every time he won a primary, he had the entire nation's attention—unfiltered by the media analysis that would invariably spin his words against him—and yet he seemed unable to hold that attention. All of the right *ideas* were there in his speeches—he supported the right policies, thanked the right people, made the right noises about victory and humility, about the challenges America faced and the ability of Americans to overcome. Most of all, McCain—unlike any other candidate—portrayed America as a successful and hopeful place, whereas most of the others, including Obama, described a country in desperate circumstances.

Yet McCain's delivery was lacking—and not because he was a poor speaker, as many seemed eager to declare. Rather, he was being given speeches that simply did not fit his character, or what he offered to America. Instead of "Straight Talk," his speeches often seemed overly flowery, as if he were trying to compete with Obama for attention. The sentences he was given to read were simply too long, for example, and too ambitiously literary for his speaking style. Every time he appeared on television, it seemed, he failed to seize the opportunity to tell Americans who he really was, what his victory meant, what they could expect from him and from their own future.

Behind the scenes, the McCain campaign was wracked by internal battles, as well as the fear—far beyond ordinary prudence—of making a mistake. Some of the campaign's best employees had even been fired for reasons having nothing to do with their performance. One such was Soren Dayton, the brilliant blogger and founder of TheNextRight.com, who was let go after he sent his friends a link—via the Twitter message service—to a YouTube video featuring Obama's incendiary pastor, Jeremiah Wright. Fearful of charges that it was inflaming the Wright controversy, the campaign told Dayton to leave. There was also a curious lack of curiosity about Obama. Few copies of his books were on hand at McCain headquarters, and some staffers seemed almost uninterested in knowing what they could about their candidate or their opponent. The Republican National Committee had been tasked with doing such "opposition research," but there was little interest in making the most of the information. Bloggers outside the campaign seemed to know more about what was going on inside of it than many of the staff and volunteers putting in fourteen-hour days. And there was a constant, palpable tension among various leaders within the organization—one not spoken about during working hours, but known to all.

Tension is a normal part of political campaigns. There are all sorts of rivalries that emerge—from policy differences to competing ambitions among employees hoping to secure the best post possible after the election. But in the McCain campaign, that tension seemed to indicate a far deeper ambivalence about how to run, and how to win. The maverick who could lead Congress to compromise on difficult issues seemed reluctant to lead his chief staffers to agree with or even speak to each other.[50] True, it is easier to lament the flaws of a losing campaign than a successful one; had McCain won, few would have celebrated Obama's effort in the glowing terms that have now been reserved for it in American political history. And McCain seemed to be doing his best. But though the wheels had not quite come off the "Straight Talk Express," as Obama liked to say, perhaps there were one too many backseat drivers.

McCain also had trouble uniting his party. While the Republican primary had not been as acrimonious, as costly or as long as the Clinton-Obama fight, old grievances against McCain among conservatives continued to surface. McCain had won more votes by the end, but other candidates—Mike Huckabee, Mitt Romney and even Ron Paul—seemed to have won far more enthusiasm. Conservative commentators opposed to McCain's liberal stance on immigration, for example, mocked him as "McAmnesty." When McCain launched his policy on climate change, which included an ambitious set of market-oriented policies more ambitious than anything any presidential nominee from either party had ever proposed before, liberal voters seemed uninterested and conservative Republicans reacted with derision. Some of these conservatives would be rallied, much later in the campaign, by McCain's selection of Alaska Governor Sarah Palin as his running mate. But until then, there was a sense that McCain had not managed to unify or even interest the Republican base.

Perhaps the tactical ambivalence of McCain's campaign reflected his personal ambivalence as a political leader. He seemed, at times, unsure whether he was an independent-minded leader acting on the basis of self-informed principles, or an opportunist who triangulated against his own party so successfully that he could not hope to lead it effectively into a bruising contest with the other side. In some ways McCain showed evidence of both tendencies: he was his own man on the issues that he knew best, but he was prepared, in other circumstances, to take stances in opposition to his own party largely for the sake of reaching out to Democrats. That ambivalence, far from building reliable support among moderates, actually undercut McCain's support among members of both parties, and would hurt him by November, when his long-touted appeal among independents would be of little avail.

As such, and despite a silent yet strong undercurrent of popular enthusiasm for McCain, he often seemed a man apart, fighting the campaign on his own. He could count on the support and enthusiasm of his family and a few die-hard loyalists, but many of his aides had abandoned him when the campaign seemed near failure in 2007. Others left because of well-publicized conflicts between his various strategists in which close associates had taken sides. Some of the losers in these internal battles left behind the man for whom they had worked for many years to sit out the contest on the sidelines. Many of those who subsequently came to the campaign to take their place had their own careers on the outside, and their own agendas. McCain was no doubt grateful for their help, but he very likely had to accept it without too many reservations, whereas their commitment to the cause was often somewhat conditional. In contrast, it was clear Obama's team was fiercely loyal to him. Many of them had been with him from the start of his campaign, and they were more willing both to take direction from him and to give their utmost to the cause to see him win. Obama's campaign was not perfect, and also suffered some degree of internal conflict, as every campaign must. But he could, at least, rely entirely on "Obama people"; McCain's people had "people" of their own.

There were constant debates among McCain's strategists, as well as among newspaper columnists and widely-read bloggers, about how McCain should position himself in the election. These led to various different slogans, advertisements, postures and positions. But the truth was that McCain was best when he felt he could be himself—when he was unscripted, shorn of the baggage of the party and the campaign and simply speaking to ordinary people. McCain's speech to the Republican National Convention in St. Paul, Minnesota upon formally receiving his party's nomination was watched by 38.9 million people, more than had watched Obama's acceptance speech at the Democratic National Convention the week before.[51] Yet the very best speech of his campaign was not written by any of McCain's trusted scribes, but was improvised by the man himself as he stood before tens of thousands of bikers at a motorcycle rally in Sturgis, South Dakota. Hearing the sound of the engines, McCain quipped: "As you may know, not long ago, a couple of hundred thousand Berliners made a lot of noise for my opponent. I'll take the roar of fifty thousand Harleys any day! Any day, my friends! This is my first time here, but I recognize that sound: it's the sound of freedom, and thank you for it!"[52] It was a noteable moment, not only for its spontaneity, but for what McCain was able to express about the fundamental difference between him and his opponent: his opponent was articulate about America's flaws, but McCain understood and expressed what Americans valued about freedom. And the bikers revved their engines in unison for the old fighter pilot.[53]

Meanwhile, Obama had no trouble attracting celebrities everywhere he went—whether the A-list of the present day or B-list has-beens looking to revitalize their careers. His policy team also seemed to add to its roster of luminaries every day, drawing in new support from the halls of academia, the political world, and the media—even from conservatives and Republicans. Again, McCain seemed to be running alone. There were, in fact celebrities willing to endorse him publicly. But the campaign decided to cancel a celebrity ad campaign in the wake of its highly successful "Celebrity" ad (see chapter 5) attacking Obama for being a candidate of hype rather than hope, similar to other Hollywood personalities more "famous for being famous" than for their achievements. McCain was left to soldier on with a skeleton crew traveling with him on the "Straight Talk Express" and the campaign airplane. He was able, and devoted, and confident, but outnumbered. He was, for much of the 2008 campaign, fighting alone.

Winning the Battles, Losing the War

As the campaign wore on, McCain continued to beat Obama and the Democrats on issue after issue. Though Obama continued to press for a rapid withdrawal from Iraq, for example, it was clear by the middle of 2008 that McCain had been right about the "surge." Civilian deaths among Iraqis declined as cooperation increased between local factions and Iraqi police, bolstered by the presence of additional American troops. American military casualties also decreased as members of the various armed groups opposed to the U.S. presence were defeated, demoralized or convinced to switch sides. Obama still refused—beyond reason—to acknowledge that the "surge" had worked, never retracting his call for speedy withdrawal even after taking office. His stubborn stance began to undermine his credibility on foreign policy and his attempts to caricature McCain as a warmonger began to backfire, even as his own willingness to negotiate with extreme, dictatorial regimes became an easy target for criticism.[54]

McCain had also prevailed against Obama and Clinton soundly on the issue of free trade. It was surprising to see Clinton, whose husband had crafted several free-trade agreements and who had once been supportive of free trade, falling into line behind the protectionist stance of labor unions and the new, left consensus in the Democratic Party. It was less surprising to see Obama in the anti-trade camp. He had voted against every single free trade agreement to come to the floor during his time in the Senate, except for a free trade agreement with the Sultanate of Oman, which ranks among the least important American trading partners. Even in his dramatic speech at the 2004 Democratic National Convention, Obama had attacked the business practice of "outsourcing" jobs to offshore companies in developing countries—a free trade in services that hurt some American workers in the short term but benefited the economy as a whole, and which created more jobs in the long term.

Similarly, Obama's repeated opposition to NAFTA and other treaties was a source of alarm to America's trading partners, including Canada. When Obama suggested renegotiating NAFTA, Canada's conservative prime minister Stephen Harper cautioned: "If any American government ever chose to make the mistake of opening that, we would have something we would want to talk about as well."[55] Later, Obama adviser Austan Goolsbee quietly informed Canada that Obama was only talking up protectionism for the sake of campaign rhetoric and that he would later reverse his policies.[56] When the revelation was leaked to the media, it proved a huge embarrassment to Obama's campaign—one that the Clinton campaign sought to capitalize upon. Meanwhile McCain remained steadfast in his support for free trade policies. He pointed out that America's troubled economy was largely being kept afloat by a booming export sector, and that his opponent's proposals would shut down the only part of the economy that was working. In time, Obama would seek to soften his stance, saying that he wanted to make free trade into "fair" trade. It was only one of many issues on which Obama had to concede the substance of the issue to his rival, though he never allowed himself to do so explicitly.

As fuel prices rose to record highs over the summer, only McCain seemed to have solutions. One of them was a federal gas tax "holiday," a temporary suspension of the 18.4-cent surcharge on each gallon of gas pumped by Americans, whose proceeds went to highway maintenance and construction.[57] Clinton immediately seized the idea and adopted it as her own. McCain knew it was only a short-term solution, but it would have at least some effect on lowering prices at the pump. Obama dismissed the idea as a "gimmick,"[58] though he had once voted for a similar measure in the Illinois legislature.[59] He also attacked McCain's newfound support for offshore oil drilling. The Arizona senator had once opposed offshore drilling, and still opposed drilling in the Arctic National Wildlife Refuge, but reversed his position. This was not a "flip-flop," McCain insisted: it was a logical response to changing facts. It was also the politically smart response, since both of McCain's opponents had opposed offshore drilling in the face of overwhelming public support for it. McCain also supported investment in alternative energy sources, and proposed a new federal competition to design a new battery for electric cars that would be more efficient than the hybrid engines currently on the market. Obama's response seemed weak; he suggested that Americans inflate their tires properly rather than search for oil on the outer continental shelf, for example. But Obama soon backtracked, caving in on offshore drilling after it was clear McCain had taken the lead on the issue.

The public trusted McCain's policy answers to the most pressing challenges facing the country. Yet they still seemed to have greater faith in Obama as a candidate: he led steadily through July with a lead of roughly 3 to 6 percentage points in national polls. That was partly a function of his favorable media coverage, his personal charisma and the effectiveness of his campaign. But it was also perhaps a sign that some Americans were losing faith in the principles underlying McCain's policies. The benefits of free trade, for example, were great—but diffuse. The costs, on the other hand, were often direct and concentrated, and easy to exaggerate in the media. The same held true for the free market, which people began to lose faith in—at least as a general principle—as stock prices, which had risen fairly steadily for an entire generation, began to stagnate and wobble. For all his talk of hope, Obama spent much time on the hustings blasting the free market and the economic policies of the Bush years, which he claimed had produced America's new-found economic problems. His message hit home with many Americans, who suddenly doubted the basic principles that had propelled the United States to global economic and political leadership in the twentieth and into the twenty-first centuries.

Americans had also traditionally backed presidential candidates with strong, security-conscious foreign policies, almost without exception. But in the aftermath of the Iraq debacle, which had not only cost thousands of American lives but also convinced some Americans that the rest of the world hated the United States, many people began to doubt the ability of American forces to carry out a tough policy towards rogue states, as well as the desirability of doing so. The tactic of confronting, isolating and defeating terror and its sponsors began to yield in public debate to other alternatives rarely seen in mainstream American political discourse. At the height of the cold war, Lyndon Johnson could mock his presidential rival Barry Goldwater by exaggerating his bellicosity (as he did to explosive effect in the infamous "Daisy" television ad), but he would never have thought to highlight his own (hypothetical) willingness to negotiate with the Soviet premier without preconditions as a selling point to the American electorate.

The 2008 election marked a turning point—a moment at which a foreign policy with many features of "appeasement" no longer seemed immediately objectionable to millions of Americans. It was a difficult time—a time when the leaders of the United States had stepped back from the shadow of their own unpopularity, when there were few to speak to the steadfast values and virtues that had made America an exceptional success in a world of stagnation, weakness and doubt. It was a time when a generation came of voting age that had grown up entirely beyond the memory of the Cold War and largely ignorant of the dangers of communism and the pitfalls of centralized planning. It was a time when America's politicians had made so many mistakes, and explained them so poorly, that many ordinary people began to lose faith in uniquely American values. And Obama offered the people hope—not ordinary hope, but the hope attached to despair, the kind of millennial hope that accompanies frustration. McCain felt Americans' pain, but Obama felt their anger. He empathized with it, and channeled it into his campaign, fanning it to a steady flame.

And McCain, who had already been castigated in the press and attacked by Obama for his mythical temper, failed to fight back when the chance presented itself. "If John McCain wants to have a debate about who has the temperament, and judgment, to serve as the next Commander-in-Chief, that's a debate I'm ready to have," Obama said often on the campaign trail, and in his acceptance speech at the Democratic National Convention, to little protest from his rival.[60] When on the defensive, McCain often failed to stand up for himself and for his policies when he was viciously and unfairly attacked. He seemed to want to avoid tit-for-tat politics at all costs, often—though not always—letting attacks by Obama slide. He also anticipated, correctly, that his attempts to respond would be judged more harshly than Obama's initial criticisms. But he failed to find a better way—to find *any* way—of responding on most occasions, much to the visible and at times vocal frustration of his supporters, who were sometimes stymied by McCain's equanimity and apparent passivity.[61] Until very late in the campaign, McCain did not attempt to tie Obama to the inept and disappointing congressional leadership of Pelosi and Reid the way Obama had linked him with Bush—with far less justification, since McCain could at least point to significant areas of disagreement with the president, while Obama had marched almost uniformly in lockstep with his party.

McCain did launch several negative attacks at Obama, one describing his relationship with former terrorist William Ayers, one linking him to Fannie Mae and Freddie Mac executives, and another attacking Obama's position on sex education for kindergarteners. The latter was considered out of bounds by many commentators—including former Bush strategist Karl Rove.[62] But McCain refused to pounce on the easiest target of all: the controversy surrounding Jeremiah Wright and Trinity United Church of Christ, Obama's place of worship for two decades. McCain's decision was based on principled as well as tactical grounds. He wanted the campaign to be about matters larger than personal associations. Moreover, he did not want to make an issue out of race in the country's first election featuring a black nominee, nor encounter a potential backlash among voters tired of negative politics (from the Republican side, anyway). But Obama himself had said that the Wright issue was "fair game"—perhaps hoping to bait McCain into attacking it, but fair game nonetheless.[63] And McCain could have made the debate into one about Obama's credibility—since he had been less than forthcoming about his knowledge of Wright's opinions—rather than the substance of Wright's views. Still, he resisted exploiting the Wright uproar, and told the North Carolina Republicans to stop using an ad that used the Wright-Obama connection to tarnish a local Democratic candidate, saying they were "out of touch with reality."[64] McCain's attempt to restrain his own party led to alarm among some conservatives, but he persisted with that restraint through the end of the election.

Another point McCain refused to press was Obama's lack of military service. Obama would be inheriting two wars, but had never shown the slightest interest in the military or even in national security issues beyond registering for the Selective Service (as required by law)—not even the crude form of interest that is implied in draft-dodging or conscientious objection. In response to public criticism of his failure to serve, Obama claimed that he had considered serving but that there had been no military conflict at the age when he had been eligible to enlist.[65] However, he certainly would have been eligible to serve in the Gulf War in 1991. In any case, conflict was certainly no prerequisite to service. What Obama was really admitting was that he felt no pressing motivation to join the armed forces, of which he was now hoping to become commander-in-chief. Yet McCain resisted the urge to attack Obama on this point, perhaps because he did not wish to politicize military service, reignite the culture wars of the 1960s, nor alienate the millions of Americans who had not served themselves.

All of these strategic choices were, to some extent, dictated by McCain's embrace of the prevailing hypothesis about moderate voters. To win, he had to reach the middle. And to do that, he had to avoid the political backlash that would surely result if he were perceived as overly conservative or as making use of racial divisions. He knew that Democrats would cast these accusations at him anyway, but he did not want to give them extra ammunition. In the fall, as Election Day drew closer, McCain did attack Obama's association with Ayers directly, but only reluctantly: he avoided mentioning it in the second presidential debate, for instance, disappointing some of his supporters—and perhaps Obama as well, who clearly seemed to have expected just such an attack. And what was most alarming of all to the conservative base of the party was that McCain—and many of his Republican allies in Congress—seemed prepared to yield to their rivals on fundamental matters of economic and political principle.

Meanwhile, the Obama campaign and the media refused to offer the same deference to McCain when it came to his age. Obama claimed on occasion that McCain was "losing his bearings,"[66] which McCain supporters took as an indirect disparagement of the 72-year-old candidate. Late-night comedians such as David Letterman also pounded McCain for his age; it became the staple of political humor for much of the campaign. Craig Ferguson, host of *The Late Late Show* on CBS, appeared on ABC's *The View* when Cindy McCain was featured as a guest host, and asked her to suggest some new joke ideas: "He's old—that's all we got... On behalf of the late night performers of America, if you could give us something, like maybe some inappropriate behavior somewhere, *something* we can work with...".[67] Few other comedians were as candid about their approach to McCain's candidacy.

While McCain refused to make political issues out of some of his rival's weaknesses, Obama rarely missed an opportunity to press home the advantage. He and his supporters portrayed McCain as a warmonger, based on a single comment he had made at a town hall meeting in which he had suggested that the U.S. might maintain a long-term presence in Iraq as it had elsewhere (see above). Similarly, Obama plucked a McCain quote about the economy in which McCain had said—correctly—that America experienced a long period of economic growth during the Bush presidency, but in which McCain also lamented the economic challenges facing American families. Obama distorted these remarks to claim that McCain was out of touch with Americans' worries about the economy. He hammered home the attack throughout the summer, renewing it with vigor during the financial crisis that struck in the fall. Worst, perhaps, Obama referred constantly—if obliquely—to tabloid-worthy rumors about McCain's temper. Obama even cited a joke McCain had once told at a town hall meeting: when asked about his Iran policy, McCain sang, to the tune of "Barbara Ann" by the Beach Boys: "Bomb, bomb, bomb, bomb bomb Iran."[68] The song had clearly been intended in jest, but Obama and his supporters referred to it as further evidence of McCain's lack of "temperament."

When McCain declined to return fire, Obama goaded him, suggesting none-too-subtly that McCain was afraid of taking him on: "[W]e've been seeing some pretty over-the-top attacks coming out of the McCain campaign over the last several days that he wasn't willing to say it to my face," Obama said.[69] Such machismo had been a feature of Obama's campaign since the primary, when he had once performed knife-digging gestures to describe Clinton's tactics.[70] His campaign had also deliberately staged its rally to celebrate winning the Democratic nomination in St. Paul, Minnesota, at the very stadium where the Republicans were to have their convention. It was an act clearly intended to project defiance and provoke the opposition. Ironically, though Obama constantly reiterated his willingness to debate McCain about "temperament" and other issues, Obama had refused McCain's offer of ten town hall meetings over the summer of 2008.

McCain generally had the better of the arguments on the issues—a reality that became clear as Obama constantly shifted his position in response to the Republican's own. Moreover, Obama was often weak when actually confronted with real adversity and opposition, whether on rare occasions from the press, or from his opponents. But McCain seemed uninterested, at times, in finding a convincing or committed response to all of Obama's charges against him. He seemed, to some supporters, not to have the will to fight back. He insisted on running a better sort of campaign—or one, at least, that would play to his strengths by focusing on actual issues, values and experiences.

But now the media was singing to Obama's tune. McCain could no longer count on any favored treatment from his former journalistic admirers. When the *New York Times* ran a front-page article implying that McCain had enjoyed an inappropriate and romantic relationship with a lobbyist—which he strongly denied—it was clear the media's fascination with

McCain had been eclipsed.[71] Paradoxically, the article may have helped McCain shore up conservative support: such was the mistrust of the *New York Times* on the right that the attack on McCain rallied Republicans to his side. As the campaign continued, the media showed little interest in comparing the records and policies of the two major candidates. Personality and persona became the only issues in the election, though it was only a few years since liberal columnists like the *New Yorker*'s Hendrik Hertzberg had bemoaned the electorate's obsession with "personality" in apparently favoring George W. Bush over Al Gore.[72]

When on offense, the McCain campaign excelled at highlighting many of Obama's weaknesses—especially once the general election campaign got under way, and hard-hitting strategist Steve Schmidt took over most of the daily management of the campaign. But the campaign still struggled to define McCain himself. One episode, the infamous "green screen" speech, told the whole story. On the day Obama clinched his party's nomination with a final victory in the Montana caucuses (though he lost the South Dakota contest to Clinton the same day), McCain gave a speech in New Orleans that would be his first opportunity to address the nation on the eve of the general election, and a chance to steal some of Obama's limelight besides. The speech was well written, the ideas solid, the new slogan—"Reform. Prosperity. Peace."—catchy enough. But McCain looked terribly uncomfortable in the hot and humid room on a late spring Louisiana evening. The building was filled to capacity, with people apparently still waiting outside. Yet somehow—whether for structural reasons, or simply because of the way the seats had been arranged—the crowd still appeared small compared to Obama's audience in St. Paul that evening. When he began to speak, McCain was already sweating—and because of his disability, he struggled to wipe his brow. His face glistening from the strain, he read from the TelePrompTer with difficulty, delivering the words jerkily and awkwardly.

But worst of all was the background behind McCain—a green screen, instead of the usual blue and yellow colors McCain had used in the primary. The hope evidently had been to highlight McCain's reformist credentials with a new color not typically used by either party. But there was a severe problem: just as Hollywood cinematographers film actors against green backgrounds so as to crop their images later and fill in the background with special effects, so, too, McCain's "green screen" allowed home video editors to substitute backgrounds of their choice behind the candidate. The green screen became an instant Internet and late-night chat show joke, with a variety of backgrounds—from safari images to hard-core pornography—filling in behind the Republican candidate.

The episode symbolized the technological superiority of the Obama campaign effort. And it also highlighted McCain's difficulty in communicating his message past the filter of the media and the left-wing "netroots." If Obama was a "blank slate" onto which voters could project their hopes, McCain was manipulated into becoming a blank screen onto which they could project their worst fears and hatred. McCain could fight—hard. He would deliver his "Straight Talk" with unfailing energy and enthusiasm. But from that point on, it was uncertain whether anyone in America would listen.

4

The Obama Insurgency

The Revolutionary Candidate

By 2007, one presidential candidate had come from rela-
tive obscurity to take the American political world by storm.
He had established a massive Internet presence, using social
networking technology and a battery of blogs to reach thousands of eager activists across the country. Through a focused, issue-oriented campaign, centered around opposition
to the Iraq War, he captured the imagination and enthusiasm
of America's youth. His volunteers were a ubiquitous presence on college campuses. His logo was everywhere. He won
every Internet poll, taking even seasoned analysts by surprise.
And he was confident of victory, despite low polling numbers
in the initial primary states.

What was even more impressive were his fundraising
numbers. In a matter of a few short months he had leapt
ahead of every other candidate in his party,[1] and received
large contributions from members of the military on active
duty, despite his anti-war stance.[2] He suddenly had the political war chest to mount a serious challenge for his party's
nomination—perhaps enough to take on and defeat the party
insiders and their pre-existing organizations. In speeches and
debates, he began making an impact on voters and attracting
support from members of both parties. He sparked controversy but also hope with his promises of a revolutionary
change in American politics.

That candidate was not Barack Obama. It was Republican
congressman Ron Paul of Texas, a former libertarian candidate for president who shook the foundations of his party in
the months leading up to the 2008 primaries. He was the first

truly "online" candidate. In the end, his massive fundraising effort, his Internet support and his armies of activists did not translate into actual votes—though he did very nearly win the Nevada Republican caucus before the determined (and unfair, some claimed) intervention of the party leadership.[3] As his defeat became inevitable, Paul disappeared from the campaign trail to return home to his congressional district, where—in contrast to the wild expectations of his supporters—he had prepared a contingency plan and filed papers to run for re-election. He ended his campaign much as he had started it: as a media phenomenon, missed by only his most devoted followers and admirers.

Why did Obama succeed where Paul had failed? In some respects, Obama had been able to benefit from a double standard. Though Paul enjoyed some sympathy from the media—especially from journalists who enjoyed the spectacle of a Republican excoriating his own party and president on the Iraq War and other matters—he still had a harder hill to climb. He was a conservative, first of all, and there was nothing "historic" about his candidacy aside from the tools he was using to pursue it. In addition, as the primaries began, some of Paul's old newsletters were unearthed that revealed racist opinions about blacks as well as bigotry towards gays and hostility towards Israel.[4] As CNN described their contents:

> The controversial newsletters include rants against the Israeli lobby, gays, AIDS victims and Martin Luther King Jr.—described as a "pro-Communist philanderer." One newsletter, from June 1992, right after the LA riots, says "order was only restored in L.A. when it came time for the blacks to pick up their welfare checks."

> Another says, "The criminals who terrorize our cities—in riots and on every non-riot day—are not exclusively young black males, but they largely are. As children, they are trained to hate whites, to believe that white oppression is responsible for all black ills, to 'fight the power,' to steal and loot as much money from the white enemy as possible."

110

In some excerpts, the reader may be led to believe the words are indeed from Paul, a resident of Lake Jackson, Texas. In the "Ron Paul Political Report" from October 1992, the writer describes carjacking as the "hip-hop thing to do among the urban youth who play unsuspecting whites like pianos."

The author then offers advice from others on how to avoid being carjacked, including "an ex-cop I know," and says, "I frankly don't know what to make of such advice, but even in my little town of Lake Jackson, Texas, I've urged everyone in my family to know how to use a gun in self defense. For the animals are coming."[5]

Despite Paul's vigorous denials and disavowals, these views all but ended the left-wing romance with his campaign. Such views were tolerated, oddly, when they came from Obama, whose first memoir, *Dreams from My Father*, was filled with racial innuendo. As the right-wing columnist Ann Coulter complained:

When his mother expresses concern about Obama's high school friend being busted for drugs, Obama says he patted his mother's hand and told her not to worry.

This, too, prompted Obama to share with his readers a life lesson on how to handle white people: "It was usually an effective tactic, another one of those tricks I had learned: People were satisfied so long as you were courteous and smiled and made no sudden moves. They were more than satisfied, they were relieved—such a pleasant surprise to find a well-mannered young black man who didn't seem angry all the time."

First of all, I note that this technique seems to be the basis of Obama's entire presidential campaign. But moreover—he was talking about his own mother! As Obama says: "Any distinction between good and bad whites held negligible meaning." Say, do you think a white person who said that about blacks would be a leading presidential candidate?

In college, Obama explains to a girl why he was reading Joseph Conrad's 1902 classic, "Heart of Darkness": "I read the book to help me understand just what it is that makes white people so afraid. Their demons. The way ideas get twisted around. It helps me understand how people learn to hate."

111

By contrast, Malcolm X's autobiography "spoke" to Obama. One line in particular "stayed with me," he says. "He spoke of a wish he'd once had, the wish that the white blood that ran through him, there by an act of violence, might somehow be expunged."[6]

In addition, the media and the public—and McCain—were willing to absolve Obama of any association with the racist and anti-American views of his pastor, Jeremiah Wright. It is difficult to imagine any other candidate receiving such generous forgiveness, and Paul certainly did not.

But the main problem with Paul was not the racial double standard: it was the fact that unlike Obama, he was willing to stand up for concrete and controversial ideas. Paul was not merely a conservative, just as Obama was not merely a liberal. They both had extreme views of politics, economics and society—Paul on the right, Obama on the left. Obama carefully concealed his positions with centrist rhetoric and what the media praised as a "calm demeanor." But Paul made no secret of his opinions. His views on the Iraq War had made his reputation, but when voters learned of his enthusiasm for returning to the gold standard, and his opposition not just to the Iraq War and the Vietnam War but even the Korean War, they tended to look elsewhere. Paul was simply too up-front with his radicalism. He had left too long and too glaring a paper trail to hide—and he did not want to hide it. He saw his candidacy as a wonderful vehicle for his ideas as well as his personal celebrity.

The same problem had halted the earlier, left-wing campaigns of presidential hopeful Howard Dean in 2004 and Senate hopeful Ned Lamont in 2006. Both were fairly moderate men of means—Dean a physician, Lamont the heir to a vast fortune—who ran on anti-war platforms, and lost. Dean captured the imagination of the Democratic base but failed to win the Iowa caucus against John Kerry's superior organization.[7] He then undermined public confidence in his leadership with his infamous "scream" during his concession speech. Lamont had ousted incumbent Joe Lieberman in the

Democratic primary for U.S. Senate in Connecticut, aided by an Internet campaign that would later serve as a model for Obama's own, as well as a backlash among Democrats against Lieberman's support for Bush's foreign policies. But Lamont lost in the general election as Republicans crossed over to vote for Lieberman as an Independent and to keep their moderate and powerful senator in Washington.

Obama was far more radical in his views than either Dean or Lamont had been. Dean, for example, favored the death penalty in certain cases, opposed ambitious gun control laws, and backed market-oriented economic policies. He had been a member of the centrist Democratic Leadership Council, along with Lieberman and other "New Democrats," which had focused for years on separating the Democratic Party from the failed orthodoxies of the unions and the far left. (Perhaps his "scream" marked the moment where the façade of Dean's highly stylized radicalism finally collapsed.) But unlike Dean, Lamont and Ron Paul, Obama was careful to obscure many of his views. He had voted "present" 129 times in the Illinois legislature on controversial issues;[8] he had spent more than a decade as a senior lecturer at the University of Chicago Law School without publishing a single academic paper;[9] he had contrived to lose many of his past records, including his Illinois senate papers and his college thesis. He remained, in his own words, a "blank slate" and a universal symbol, a radical with a moderate way of presenting himself, able to avoid causing lasting offense or offer grounds for serious objection. He was the perfect candidate for the Internet age, and he was able to reach beyond its insular world.

Transforming Obama

Of all its remarkable achievements, the greatest success of the Obama campaign was the way it transformed a weak candidate—with little experience, few apparent policies, and undeniably extreme views—into a winner. Obama could give inspiring speeches—though it was often difficult to remember anything particular that he had said, so plain were his political bromides—but he had little else to offer besides potential. In his first campaign for political office in 1996, Obama won a seat in the Illinois state senate by disqualifying his rivals—including incumbent and mentor Alice Palmer—through challenges to their ballot signatures. The only fault with many of the signatures, obtained from residents of Chicago's impoverished South Side, was that they had been printed instead of signed in cursive writing.[10] In launching his signature challenges, Obama had law, if not justice, on his side. Viewed charitably, his move was an attempt to ensure the integrity of the primary election; viewed more cynically, it had more in common with the literacy tests once administered to black voters in the Jim Crow South to keep them from voting. Either way, it was hard-edged politics, the Chicago way, for the sole purpose of Obama's personal political advancement.

Once he arrived in Springfield, the Illinois state capital, Obama achieved little as a legislator until the Democratic machine, led by Illinois Senate president Emil Jones, Jr., decided to "make" him a U.S. senator.[11] Suddenly, he managed to sponsor twenty-six bills that passed into law in his final year in the state capital—an astonishing achievement made possible only because Obama's name was affixed to legislation that others had been working on. Once in Washington, he paid back his political patrons by requesting close to $1 billion in special appropriations—"earmarks," or "pork"—to be spent in their districts back home. Many of those appropriations were spent in the richest areas of the state, where Obama's wealthy contributors lived. Meanwhile, Axelrod—still working for the Daley operation in Chicago, even as he advised Obama—stepped forth to justify political wheeling and dealing as a better form of politics. Government in the style of trading votes for favors, Axelrod wrote in the *Chicago Tribune*, was not corruption, but in fact a "well-oiled machine."[12]

In three years in Washington, Obama had made no impact whatsoever on policy debates, nor had there been much evidence of his effort to do so. He failed to advance the issues he had promised to fight for, such as a middle class tax cut, which he had promised Illinois voters he would pursue in Washington; instead, he voted repeatedly—ninety-four times, according to the McCain campaign—to raise taxes.[13] He achieved little on his own, but had no trouble claiming credit for the work others had done. The *Washington Post*—in a rare departure from its overwhelmingly favorable coverage of Obama, though couched in an article also criticizing Clinton—noted how he had tried to steal the limelight on immigration reform from McCain and others who had actually worked on the legislation:

> After weeks of arduous negotiations, on April 6, 2006, a bipartisan group of senators burst out of the "President's Room," just off the Senate chamber, with a deal on new immigration policy.

> As the half-dozen senators—including John McCain (R-Ariz.) and Edward M. Kennedy (D-Mass.)—headed to announce their plan, they met Sen. Barack Obama (D-Ill.), who made a request common when Capitol Hill news conferences are in the offing: "Hey, guys, can I come along?" And when Obama went before the microphones, he was generous with his list of senators to congratulate—a list that included himself.

> "I want to cite Lindsey Graham, Sam Brownback, Mel Martinez, Ken Salazar, myself, Dick Durbin, Joe Lieberman . . . who've actually had to wake up early to try to hammer this stuff out," he said.

> To Senate staff members, who had been arriving for 7 a.m. negotiating sessions for weeks, it was a galling moment. Those morning sessions had attracted just three to four senators a side, Sen. Arlen Specter (R-Pa.) recalled, each deeply involved in the issue. Obama was not one of them...

> In 2007, after the first comprehensive immigration bill had died, the senators were back at it, and again, Obama was notably absent, staffers and senators said. At one meeting, three key negotiators recalled, he entered late and raised a number of questions about the bill's employment verification system. Kennedy and Specter both rebuked him, saying that the issue had already been resolved and that he was coming late to the discussion. Kennedy

115

dressed him down, according to witnesses, and Obama left shortly thereafter.

"Senator Obama came in late, brought up issues that had been hashed and rehashed," Specter recalled. "He didn't stay long."[14]

No major legislation bore Obama's name; he had taken no controversial stances, nor had he fought for any causes worth notice in his political or even during his legal career. As an attorney representing some of his more radical clients, such as ACORN, he had taken a back seat to other litigators, as he had done on most of his cases, rarely doing more in court than standing up and announcing his name before sitting down and letting others take over.[15] In his time in the state senate, his accomplishments on behalf of his Chicago constituents were minimal. He did support state subsidies to private developers—such as convicted felon "Tony" Rezko, one of Obama's main early fundraisers—to build public housing projects. But these were so poorly built, and fell into such disrepair, that residents suffered mice infestations and sewage backing up into their kitchens only a few years after the buildings had been completed.[16] Obama also obtained millions of dollars in state earmarks to contributors and supporters, including $100,000 for a garden planned by a former campaign volunteer.[17] The garden was never built, and Obama failed to follow up on what was done with the money. His record, viewed in comparison to more energetic and conscientious legislators, was one of self-dealing and neglect.

Adding to the problem was Obama's strange distance from the lives and lifestyles lived by most Americans. He had attended elite private schools for his entire educational career, though he refused to support school choice and voucher initiatives that would have given poor children in his South Side neighborhood the same opportunities. He moved straight from the offices of the *Harvard Law Review* to the rarified world of corporate law in Chicago. He was reluctant to participate in open displays of patriotism, refusing to wear a "flag pin" on his lapel:

> The truth is that right after 9/11, I had a pin. Shortly after 9/11, particularly because as we're talking about the Iraq war, that became a substitute for, I think, true patriotism, which is speaking out on issues that are of importance to our national security. I decided I won't wear that pin on my chest. Instead I'm going to try to tell the American people what I believe what will make this country great and hopefully that will be a testimony to my patriotism.[18]

He exhibited expensive tastes, making use of a 1,000-bottle wine cellar in his Chicago home,[19] and buying suits "off the rack" at the expensive Burberry designer store.[20] He attempted to empathize with the financial concerns of ordinary Americans by complaining about the price of "arugula"—a gourmet lettuce leaf many Americans had never heard of. He famously described rural American voters as "bitter," claiming that it was their alienation from contemporary life that made them "cling to" guns, religion, and conservative political views.[21]

Turning a man like Obama into a viable candidate for president was a great challenge. Even his supporters in the media worried whether Obama, for all his intellectual gifts, was simply "too liberal"—much like his predecessor in Illinois, Senator Adlai Stevenson, had been.[22] But Obama had a talent with the spoken word that few others could match. And in some respects, the making and rehabilitation of Obama was not so much a task of changing the man himself as changing his opponents. The Obama campaign succeeded in turning Hillary and Bill Clinton—once beloved by African-Americans—into racists. It succeeded in turning maverick John McCain into a clone of George W. Bush—or worse—in the eyes of American voters who had until very recently been inclined to admire and respect him.

Yet the real transformation was to take Obama's greatest weakness—his apparent lack of convictions—and turn it into his greatest strength. Through a combination of personal talent—key insight into national debates, a soaring rhetorical style and natural charisma, among other gifts—plus disciplined campaigning, Obama's blank slate became a national canvas—quite literally. He not only won followers, donors and volunteers but inspired a vast and creative iconography: YouTube videos based on his speeches; colorful propaganda posters in the "Big Brother" or communist-chic style; even chants, songs and marches by youth groups and gospel choirs.

Obama also had a feeling for movement politics, and Americans' nostalgia for the consummate political experiences of the 1960s that many had experienced but many others had only discovered through pop culture and public education. Obama had not actually lived through the civil rights or anti-war movements of the time. He had come of age in the 1980s, when young left-wing Americans reached back to the 1960s or across the ocean to the South African anti-apartheid movement for inspiration. He knew the passion and the rhythm of these movements, if only by proxy. He knew he could not re-create them—but he could re-create their spirit, at least as they appeared in the American imagination. And he knew there was an entire generation of Americans who shared his nostalgia, who were ready to accompany him on a journey to Washington that they had only seen on black-and-white film, and who were eager to cast themselves in a new sequel, with him in the principal role. He offered us something we eagerly craved, and which no other candidate could: the thrilling illusion of authenticity.

A New Faith

Candidate Obama as a "blank slate" would not have been as formidable had he not succeeded in projecting himself as a symbol of so many other things. He was both black and white—though he had, by his own admission, spent much of his adult life exploring the former side of his identity. He was born a Muslim, became an atheist and then converted to

118

Christianity; later, he sent his daughters to a Jewish nursery school.[23] He had worked as both a community organizer and a corporate lawyer; he had grown up in Hawaii in the outer orbit of American life, then rapidly climbed the inner circles of elite urban American society. He represented, and stood for, everything in general, and yet nothing in particular.

These were merely the superficial markings of the man. But Obama was always able to infuse them with associations and ideas that Americans would recognize. He was constantly aware of how best to tie the various elements of his personal and political background together in his rhetoric. He did not always succeed: he occasionally spoke disparagingly or inaccurately about his white relatives, for example, calling his grandmother a "typical white person" on a Philadelphia radio show,[24] and mistakenly claiming that his grandfather had liberated Auschwitz (freed, in fact, by the Soviet Red Army; his grandfather had been among the Americans to liberate Buchenwald).[25] He also had few actual connections with his African family. One half-brother was found living in penury in the slums of Nairobi;[26] another newspaper reported that Obama had not fulfilled the promises he had made on a 2006 visit to contribute to the welfare of his father's native village;[27] and one of Obama's paternal aunts was discovered to be illegally living in the United States in public housing in Boston.[28] Yet despite these occasional hints of confusion or inauthenticity, Obama understood that more and more Americans could relate to the experience of growing up with a patchwork of identities. And he could relate to the essential rootlessness of contemporary American life. McCain had lived an even more transient life as a military son and military father. Yet his movements were not rootless, but deeply grounded in a particular commitment to the country he served—a commitment not widely shared among the members of the nation's cosmopolitan elite. He was certainly a "modern" candidate, as evident in his enthusiasm for popular movies and rock 'n' roll, including the 1970s Swedish band Abba, which apparently topped his list of favorites on his iPod.[29] But McCain seemed unable to connect to the same "post-modern" sensibility, the same sense of rootless searching, that Obama shared with millions of young Americans.

At the same time, Obama was able to establish the palpable illusion of intimacy with the public—even in mass audiences. This was indeed a rare oratorical gift. Obama's best speech of the entire campaign was perhaps the one he delivered at a black church on the South Side of Chicago on Father's Day. Before speaking, Obama slumped in his chair, his hands folded awkwardly in his lap. After speaking, he swayed unevenly with the congregation to the rhythm of a gospel hymn. But when he spoke—when he *spoke*—he stood straight and his motions became fluid. His gestures melded with his voice. He did not quote extensively from the Bible, as one might have expected him to do in a sermon at a church, other than a quick reference to a passage from the Sermon on the Mount—hardly unusual or imaginative political fodder. There was also a deep if unintended irony in hearing a man who had left his two young daughters at home to campaign incessantly for two years preach to an enraptured audience about the importance of reading to one's children. But his words—or his speechwriter's words—went straight to what the audience *felt* and what they wanted to hear. And that was all that mattered. Even to a skeptical observer, the experience was impressive.

Perhaps Obama's most important rhetorical instinct was his sensitivity to conservative impulses. Despite his radical beliefs, Obama—like Bill Clinton before him—had developed the skill of listening to people from the other side of the political divide, and appearing to understand and empathize with them, without necessarily agreeing with them. It was a skill he had possessed for a long time. Speaking to an interviewer in 1990, when he had been elected the first black president of the *Harvard Law Review*, he said of his fellow students: "These are the people who will be running the country in some form or other when they graduate. If I'm talking to a white conservative who wants to dismantle the welfare state, he has the respect to listen to me and I to him. That's the biggest value of the *Harvard Law Review*. Ideas get fleshed out and there is no party line to follow."[30] It was a style he would continue to emulate throughout his political career. For example, he would often acknowledge conservative critiques of left-wing ideas and even admit their relevance. But he would not explain whether or how those ideas had changed his own—which, quite often, they had not.

His speeches and policies often appealed to that most poignant of conservative impulses—in style, if not in substance: nostalgia for a better past. It did not matter, to some admirers, that the past Obama sought to recover was built of left-wing policies such as the New Deal and counterculture fantasies about America rather than hard realities. He shared something of Bob Dylan—an artist who became a legend in his own right, but who had spent his early career imitating famous folk and country singers like Woody Guthrie and Hank Williams. People who heard Dylan loved the fact that they were hearing something familiar that managed, somehow, to sound new. And just as Dylan's inspirational songs were often elusive, or simply aggressive in their actual lyrical content, people ignored the substance of what he was saying and embraced him as a unique genius, a generational prophet.

Likewise, everything about Obama seemed to imitate a familiar part of American history—and quite self-consciously so. He launched his campaign at the Old State House in Springfield, Illinois, to draw comparisons with Abraham Lincoln; he timed his acceptance speech at the Democratic National Convention to coincide with the 45th anniversary of Martin Luther King, Jr.'s "I Have A Dream" speech in Washington. The press played along eagerly, with *Time* magazine (after the election) grafting Obama's face onto an old photograph of Franklin Delano Roosevelt on its cover for the week of November 24, 2008, and wondering whether Americans would get a "new New Deal." The Kennedy family chimed in with assurances that Obama represented the late John F. Kennedy's legacy.[31] And so on.

121

But perhaps the best parallel to Obama was William Jennings Bryan. For in Obama, the Democrats had found a candidate who, for the first time since Bryan, could articulate the simple language of faith. The content of Obama's faith remained elusive; unlike Bryan, Obama was not an actual religious leader, nor did he quote religious texts or beliefs with any familiarity or regularity. But he appealed to the messianic fervor of millenarian evangelical Christianity, just as Bryan had in his famous "Cross of Gold" speech to the Democratic National Convention in 1896. Obama evoked belief—not in any particular religion or set of values, nor even in America, but in himself, offering Americans the possibility of believing in *themselves* through him, too. It was an approach that some found distasteful—disparaging him as the "Obamessiah" or "The One," after the fictional lead character in the popular Matrix film trilogy—but which captured the imaginations of many others and inspired not merely support or loyalty, but devotion.

"Yes We Can"

There were, however, severe stumbles in Obama's campaign that would easily have toppled other presidential candidates. Some of his early policy positions, for example, were rather naïve: a promise to remove American missile defense systems in Europe and redirect the money towards domestic spending;[32] radical attacks on free trade agreements and their impact; commitments, in principle, to single-payer health care;[33] and drastic interventions for environmental problems such that the coal industry would go "bankrupt" if it built new plants.[34] Over time, Obama updated his policies, but refused to admit having done so. The press ordinarily grilled candidates over such intellectually dishonest maneuvering; not so, this time.

Some of Obama's more serious failures occurred when his campaign attempted to appropriate the iconography that had been produced by his most adoring supporters. In one infamous case, Obama spoke at a mayors' conference in June 2008 at a podium decorated with a faux presidential seal that had been remade in the campaign's blue-and-white colors and adorned with the Latin version of "Yes We Can," the campaign motto: "Vero Possumus." The campaign, apparently obsessed with the fear of racial prejudice, seemed to want voters to become used to seeing Obama in presidential mode, so that when they entered the privacy of the voting booth they would not yield to skepticism about the possibility that a black man could govern them. To that end, the campaign also put a mock presidential seal on the campaign website and marked some of the items Obama personally used—such as his seat on the campaign plane—with the label "President."[35] But the rest of the country, apparently not aware of its latent racial prejudices, saw the mock presidential seal as evidence of astounding hubris, and the tactic backfired. The seal was never used again at any Obama event.

Obama also seemed guilty of supreme overconfidence at times. He walked into a shocking defeat in the New Hampshire primary at the hands of a struggling Clinton campaign, delivering a speech at his concession rally that had clearly been meant for use in the event of victory. It was as if he and his campaign had refused to consider the possibility of losing. Obama also lost every other primary in a major state, save his home state of Illinois. In New York, California, Ohio, Pennsylvania and Florida (where neither candidate campaigned because the state had violated party rules by bringing the date of its primary forward), Clinton won the backing of the popular majority of Democrats. On each of these occasions, where Obama also seemed to have expected victory, his speeches sounded wooden. Rather than his usual charisma and confidence, he exuded discomfort, even frustration. He turned at sharp forty-five degree angles to face the TelePrompTer screens, using them as a crutch to muddle through the text; he furrowed his brow, intoning lines in steady anger that were meant to have been delivered in thunderous, inspiring tones.

Yet there was, by then, a self-correcting element in Obama's campaign—aside from the endless positive spin he enjoyed in the media: his supporters, who would adapt his message and respond to changing circumstances the way the campaign had sometimes failed to do. After the New Hampshire debacle, for instance, hip hop music star Will.I.Am of the Black-Eyed Peas took Obama's stiff, losing speech and used it as the lyrical background to a new folk-rock video entitled "Yes We Can" that featured other like-minded celebrities and became an overnight, overwhelming Internet sensation. (As of this writing it has gathered over 15 million full views on YouTube.)

The sensation did not end there. Hollywood celebrities embraced Obama as one of their own. Graphic artists created Obama posters. Bloggers created responses to Republican attacks and media criticisms. Republicans undertook similar efforts to support their own candidates, but these efforts were fewer in number and far weaker in effect. The mainstream media began paying attention. Soon, the Obama campaign began incorporating elements of what its supporters were doing, and giving them the tools to continue doing it. At the social networking website my.barackobama.com (with the unfortunate abbreviation "myBO.com"), for example, supporters could create their own blogs and advocate for Obama based on their own personal views, interests and opinions. They could, in effect, fill in the "blank slate" of Obama's character in whatever way they chose—a form of "microtargeting" in which the campaign did not have to identify groups of potentially sympathetic votes, but simply wait for supporters to do it on their own.

Obama's social networking technology created a vast amount of enthusiasm and cash—and also a set of highly contradictory messages that the campaign could not (or would not) control. A handful of the bloggers attracted by Obama, for example, were outright antisemites or far-left radicals who occasionally caused the campaign some embarrassment.[36] A few were removed or deleted from the site, but many more remained. With closer media scrutiny, Obama might have struggled to explain these views and why he had not instructed his campaign to monitor them more closely. But he was rarely ever taken to task for what his supporters said or did—a development that his technology team welcomed as a sign of the maturation of the media. It was true that there were instances of bloggers who opposed Obama using the site to attack his positions—a phenomenon that added credibility to the campaign's claim that they could not be expected to control the message. In any case, Obama was able to exploit the benefits of this method of campaigning without suffering the costs that a less forgiving media might have imposed. And the benefits were huge: not only did his online operation generate huge cash inflows, often several times the amount of expenditure on advertising, but it also gave his supporters a sense that they had a stake in the campaign and its success. People saw themselves in Obama, and saw his cause as their own, in a way not encountered before in contemporary American presidential politics.

Race and the Race

Another of Obama's strengths was race—though the campaign and the media, both domestic and international, obsessed about the possibility that it would prove a weakness. The America of 2008 was ready for a black president. It had been ready, in fact, for a very long time. Previous black candidates—Al Sharpton, Jesse Jackson, Carol Moseley-Braun—had tried, and failed, but they had all—like Ron Paul, Howard Dean and Ned Lamont—been up-front with their radicalism. And so a black candidate who was moderate or conservative may have had a chance in previous elections, had circumstances been different. The media aura that surrounded Obama never graced Condoleezza Rice or Colin Powell, for instance, who were both mooted as presidential contenders in their day, the latter quite seriously. What made Obama special was that he came from the left. That was his triumph, even if masking his ideological roots had been his dominant tactic. He made it seem that finally the left wing of the Democratic Party could overcome years of wandering in the intellectual and political wilderness. At last, it could transcend decades of having disappointed the hopes of African-Americans, whose cause the Democrats had purported to represent since the 1960s.

There were new opportunities for Obama to exploit in an increasingly multicultural America. Admittedly, there were old challenges to surmount as well. At the campaign's start, African-American scholar Shelby Steele wrote a book with the (retrospectively) unfortunate title: *A Bound Man: Why We Are Excited About Obama and Why He Can't Win.* Wrong in its ultimate predictions about the outcome of the presidential race, the book nonetheless contained several important insights. One was that Obama, like television star Oprah Winfrey (who became a prominent Obama supporter), was a black person who appealed to the white American majority partly because he was a racial "bargainer"—a man who offered reconciliation and redemption to whites for the lingering "original sin" of racism. Obama privately felt whites were typically prejudiced, or admitted his feelings to small groups of people and in intimate settings, but he did not openly question their lingering prejudices. Instead, he showed understanding towards their grievances, and offered them credit for their repentance and progress. Before black audiences, Steele observed, Obama often affected a different approach—that of the black "challenger," the man cast as the undying enemy of persistent white supremacy. Such was the philosophy of Obama's chosen church and pastor, a xenophobic and fatalistic approach to black identity that recycled endless feelings of victimization. In churches and before inner-city audiences, Obama also adopted "black" modes of speech (as white politicians often did as well, somewhat patronizingly), and offered the same cynical-yet-hopeful, tragic-comic view of the world in which history was destined to repeat its miseries, but hope and salvation could always come in a dazzling messianic moment. These were the contradictions of the man—a man who, like Steele, had been born to one white and one black parent, with one foot in either world and careful insights into the boundaries—and hence the identities—of both.

Steele's pessimistic prediction was that Obama would fall between the cracks and contradictions of these two roles and of his own complex racial identity, which naturally resisted such neat and mutually exclusive categories. His recommendation was that Obama simply be himself and transcend both the role of the "bargainer" and the "challenger." That, Steele claimed, was the only way Obama could win—but he doubted that he would. The day after Obama's victory, Steele acknowledged that he had been wrong about Obama's prospects, but credited Obama's "bargaining" approach for his victory:

> Obama's post-racial idealism told whites the one thing they most wanted to hear: America had essentially contained the evil of racism to the point at which it was no longer a serious barrier to black advancement. Thus, whites became enchanted enough with Obama to become his political base. It was Iowa—95% white—that made him a contender. Blacks came his way only after he won enough white voters to be a plausible candidate…
>
> But there is an inherent contradiction in all this. When whites—especially today's younger generation—proudly support Obama for his post-racialism, they unwittingly embrace race as their primary motivation. They think and act racially, not post-racially. The point is that a post-racial society is a bargainer's ploy: It seduces whites with a vision of their racial innocence precisely to coerce them into acting out of a racial motivation. A real post-racialist could not be bargained with and would not care about displaying or documenting his racial innocence. Such a person would evaluate Obama politically rather than culturally.
>
> Certainly things other than bargaining account for Obama's victory. He was a talented campaigner. He was reassuringly articulate on many issues—a quality that Americans now long for in a president. And, in these last weeks, he was clearly pushed over the top by the economic terrors that beset the nation. But it was the peculiar cultural manipulation of racial bargaining that

brought him to the political dance. It inflated him as a candidate, and it may well inflate him as a president.[37]

But there were moments in the campaign when Obama had been forced to confront his past role as a "challenger," when evidence of his radical past bubbled to the surface, as it did eventually in the controversy that erupted over Jeremiah Wright and Trinity United. Obama's response—a speech on racial reconciliation—incorporated both the "bargainer" and "challenger" roles. He acknowledged white fears, but asserted the importance of black grievances. That was enough to allow him to ride out the storm, but it did cause Obama some lingering political damage.

For much of the rest of the campaign, Obama had, as Steele noted, resorted to full-time "bargaining." But he did not simply abandon the "challenger" mode: he merely, and cleverly, re-shaped it. Instead of leading the attack, he left accusations of racism to his surrogates and subordinates, while he assumed the role of the victim. One frequent refrain was Obama's prediction—never realized—that he would be attacked by Republicans because of his race. At a fundraiser in June 2008, for example, he told his audience: "We know what kind of campaign they're going to run. They're going to try to make you afraid. They're going to try to make you afraid of me. He's young and inexperienced and he's got a funny name. And did I mention he's black?"[38] He had used the same tactics in the primary election, sending surrogates to pounce on every stray remark by Hillary or Bill Clinton that could possibly be construed as racist, from Hillary crediting Lyndon Johnson with the successes of the civil rights movement, to Bill calling the story of Obama's opposition to the Iraq War a "fairy tale," to Hillary noting the fact of her increasing support among white Americans. As *The New Republic*'s Sean Wilentz observed:

> A review of what actually happened shows that the charges that the Clintons played the "race card" were not simply false; they were deliberately manufactured by the Obama camp and trumpeted by a credulous and/or compliant press corps in order to

strip away her once formidable majority among black voters and to outrage affluent, college-educated white liberals as well as college students. The Clinton campaign, in fact, has not racialized the campaign, and never had any reason to do so. Rather the Obama campaign and its supporters, well-prepared to play the "race-baiter card" before the primaries began, launched it with a vengeance when Obama ran into dire straits after his losses in New Hampshire and Nevada—and thereby created a campaign myth that has turned into an incontrovertible truth among political pundits, reporters, and various Obama supporters.[39]

Much of America, at least outside the Democratic Party, rejected Obama's appeal to race. When he tried it in the general campaign, voters gave it little credit at all. But among Democrats, where identity politics had long been a staple of political debate, it was a crude yet brilliantly effective tactic.

The trick was to misconstrue remarks that Hillary and Bill Clinton had made such that if black voters weren't quite convinced that the Clintons were racist, they did at least believe Obama was being victimized, and swung solidly behind him in response. At Harvard Law School, one black female Hillary supporter explained why she had switched to Obama: "Clinton went a little crazy," she said. The implication was clear: Clinton had not committed a single act of racism, but the accusation itself was enough to warrant suspicion about her *thoughts*. Another student, a black woman who had until then guarded her political opinions closely, began wearing a "Women For Obama" button to class after racial controversies surrounded the Clintons. Cinque Henderson, another contributor to *The New Republic*, describing herself as one of the last black Clinton supporters, offered this account of Obama's victory in her home state of South Carolina:

> It's worth remembering that the majority of blacks still think O.J. Simpson is innocent. And, in times like these, when a black man is out front in the public eye, black people feel both proud and vulnerable and, as a result, scour the earth for evidence of racists plotting to bring him down, like an advance team ready to sound an alarm. Barack needed only a gesture, a quick sneer or nod in the direction of the Clintons' hidden racism to avail himself of the twisted love that rescued O.J. and others like him and

129

to smooth his path to victory, and, therefore, to salvage his candidacy. After Donna Brazile and James Clyburn started to cry racism, Barack was repeatedly asked his thoughts. He declined to answer, allowing the charge to grow for days (in sharp contrast to how he leapt to Joe Biden's defense a month earlier). But, while he remained silent about the allegations of racism, he gave speeches across South Carolina that warned against being "hoodwinked" and "bamboozled" by the Clintons. His use of the phrase is resonant. It comes from a scene in Malcolm X, where Denzel Washington warns black people about the hidden evils of "the White Man" masquerading as a smiling politician: "Every election year, these politicians are sent up here to pacify us," he says. "You've been hoodwinked. Bamboozled."

By uttering this famous phrase, Obama told his black audience everything it needed to know. He was helping to convince blacks that the first two-term Democratic president in 50 years, a man referred to as the first black president, is in fact a secret racist. As soon as I heard that Obama had quoted from Malcolm X like this, I knew that Obama would win South Carolina by a massive margin.[40]

The Clintons made rather poor victims, partly because they had used identity politics to their own benefit for so many years, and partly because they really had made some genuine contributions to the black community. Bill Clinton had chosen, after all, to locate the offices of his charitable foundation—the focus of his post-presidential activities—in Harlem. And Hillary had played the gender card to the hilt—even apparently staging a confrontation with a man holding a sign at a rally reading "Iron My Shirt," as if to demonstrate her heroism in battling male chauvinism.[41] But there was little the Clintons could do when the tables were turned against them.

Bill Clinton, for one, began lashing out at the media, which had once loved him but suddenly abandoned him. His critiques, while accurate, were pilloried by the Obama campaign and sympathetic journalists, making matters that much worse for his wife's presidential ambitions. One of the remarks for which the Clintons suffered most was Bill Clinton's comparison of Obama's victory in South Carolina to that of

Jesse Jackson in 1984, which relied heavily on black support but did not help him win the party's nomination in the end.[42] That remark, to Obama's supporters, was the smoking-gun proof that the Clintons were using racial politics: they were, the argument went, belittling Obama's victory by claiming it had only come about because of black support. Later, when Clinton was interviewed by a Pittsburgh radio station about the incident, he said:

> We were talking about South Carolina political history and this was used out of context and twisted for political purposes by the Obama campaign to try to breed resentment elsewhere. And you know, do I regret saying it? No. Do I regret that it was used that way? I certainly do. But you really got to go some to try to portray me as a racist.[43]

As the interview ended, Clinton was heard to say to someone in the background: "I don't think I should take any shit from anybody on that, do you?" But he would take even more. In late May, another associate of Obama's, Father Michael Pfleger, mocked the Clintons in a guest sermon at Trinity United in which he imitated Hillary, pretending to cry: "I'm white. I'm entitled. There's a black man stealing my show."[44] It was Pfleger's performance, and not anything Wright had previously said or done, that ultimately precipitated Obama's departure from the church. However reluctant he may have been to renege on his previous pledge to remain firmly rooted at Trinity despite the radicalism of its leader (see below), Obama could not in the end ignore the potential political consequences of alienating Clinton's supporters. Bill Clinton, meanwhile, lamented that Obama continued to get away with using surrogates to "slime" his wife's candidacy.[45] There was little he could do; the die had been cast.

The controversy surrounding Jeremiah Wright, the founder and pastor emeritus at Trinity United Church of Christ on Chicago's South Side, nearly ended Obama's campaign. Information about the church was freely available on the congregation's website, and had been discussed on the Internet for months—even before Obama had launched his campaign.

131

Its creed championed "the Black Value System," required "Disavowal of the Pursuit of 'Middleclassness'," and encouraged congregants to tithe "a Portion of Personal Resources for Strengthening and Supporting Black Institutions."[46] It also preached a version of liberation theology mixed with black nationalist ethics. This was powerful, controversial stuff—the sort of radical politics mixed with racist innuendo that could quickly destroy a campaign and a candidate's political career.

For months, the media ignored the church. And then, finally, ABC News uncovered videotape of Wright's first sermon after 9/11, which had been openly available through the church store. It featured Wright echoing Malcolm X's infamous conclusion about the Kennedy assassination—that it was "America's chickens coming home to roost"—as well as Wright referring to the country as the "U.S. of K.K.K.A."[47] Other sermons featured rhetoric that shocked the nation: "The government gives them the drugs, builds bigger prisons, passes a three-strike law and then wants us to sing 'God Bless America.' No, no, no, God damn America, that's in the Bible for killing innocent people."[48] The controversy did not end there. Despite his fulminations against the American government, Wright had accepted more than $15 million in federal funds for faith-based community service initiatives.[49] And he had become quite wealthy while preaching against the values of "Middleclassness," earning a healthy salary and a new home paid for by the church.[50]

At first, Obama tried to duck the controversy, as if it were beneath him to have to respond. But there was simply no denying the close ties that bound him—or rather, through which he had bound himself—to Trinity. He had converted to Christianity there; he had been a member for two decades; he had been married there; he had his two daughters baptized there. He had given the church $22,500 in 2006[51]—a year in which he had already begun preparing his presidential run, and clearly knew of the potential impact the church's image could have on his campaign. He even named his second memoir, *The Audacity of Hope*, after one of Jeremiah Wright's sermons. He was going to have to respond.

Obama chose his favorite medium—not a press conference, where journalists could ask questions about the church, or even a public meeting, but a speech, pure and simple, in front of an eagerly attentive press corps. His "great race speech," as some referred to it, lasted for a full 38 minutes and was instantly pronounced a success by Obama's praise-singers in the press. MSNBC anchor Chris Matthews—who had earlier made his love of Obama apparent by acknowledging that he "felt this thrill going up my leg"[52] when Obama spoke—declared: "a speech worthy of Abraham Lincoln....what I personally view as the best speech ever given on race in this country...This is the kind of speech that first graders should see, people in the last year of college should see before they go out in the world."[53] Maureen Dowd of the *New York Times* called it "momentous and edifying." Similar reactions were echoed throughout the left-leaning media, which had largely ignored or panned Republican Mitt Romney's sweeping speech on religion in America several months before.[54]

The message of Obama's speech was simple. He condemned Wright's statements, but refused to dissociate himself from the man or the church:

> I can no more disown him than I can disown the black community. I can no more disown him than I can my white grandmother—a woman who helped raise me, a woman who sacrificed again and again for me, a woman who loves me as much as she loves anything in this world, but a woman who once confessed her fear of black men who passed by her on the street, and who on more than one occasion has uttered racial or ethnic stereotypes that made me cringe.[55]

Obama's rhetorical use of his grandmother here struck some observers as ungracious. Nevertheless, she was essential to his theme: race is an issue all Americans must grapple with, he argued, one "that I believe this nation cannot afford to ignore right now." Wright's statements were wrong in "that he spoke as if our society was static; as if no progress has been made." But his words could be understood, Obama explained, as the manifestation of black frustration with America's broken promises. Obama also said that he understood the "resentment" of white Americans who did not feel they had benefited from racism and were often asked to make sacrifices for the sake of racial redress. The challenge, Obama asserted, was to "move beyond some of our old racial wounds...on the path of a more perfect union." And to do that, black Americans would have to learn to take more responsibility for their lives; white Americans would have to contribute more towards "investing" in "health, welfare, and education"; and all would need to join together for the betterment of the whole, and each other.

Obama's speech was indeed well-written, and well-delivered. But throughout the entire 38-minute oration, he never once offered an apology, nor any specific desription of what the church had meant to *him*; no Biblical quotations or insights, nor any requests for, or offers of, Christian forgiveness. In a sense, Obama was prescribing his own policies, and his own campaign, as the solution to America's racial problems. He had shunted responsibility for Wright's racist and quisling sermons onto the rest of the country, and onto the "corporate" monsters that were "the real culprits." There were other problems, too: constitutional law lecturer that he was, Obama had provided incorrect information about the U.S. Constitution in the very first paragraph of the speech. The Framers had not, as Obama claimed, "traveled across an ocean" to write the document, nor did they meet "at a Philadelphia convention that lasted through the spring of 1787," but one that began and ended in the sweltering summer of that year.

The conservative columnist Charles Krauthammer described Obama's race speech as a "brilliant fraud." Obama had not, he observed, answered key questions about whether he knew of—or distanced himself from—*all* of Wright's remarks, including his claim that the American government had invented HIV to kill black people, or that president Roosevelt had known about the Pearl Harbor attacks, among others. "His defense," Krauthammer observed, "rests on two central propositions: (a) moral equivalence and (b) white guilt." He concluded:

> This contextual analysis of Wright's venom, this extenuation of black hate speech as a product of white racism, is not new. It's the Jesse Jackson politics of racial grievance, expressed in Ivy League diction and Harvard Law nuance. That's why the speech made so many liberal commentators swoon: It bathed them in racial guilt while flattering their intellectual pretensions. An unbeatable combination.

> But Obama was supposed to be new. He flatters himself as a man of the future transcending the anger of the past as represented by his beloved pastor. Obama then waxes rhapsodic about the hope brought by the new consciousness of the young people in his campaign. Then answer this, Senator: If Wright is a man of the past, why would you expose your children to his vitriolic divisiveness? This is a man who curses America and who proclaimed moral satisfaction in the deaths of 3,000 innocents at a time when their bodies were still being sought at Ground Zero. It is not just the older congregants who stand and cheer and roar in wild approval of Wright's rants, but young people as well. Why did you give $22,500 just two years ago to a church run by a man of the past who infects the younger generation with precisely the racial attitudes and animus you say you have come unto us to transcend?[56]

The answers never came. Yet few in the media doubted that Obama had saved his election—and perhaps changed America.

But Krauthammer's contention that the speech was a fraud was proved substantively correct a few weeks later, when Wright appeared at the National Press Club in Washington, D.C. to defend his views. He clearly relished the public controversy, resented Obama's subtle rebukes, and was determined to have his moment of confrontation with his critics. After an opening speech in which he offered to explain the "black religious experience" to those assembled, he indulged the prepared questions of journalists in a rambling

135

session that confirmed all of the worst impressions about his beliefs.[57] It was no longer possible to ignore Wright—though many media outlets did, with the *New York Times* refusing to print any of Wright's incendiary remarks until Obama finally distanced himself from both the pastor and the church.[58] That moment only came in late May, when Father Pfleger—a white preacher, whom Obama could ostensibly afford offending without separating himself from the black community—attacked Hillary Clinton from the pulpit (see above). Wright's views—his racism, his hatred of America and its government, his evident hostility towards Israel—none of these were enough to induce Obama to leave, but the prospect of an angry rebellion by Clinton supporters at the Democratic National Convention was enough to make the political cost of his membership clear.

What was even more striking was that aside from a few intrepid investigative reporters, and the odd columnist willing to risk public opprobrium for political correctness, the media accepted Obama's version of events. The public was expected to believe that he was not in church at any time that Wright expressed his offensive views, despite having told an interviewer in 2004 that he attended every Sunday.[59] This was not the Reverend Wright he knew; he prayed in the church and donated to it without endorsing its beliefs; he was entitled to some amount of understanding, for he needed to establish his political credentials in the local community; and so on. They declared Obama's race speech a triumph, even if they had to accept the fact—after it was waved in their faces—that Wright was an extremist. They separated Obama from Wright—just as they had separated Obama from "slumlord" Tony Rezko when Hillary Clinton brought up Obama's association with his soon-to-be convicted former fundraiser; just as they would separate Obama from his early supporter and colleague William Ayers, the former Weather Underground terrorist who had hosted a fundraiser for Obama early in his political career; just as they would later separate Obama from the corruption of Illinois governor Rod Blagojevich and the rest of the Chicago political machine whose machinations were revealed by federal prosecutors weeks after all the votes had already been counted.

Obama's absolution went far beyond mere media favoritism—though that, too, went quite far—and to a deeper theme in American consciousness about race: the belief in his exceptional potential. In a country that had long burdened African-Americans with the symbolic stewardship of the nation's moral conscience, Obama was that hoped-for paragon whose ascent would confirm both the effectiveness of affirmative action policies, and their obsolescence; who would validate the left-wing dream of a government that could arrange ideal social outcomes, and affirm the conservative belief in self-reliance; who could relate to the vast popular culture to which African-Americans had contributed so much, but relate to the "high culture" beloved by the intellectuals and patronized by the wealthy. Many of the more ambitious interventions to address racial inequality in America, such as busing and affirmative action, had failed, but all had justified themselves by pointing to individuals who had succeeded, despite the odds and against all the evidence. Obama was such an exception, and he answered the deep need to believe in the potential of the needy but exceptional black individual—viewed in implicit and insulting contrast to black Americans as a whole—whose rise would both carry and cure the nation's sins. Few were willing to look past race and see the individuals beyond the paternalistic policies, or the great achievements of black Americans absent the yoke of the state. That was too much transcendence to ask of ordinary Americans, if the journalists who acted as the self-appointed arbiters of the nation's moral conscience were to be trusted at their word.

The widespread belief—which crossed party and ideological lines—in the transformative potential of the exceptional individual manifested itself in Obama with particular sharpness. That was partly because of Obama's symbolic appeal as a man of many origins and partly because he had proven—or seemed to have proven—his potential in the past, at the *Harvard Law Review* if nowhere else. Obama was also able to articulate—magnificently and convincingly, if not always accurately or fully—the dilemma of his personal position vis-à-vis Wright and other compelling moral and political questions surrounding race. He did not always provide answers—in fact, he rarely did except when forced to by circumstances—but many Americans liked the way he put the questions. It was not just that Obama's words were rhetorically impressive; he also offered Americans an escape from the difficult and real dilemmas that they were faced with by articulating the burden of dealing with them. Through him, through his words, the country would be absolved, he seemed to say. It was a messianic offer, made in the erudite language of the academy, and in the stirring cadence of the African-American church—and America's establishment bought it.

In the short term, however, the Wright scandal had a detrimental effect on Obama's campaign, measured in lost votes and primary contests. For the rest of the Democratic contest, Obama would fail to win a primary in any state without a large black electorate or a caucus system that could be influenced by well-organized volunteers. He literally crashed across the finish line, losing yet another primary on the day he won the nomination in June, creating some doubt as to whether he still had the popular appeal to pull off a win in the general election. And yet the belief in Obama as an almost mythological figure, the leader of an epic struggle against America's unnamed demons and towards its unknown destiny, continued. Enough people still saw themselves in him, still contributed to him and wanted him to win.

The Real Hillary Clinton

Barely a year before Obama had been elected president, such an outcome seemed quite unlikely. The year 2008 was supposed to be Hillary Clinton's year; she had been favored in early polls and seemed the Democrat best positioned to

138

win the nomination. She had name recognition; she had an active organization of donors and supporters; she had policy achievements to point to. She had also been re-elected in her adopted state of New York, which embraced her in 2000 despite deep misgivings about her throughout the rest of the country. In just eight years, she had managed to build a secure home base there and a loyal following. She would also be the first viable female presidential candidate in American history and promised her supporters that she would shatter that final "highest glass ceiling"[60] of American leadership once and for all.

Yet when the primaries began, Clinton found herself outflanked on the left—not just by Obama, but by former South Carolina senator John Edwards, who had been the vice-presidential nominee in 2004 and had run, unsuccessfully, alongside John Kerry. Edwards retained a sunny disposition that many voters found appealing, and he played up populist themes on the campaign trail in a bid to shock the frontrunners and claim the lead in the primary race (revelations of an extramarital affair, carried on while his wife was fighting cancer, were still far away in Edwards' future; mainstream media outlets covered up the story for months). As 2008 drew nearer, Clinton found her lead suddenly slipping as she was dogged by her two rivals and by an activist Democratic base—the "netroots"—eager to nominate a reliably anti-war candidate and overturn the New Democrat centrism that had held sway in the party since the 1990s. Left wing Democrats believed that the party had already had a chance to nominate a moderate—or, at the very least, someone with national security experience who had supported the Iraq War—in 2004, and lost. Now, they wanted a "real" Democrat, a candidate who could put clear blue water between the two parties and offer something truly different, not merely the same policies as the Republican Party at a discount.

Clinton was vulnerable in many ways. Firstly, she had backed the Iraq War—ostensibly, and somewhat credibly, because she had believed the Bush administration's intelli-

139

gence assessments about the likelihood that Saddam Hussein was producing and stockpiling weapons of mass destruction. She may also, however, have taken a different lesson from Kerry's failure than the party activists—namely, that a Democrat who looked weak on defense could not hope to win while the country was at war on two fronts. Yet Clinton was also vulnerable on the issue of free trade, which she had supported during her husband's administration, but which was the bugbear of the unions and many of the core activists of the left. She was also a symbol of the party establishment in a year when Americans seemed open to anti-establishment leaders and ideas. So when Obama, Edwards and other candidates began gaining traction on the left, Clinton began to play catch-up. She opposed free trade agreements like NAFTA. She denounced the Iraq War, blaming Bush for false intelligence and costly mismanagement in the war's aftermath.

But the Democratic base wasn't buying it. And soon Clinton found that her one best trump card—the historic nature of her candidacy as a woman—was over-trumped by Obama's own historic appeal. Hillary counted on a loyal army of activists, including many women who had been inspired by her example. But feminism had largely run its course as a motivating force in American politics—at least for the generation—and had already provoked a strong backlash, not just from men but particularly from women. The movement was confused, uncertain whether it could or should place the hopes of all women in a single woman who had, after all, risen to prominence initially not just because she was a sharp lawyer but because she was married to the president.

The special nature of Obama's historic run did not provoke the same backlash—partly because so few black candidates had ever stood a serious chance at the national level before, and also because of the historic tendency in America to place equal rights for black men ahead of those for all women. It was a priority measured in the distance between the Fourteenth Amendment to the U.S. Constitution (1868), and the Nineteenth (1920), between the end of the Civil War and the end of the First World War. It was, perhaps, a theme deeply ingrained in the American psyche: in its treatment of black people, America had traveled a rather unique road, whereas in its treatment of women the United States was simply a nation like any other.

Clinton tried to counter the unique nature of Obama's candidacy by claiming ownership of his historic claims as well as hers. She frequently congratulated the Democratic Party on having both an African-American and a woman as its front-runners.[61] But these attempts had the ring of condescension (as well as self-congratulation) and Clinton found herself trapped: the only way to fight against Obama's advantage in the identity politics battle would be to step completely outside the realm of identity politics. And that was something neither she nor her party was willing to do.

It was a bitter irony for Clinton, because while the media obsessed about whether Obama was encountering racism among white voters, few anticipated—or noticed—the degree to which sexism had become an obstacle to Clinton on the campaign trail. Male reporters and columnists often seemed to show particular glee in writing about Clinton's various shortcomings and mistakes; moderators in debates were far harsher with her than her rivals. As the *New York Times* reported of her debate with Obama in Cleveland in late February:

> Mrs. Clinton wanted the world to understand that the press is tougher on her than on Barack Obama. And she made her case by citing a sketch on last week's "Saturday Night Live" that showed mock debate moderators grilling her stand-in, Ms. Poehler, but fawning over the Obama character...

> And for the rest of the evening, the MSNBC debate did look a bit like the "S.N.L." parody....

> Mrs. Clinton was under attack, but the toughest blows came not from Mr. Obama but from Mr. Russert, who fiercely questioned her about her past positions on Nafta, Iraq and even a campaign promise from 2000, in her first Senate run...

When Mrs. Clinton insisted on adding to her remarks about Iraq when it was time for a break, the usually unflappable Brian Williams looked affronted. "Television does not stop," he said sharply. "Can you hold that thought until we come back from a break?"

...Tuesday night, even fate seemed to support her point about the favoritism surrounding Mr. Obama: after the first break, MSNBC showed a second unflattering clip of Mrs. Clinton mocking Mr. Obama's inspirational speeches, which to viewers, at least, might seem like the network was piling on. Mr. Williams sheepishly explained that the clip was shown in error and that his producers had intended to give Mr. Obama's embarrassing video moments equal time. He then went on nevertheless to ask Mr. Obama to comment on Mrs. Clinton's video, giving him yet another chance to show off his grace and even temper. "Well, I thought Senator Clinton showed some good humor there," he said with a twinkle. "I would give her points for delivery."[62]

Clinton did her best to make things worse—often by exploiting claims of sexism in a crude manner, as in the "Iron My Shirt" episode (see above). She also undermined her own credibility in a few notorious gaffes. The worst of these—both in terms of its egregiousness, and its timing, since it came just as Clinton was beginning to regain ground lost to Obama—was the so-called "Tuzla dash." Clinton, in an attempt to burnish her foreign policy credentials, claimed that when she had visited Bosnia as First Lady with her daughter in 1995, she had landed "under sniper fire" and had been forced to duck as she left her aircraft.[63] But video footage of her visit showed no such gunfire; instead, it portrayed the smiling First Lady as she greeted local residents and posed with troops in the field.[64] When she foolishly insisted on her original version of the story—perhaps genuinely believing it to be true—the media eagerly piled on the criticism.

Later in the campaign, during the general election, few reporters thought to make much of Democratic vice-presidential candidate Joe Biden's own tall tales of visiting war zones under hostile fire. "That's just Joe being Joe," was the typical response, even though Biden had a pattern of repeating such stories in print and off-the-cuff, all of which involved death-defying courage uncommon in the ordinary politician. Biden's whoppers were laughed off as machismo, but Clinton's story was taken as evidence of her dishonesty—a suspicion that had been planted during her eight years as First Lady, amidst the numerous scandals that surrounded the White House. Her comments were, of course, legitimate grounds for attack—it is never a good idea to invent experiences in the middle of an election—but she still received far harsher treatment than other, male candidates. And the "Tuzla dash" episode reinforced the sense that Obama had a monopoly on political authenticity, while Clinton was merely a politician—one capable of "stooping to anything," in the words of one Obama adviser.[65]

It was true that the unfairness and abuse helped Clinton to some degree—though not, probably, as much as it hurt her—by encouraging sympathy from female voters and by tempting Clinton to have done with the sham of identity politics once and for all. After almost breaking down in tears in New Hampshire on the weekend before the fateful primary vote, she recovered her composure and went on to win a massive and unprecedented victory, overcoming a double-digit deficit in the polls.[66] Critics and Obama supporters charged that her emotional display had been staged—and perhaps there was reason to suspect it might have been. But the reason voters related to her in that moment was that the façade of posturing, of identity politics, and of campaign-related triangulations finally seemed to have cracked, revealing the real woman behind the persona.

That moment—and that win—launched a bitter battle of attrition that lasted another five months. It was a long fight that Clinton, as the presumed frontrunner in the primary race, had not budgeted for—and that her opponent, planning a long-shot campaign that would have to take each victory as it came, had planned meticulously. Clinton's prior overconfidence became an extreme strategic disadvantage: her campaign had not prepared properly to contest the caucus states,

143

and found itself desperately short of staff and funds in sparse rural areas where Obama had managed to recruit and deploy full field offices, and where a few well-organized activists could make a difference.

Still, Hillary won many of the major Democratic contests, while Obama's victories were largely confined to states that had traditionally gone to Republicans in the general election—the mountain west and the deep South. His chances to flip some of these traditionally "red" states into the "blue" column would eventually be far better than most had anticipated, but at the time his victories in the general election were far from certain. And in the more populous states, Hillary managed to out-muscle even Obama's vaunted organization. She may even have benefited from Republicans crossing over to vote for her—either out of pure conviction or in response to the "Operation Chaos" effort of conservative radio host Rush Limbaugh, who aimed to prolong the Democratic fight by boosting Clinton's votes. Regardless, though Clinton lacked Obama's technological edge and was desperately short of cash, she finished the last few months turning out substantially more voters than her rival. Overall, if the votes from the disputed early-voting states of Michigan and Florida were included, Clinton had actually won more votes than Obama, and more votes than any primary candidate in the history of American elections.

As the Democratic primary ground onwards, Clinton also found a new voice, as the depth of Obama's radicalism became apparent. She no longer had to tack left as her opponent careened to the edge of the political map; now she could return to the middle and hold it. Clinton may have been the darling of liberal New York, but she was also a former Goldwater Girl from the Republican suburbs of northwest Chicago. And now, she suddenly found her voice as the representative of the ordinary, working-class Americans in the heartland that had been disappointed by Republican governance and written off by the Democratic elite. It was almost as if Hillary Clinton had found her true constituency, tapping into the lessons of her early political experiences in Arkansas, connecting to voters in "flyover country" typically disregarded by the Beltway elite. She found new support, and new respect.

What Was Lost

But Clinton's successes came too late to make much of a difference in the end. By the time the race began winding to a close in May, it seemed that Obama had managed to overcome every safeguard intended to protect American democracy from the rise of a charismatic demagogue. Had the Democrats used a winner-takes-all system for each state contest, as the Republicans do, she would have easily and quickly defeated Obama.[67] But she did not win the overall nomination, both because of the Democrats' system of proportional representation in the primaries, and because of the curious system of "superdelegates." These were elected officials and party bigwigs who each held an at-large vote at the Democratic National Convention. Their role was to act as a firewall in the event of a radical, insurgent candidacy, such as the Kennedy campaign in 1980, which nearly unseated President Jimmy Carter and weakened him for the general election against Ronald Reagan. They possessed just enough votes— roughly 20 percent as of the 2008 election—to play the role of kingmakers in a close contest, which they had done in selecting Minnesota senator Walter Mondale over Indiana senator Gary Hart in 1984.[68]

Because of Clinton's prominence in the party, and her assiduous lobbying of every one of its constituencies, most of the superdelegates who had declared a preference for one candidate or another at the start of the primary season had been in the Clinton camp. But over time, they began to shift, as more and more superdelegates declared for Obama, and Obama even began poaching some of Clinton's superdelegate votes. One reason for the shift was Obama's success in a string of caucuses in February and March; the party insiders wanted to be on the winning side no matter who was the eventual nominee, and Obama's chances drastically improved during that run. Racial politics were another factor. Congressman John Lewis, the black former civil rights leader and long-time Clinton supporter, switched over from Hillary Clinton to Barack Obama, citing the wishes of his constituents but also admitting that he did not want to find himself on "the wrong side" of history if a black candidate for president became a viable contender.

But another reason that so many superdelegates switched was simply that Obama had outbid Clinton for their votes. Behind the public spectacle of voting, superdelegates—especially those holding public offices—were jockeying for campaign funds. Obama had distributed far more cash ($694,000) to superdelegates than Clinton ($195,000), by a factor of 3.5 to 1.[69] Effectively, he had bought their support—and this during the years leading up to 2008, when Clinton had not yet run into the cash crunch she would encounter after "Super Tuesday," the multi-state primary contest on the first Tuesday in February. The system of superdelegates, which had been designed to keep the Democratic Party safe from its own excesses, collapsed in the face of Obama's rhetorical and financial challenge.

An additional factor in Obama's victory was the highly slanted media coverage his campaign benefited from. Few journalists showed any interest at all in exploring his weaknesses, and when they did so they were subjected to vociferous complaints from the Obama campaign. For example, Obama aides asked CNN not to air a documentary on the *Anderson Cooper 360°* show about his first political race in Chicago, when he had all of his Democratic opponents disqualified. The network aired it anyway—but it was a rare departure from their general practice of sheltering Obama from criticism. On another occasion on the same program, fellow guest Joe Klein of *Time* magazine attempted to prevent Clinton surrogate Lanny Davis from referring to or quoting the sermons of Jeremiah Wright. Davis later recalled:

When I said on CNN recently that concerns about the Wright - Obama issue were "appropriate" to continue to be discussed, my friend Joe Klein of Time Magazine said, "Lanny, Lanny, you're spreading the poison right now" and that an "honorable person" would "stay away from this stuff."

Attacking the motives of those who feel this discomfort about Senator Obama's response or non-response to Reverend Wright's concerns is not just unfair and wrong. It also misses the important electoral point about winning the general election in November: this issue is not going away...

One thing is for sure: if Senator Obama doesn't show a willingness to try to answer all the questions now, Senator McCain and the Republican attack machine will not waste a minute pressuring him to do so if he is the Democratic Party's choice in the fall.[70]

Davis was wrong about McCain's willingness to use Wright as an issue—which suggests that much of the hysteria that Democrats had developed about unscrupulous Republican campaign tactics was overblown. But he was right about the unwillingness of journalists and mainstream media outlets—including the *New York Times* and the *Los Angeles Times*[71]—to fully air Wright's incendiary views. The *Los Angeles Times* would continue its self- censorship through the November election and beyond, refusing to release a video recording of Obama at a farewell party for former Palestine Liberation Organization (PLO) spokesman Rashid Khalidi, citing an agreement with its sources as the dubious justification for its actions.[72] In silencing the facts about Wright and other Obama associates, the media deprived the public of the chance to learn the full story of Obama's background. On this issue, as on many others, journalists seemed to be taking their editorial cues from left-wing blogs or from the Obama campaign's talking points, barely reporting the Clinton campaign's responses without bracketing them safely within skepticism and criticism.

When George Stephanopoulos—hardly an independent voice, to be sure, as he had been Bill Clinton's press secretary in his first term at the White House—finally challenged Obama in a debate sponsored by ABC News, virtually the entire media turned against him. Stephanopoulos brought up many of the points that had been hotly debated around the "blogosphere," and repressed by the mainstream media for months, including questions about Wright and Ayers. Obama, embarrassed by his clumsy and revealing answers, refused to participate in a single additional debate after that, rejecting Clinton's further challenges. And few journalists thought to complain—they had already chosen their favorite, abandoning whatever defenses the Fourth Estate had once maintained to guard the democratic process.

In the rush to nominate Obama to the presidency, the Democratic Party even disavowed its mantra, which had been its mainstay for the eight years of the Bush presidency: the principle that "every vote counts." This idea represented the commonly-held belief among Democrats that Bush would have lost in 2000—and again in 2004, according to some true believers—if certain voters had not been excluded from the voters' rolls, if ballots had been counted by hand instead of by machine, or if Democrats had trusted the voting process enough to turn out in large numbers. Conspiracy theories aside, it was an important principle, essential to public faith in the electoral process even in well-established democracies like the United States.

But in Florida and Michigan, where the state legislatures had hoped to boost the importance of their local primaries by moving them earlier in the schedule in violation of party rules, the Democrats refused to accredit the delegates that had been elected. Effectively, the party hierarchy had disenfranchised the voters of both states—and in Florida, of all places, where Democratic voters felt they had already been disenfranchised once before in recent memory. The party's decision, in turn, created a real chance that Democratic voters could stay home in disgust or even vote for McCain, pushing both electoral-vote-heavy states into the "red" column. So the party's rules committee decided to hold a last-ditch meeting in May to resolve the problem.[73] In a show of Obama's growing strength among the party's leaders, delegates in both states were given half-votes at the convention. In Michigan, they were awarded to the candidates on a compromise basis, though Obama had not been on the ballot: he had wisely decided to pull out of the contest, hoping (correctly) that this would give him greater credibility later in the process. Effectively, this meant assigning four delegates who would have represented Clinton votes to Obama. Harold Ickes, who had represented Clinton on the committee, warned that the Clinton campaign reserved the right to fight the issue out on the floor of the national convention in Denver. He told CNN later: "[T]hey hijacked—you know, they just plain reached in and grabbed four delegates from Hillary. It's unheard of and unprecedented in this party. To take delegates from a candidate and give them to another candidate is quite incredible."[74]

The Democratic Party's display of disenfranchisement caused an outcry among some of Clinton's supporters, who declared that they would not support Obama. Some formed an organization, called PUMA—"Party Unity My Ass"—to protest what they saw as the deliberate sabotaging of Clinton's campaign. Over the next several weeks, Obama worked hard to undercut that opposition by winning over Clinton herself, who had a large campaign debt to pay and a political career to salvage. Whatever happened behind the scenes—and there were plenty of difficult negotiations—was later presented, inevitably, as the fulfillment of party unity. By the time the general election drew near, the two had even publicly buried the hatchet at a joint rally in the town of Unity, New Hampshire.

Thus the last safeguard—the principle of counting actual votes for an opponent—was abandoned in the face of Obama's superior political maneuvering, as well as his disciplined organization and his constant, consistent media support. Clinton had won the majority of the votes, and had even out-campaigned Obama in the closing weeks of the campaign, but she had lost when and where it had counted.

149

Now Obama's full persona was unleashed, and the extravagance of his belief in self-salvation—"my individual salvation is not going to come about without a collective salvation for the country,"[75] he once told an interviewer—unfurled in messianic tones as he wrapped up the Democratic nomination.

For the first time, America was faced with a cult of personality, a movement that saw its leader as the fulfillment not just of their hopes but of their selves. Some even began describing Obama in religious tones; even Obama himself indulged in prophetic language more frequently. At his speech in St. Paul, Minnesota celebrating his victory in the Democratic primaries, he claimed that history would remember the moment of his own nomination as the time "when the rise of the oceans began to slow and our planet began to heal."[76]

This was the stuff of easy parody. But late-night comedians did not dare poke fun at him; when they did, audiences fell silent. Jon Stewart of the *Daily Show* at least attempted to joke about the Democratic nominee; when his audience offered little more than a few chuckles, he chided them: "You know, you're allowed to laugh at him."[77] Obama was not just a man people were afraid to laugh at. He was a man no one wanted to laugh at. He was a walking caricature, an imitation of themes in American history and Christian iconography. His propaganda—or that produced by his fans—even occasionally echoed Soviet imagery, without the Gulag but also without the irony of contemporary communist chic. He was a talented politician, but also in many ways an empty one, ripe for criticism. And yet America had suddenly, inexplicably lost its sense of irony. Strangely, no one was laughing.

5

The Fall

No Surrender?

And so the general election began. Obama's offer of "Change We Can Believe In" swept the nation, and McCain's "Straight Talk Express" struggled to keep pace. It was to be a test not only of whether McCain's words could overcome Obama's, but also of whether McCain himself still believed in them—in the ideas and principles he had long stood up for, but which seemed to be fading quickly from the American political consensus. If anyone could defend the mission of U.S. foreign policy, the idea of a free economy, and the values of traditional conservatism—the "three-legged stool" upon which much of the Reagan revolution was perched—it was McCain, the last man standing as Americans turned against their Republican president. These were still ideas he held dear. But his success depended, he believed, on his ability to reach beyond the narrow constituency that still knew it supported these principles, while still motivating that constituency to vote in large numbers. The campaign was to be a contest not merely of words, but of convictions and confidence.

Faced with the challenge of running against Obama's historic campaign, McCain made several strategic choices that would define his own run for president in the general election. The first was that he would not, as Hillary Clinton had done, emphasize the "experience" argument. It had not worked for Clinton precisely because the Democratic base was tired of "experience." The left wanted a departure from the centrism of the New Democrats and a break with the Clinton establishment. It also believed that the "experience" argument had not worked for Kerry in 2004. Even George

W. Bush, after all, had won the presidency while lacking experience in important areas like national security (his service in the Texas Air National Guard notwithstanding) and foreign policy.

For McCain, there were two additional drawbacks to the "experience" approach. One was the candidate's own age. He was not the oldest candidate ever to have been nominated to run for the presidency. That honor belonged to former senator Bob Dole, who ran (unsuccessfully) against Bill Clinton in 1996. But if he won, McCain would be the oldest man ever to take the oath of office. Emphasizing his experience would be a way of highlighting his age—something the Obama campaign had been eagerly, and not too subtly, doing for months. Another reason for McCain to avoid the "experience" approach was that despite his twenty-five years in Washington, and his many years in the Navy before that, he had little executive experience. After returning from Vietnam, he had commanded the largest flight squadron in the Navy and restored all of its aircraft to working condition—a feat of management that had previously been considered almost impossible under the circumstances.[1] That spoke well to McCain's management potential, but he had never held a public executive office, nor did he have experience in business or a related field.

Obama had even less to offer in terms of executive experience than McCain. His only management experience was his unremarkable year at the helm of the *Harvard Law Review* and his service as head of a charitable board, the Chicago Annenberg Challenge, that included former terrorist William Ayers.[2] Obama's Annenberg project was, moreover, a failure, wasting millions of dollars on ineffective interventions in public schools that were aimed more at inculcating political radicalism than promoting educational excellence. Not only did Obama wish to avoid drawing attention to his participation with Ayers, but also to the essential uselessness of the project: an independent evaluation concluded that there were "no statistically significant differences between Annenberg

152

and non-Annenberg schools in rates of achievement gain, classroom behavior, student self-efficacy, and social competence."[3] So the McCain campaign decided to pursue Obama's *inexperience* vigorously, but without drawing too many comparisons to McCain's own experience.

That strategy, however, yielded little. Aside from the marginal advantage McCain held in this area of comparison, the public simply wasn't in the mood: in a year of public frustration with Washington in general and Republicans in particular, inexperience looked like a selling point to many voters. So instead, McCain chose to take the fight directly to Obama's central and strongest claim: that he represented "change." His campaign focused on pointing out the myriad ways in which Obama was just another ordinary politician—from his failure to lead on any particular issue, to his apparent fondness for pork-barrel projects and his refusal to reveal the full truth of his associations with controversial figures like Wright, Rezko and Ayers. And McCain also focused on his own record of fighting for change—"real" change, as opposed to the rhetorical sort. In this approach, he risked being outrun: it would be hard to "out-Obama" the man himself, especially when the media and the popular imagination seemed to treat the very idea of "change" as an Obama campaign trademark. But McCain was counting on the hope that Obama's brand of change would be too radical for the electorate, for whom the last eight years had in many ways been a time of too *much* change in America. The country had lived through two economic downturns, a housing boom and bust, a massive terror attack, two wars, several natural disasters and at least two shifts in congressional power during the eight years of Bush's presidency. For many, stability may have been a welcome thought.

McCain's proposed alternative to Obama's "change" was "reform." The term had long been a favorite of McCain's; its revival was partly inspired by an article by the political analyst Yuval Levin, who suggested that "reform" was a way to tie together the various different strands of McCain's diverse

153

policy proposals.[4] It was a word that hearkened back to the progressive era of the early twentieth century, and to McCain's Republican hero Teddy Roosevelt. Roosevelt was a man who symbolized the boldness and adventure of the American spirit but who also believed in restraining the forces of greed, or turning them to social and environmental good. Unlike "change," which was simply open-ended (albeit less radical than Ron Paul's "revolution"), "reform" contained the conservative reassurance that those institutions and ideas that still worked could be preserved. In addition, unlike the Republicans of the recent past—the "revolutionaries" of Gingrich's 104th Congress, or the big-government conservatives of the Bush years—McCain promised neither to eliminate nor expand government, but to improve its performance.

That strategy would require McCain to attack Obama's version of "change," which he did in his very first speech of the general election:

> The right change recognizes that many of the policies and institutions of our government have failed. They have failed to keep up with the challenges of our time because many of these policies were designed for the problems and opportunities of the mid to late 20th Century, before the end of the Cold War; before the revolution in information technology and rise of the global economy. The right kind of change will initiate widespread and innovative reforms in almost every area of government policy— health care, energy, the environment, the tax code, our public schools, our transportation system, disaster relief, government spending and regulation, diplomacy, the military and intelligence services. Serious and far-reaching reforms are needed in so many areas of government to meet our own challenges in our own time...
>
> The wrong change looks not to the future but to the past for solutions have failed us before and will surely fail us again. I have a few years on my opponent, so I am surprised that a young man has bought in to so many failed ideas. Like others before him, he seems to think government is the answer to every problem; that government should take our resources and make our decisions for us. That type of change doesn't trust Ameri-

cans to know what is right or what is in their own best interests. It's the attitude of politicians who are sure of themselves but have little faith in the wisdom, decency and common sense of free people. That attitude created the unresponsive bureaucracies of big government in the first place. And that's not change we can believe in.[5]

McCain continued the refrain—"That's not change we can believe in"—throughout the speech. Unfortunately, his remarks were overshadowed by the debacle involving the green screen behind him (see chapter 3), and he kept delivering the tag line with a quirky smile, as if he were uncomfortable attacking Obama quite so directly.

It was possible that McCain could have hoped to steal back some of the spotlight and political momentum if his campaign had managed to find a coherent message. But "reform" just wasn't enough. It was "change" without the charisma, a depressingly modern response to a post-modern moment. As Nietzsche might have observed, the old Apollonian god of wise stewardship had been kicked over amidst the Dionysian revelry around Obama's ecstatic and amorphous festival of "hope" and "change."

It became increasingly clear at the close of the primaries that McCain and his strategists were prepared to let the entire 2008 election become a referendum on Obama rather than a real contest between two candidates and two sets of ideas and principles. In part, they were simply acknowledging reality. The historic nature of a race that featured the first African-American candidate, plus Obama's massive edge in fundraising and his cheerleaders in the media, meant that Obama's personality—elusive in its details, perhaps, but grand in its themes and symbols—would dominate the race and the agenda of national debate.

That passive approach may have been more cost-effective and even more sensible. But it also meant that McCain, having won the Republican nomination after a tremendous effort and against extraordinary odds, would only mount a half-hearted challenge for the presidency—half a presidential campaign, in effect. McCain often vowed "no surrender," in a stirring refrain that concluded many of his speeches, but he entered the general election as a man who seemed unsure not only how he was going to win, but why he wanted to win in the first place, and what was at stake—in terms of principles, values, and policies—for America.

The McCain Surge

Yet McCain *was* prepared to fight, to the extent that he could take advantage of Obama's weaknesses, and in July 2008 he began to mount a "surge" of his own, based on several mistakes by the Obama campaign and the emergence of a foreign policy crisis unforeseen by either campaign. Obama had remained firmly in the lead throughout the summer, with little movement in the polls. Though the race was extremely stable, McCain and the Republican National Committee (RNC) continued to blast Obama for only having visited Iraq once since arriving in the Senate, as against McCain's own eight visits to the region. The RNC even put an "Obama Iraq Clock" on its website, counting down the days, hours and minutes since his last visit to the country. Initially the Obama campaign insisted that it would not be goaded into changing its schedule, but eventually it relented and Obama scheduled a trip to Iraq. It was a moderately successful visit, with the campaign producing video footage of Obama playing basketball with the troops and sinking a basket from what looked like distant three-point territory. Obama also visited Israel, causing a minor sensation when his prayer note in the Western Wall was leaked to the media (some reports suggested that his aides had leaked it themselves). All went well, and reassured Obama's supporters of the strength of their candidate on two critical foreign policy issues.

On the way back, Obama had scheduled a visit in Europe, including visits to France, the United Kingdom and Germany. There were state visits to arrange, as well as visits to wounded American soldiers recuperating at U.S. bases in

156

Germany. But the highlight was Obama's address to a massive rally in Berlin. The primary audience, of course, was back home in America, as the campaign hoped to show Americans just how popular their potential president was overseas and to convince voters that Obama could repair relations between the United States and the rest of the world.

The rally ran into problems early in the planning stages. Obama had wanted to stage it at the Brandenburg Gate, where JFK had made his famous "Ich bin ein Berliner" speech and Reagan had declared: "Mr. Gorbachev, tear down this wall!" It would fit Obama's by-now-familiar habit of comparing himself to famous presidents (something he would do, *ad infinitum*, en route to his inaugural ceremony in January 2009, and beyond as well). But German Chancellor Angela Merkel publicly, though politely, refused.[6] Obama was, after all, simply an American politician; "No German [chancellor] candidate would think of using (Washington's) National Mall or Red Square in Moscow for rallies, because it would be considered inappropriate," she said.[7] So Obama relented and the rally was held within sight of the Brandenburg Gate, at the Victory Column—erected, rather ironically, by Otto von Bismarck and moved to its current location by Adolf Hitler.

The cheering crowds on a sunny central European day in late July were a triumph. According to estimates, over 200,000 people saw Obama speak that day,[8] including people from all over Germany and Europe, as well as American expatriates eager to experience a campaign from home up close. The speech was full of platitudes: "The walls between old allies on either side of the Atlantic cannot stand. The walls between the countries with the most and those with the least cannot stand. The walls between races and tribes; natives and immigrants; Christian and Muslim and Jew cannot stand. These now are the walls we must tear down."[9] However, the visuals were arresting—the cheering throngs, waving American flags on foreign soil, among people that many Americans (with some justification) believed still resented them because of their current leader, even though several European countries had recently elected conservative leaders of their own.

But before Obama could put those images to good effect in campaign advertisements, the McCain team stole a march on him and used them to put together an ad of their own. Called "Celebrity,"[10] the ad flashed images of Paris Hilton and Britney Spears—two stars largely "famous for being famous"—before cutting to wide shots of Obama at the Victory Column. Over the sound of a crowd chanting, "Obama, Obama," the voiceover intoned: "He's the biggest celebrity in the world. But is he ready to lead? With gas prices soaring, Barack Obama says no to offshore drilling? And says he'll raise taxes on electricity? Higher taxes, more foreign oil. That's the real Obama."

The ad aroused instant indignation from the Obama campaign and its supporters. Some of Obama's loyal followers in the media accused McCain of racism. *New York Times* columnist Bob Herbert even suggested that McCain had included images of the leaning tower of Pisa and the Washington Monument as phallic symbols with racial undertones.[11] Both structures, however, turned out to be the Victory Column, chosen as the venue by Obama himself. Obama, too, climbed in, suggesting that the ad was racist: "What they're going to try to do is make you scared of me. You know, he doesn't look like all those other presidents on the dollar bills."[12] But that counter-attack backfired. According to an opinion survey by Rasmussen, only one in five Americans thought the "Celebrity" ad was racist, while more than half found Obama's response racist.[13] The ad was extremely effective, both in highlighting Obama's lack of substantive experience and his inability to take criticism. And there was more: soon the story emerged that Obama had skipped a visit to wounded soldiers in Germany, ostensibly because the military would not allow his campaign to bring a camera crew into the hospital.[14] That report caused public outrage at home. Overall, the entire European leg of the trip had caused Obama more harm than good.

McCain made even greater strides a few weeks later in responding to Russia's sudden invasion of the former Soviet republic of Georgia in August. The issue was the fate of two secessionist "republics," South Ossetia and Abkhazia, which contained a large number of ethnic Russians and where there had been a history of conflict with the central Georgian government. As Georgia sought admission into NATO, much to the frustration of the Kremlin, Russia began strengthening ties to the two republics. In the course of the ongoing mediation process around the dispute, Russia managed to deploy its own troops as "international" peacekeepers there, and tensions built until Georgia finally sent troops to quell an apparent uprising by separatist forces. On August 8, 2008—while the rest of the world's leaders were distracted by the opening ceremonies of the Olympics in Beijing, China—Russia invaded with overwhelming force. In the course of the fighting, thousands of civilians were killed. According to many western analysts, the war had been a crisis prepared well in advance by former Russian president (now prime minister) Vladimir Putin, the better to showcase Russia's renewed, belligerent might. The attack also sent a signal to NATO about its plans for missile defense systems in Eastern Europe as well as its ambition of admitting more former Soviet republics and Eastern bloc states to membership.

The responses by the McCain and Obama campaigns to the Georgian conflict could not have been more different. McCain's statement referred specifically in its title to "Russia's Aggression in Georgia," and began:

> Today, news reports indicate that Russian military forces crossed an internationally-recognized border into the sovereign territory of Georgia. Russia should immediately and unconditionally cease its military operations and withdraw all forces from sovereign Georgian territory. What is most critical now is to avoid further confrontation between Russian and Georgian military forces. The consequences for Euro-Atlantic stability and security are grave.[15]

159

McCain put the responsibility for the crisis where it belonged, and called for an immediate withdrawal by Russian forces. Obama's statement on the "Grave Situation in Georgia," in contrast, appeared wishy-washy, casting both sides in morally equivalent terms:

> I strongly condemn the outbreak of violence in Georgia, and urge an immediate end to armed conflict. Now is the time for Georgia and Russia to show restraint, and to avoid an escalation to full scale war. Georgia's territorial integrity must be respected. All sides should enter into direct talks on behalf of stability in Georgia, and the United States, the United Nations Security Council, and the international community should fully support a peaceful resolution to this crisis.[16]

McCain's statement made a far stronger impact—so much so that it was acknowledged by Georgian president Mikheil Saakashvili at a rally in the capital city, Tbilisi.[17] In fact, McCain's response was so much more effective than the one issued by Obama—then on vacation at a Hawaii beach house—that the Democrat felt compelled to issue a second, tougher statement,[18] as did President Bush, whose initial remarks had been more cautious. McCain's stand was welcomed by other former communist countries threatened by Russia's new imperial ambitions, and raised doubts about whether Obama's lack of resolve was simply the result of inexperience or the sign of an underlying foreign policy weakness. Certainly his initial bearing suggested a desire to handle the crisis according to the philosophy of diplomacy that he had articulated during the campaign. But against the test of a real-world challenge, Obama's approach was found wanting.

McCain also began to mount a strong challenge to Obama's supposed religious appeal. Whereas McCain's natural speaking style was somewhat stilted and straightforward, punctuated a awkwardly with a rhetorical crutch, "my friends," Obama's use of religious cadences and millenarian themes attracted evangelical voters like no other Democrat had since Jimmy Carter. He spoke frequently in churches and often told audiences and journalists about the importance of

160

his own church to his life. Even after the Wright scandal broke, he continued to emphasize his religious sensitivity. His campaign began a determined effort to reach out to evangelicals—something Kerry's campaign had done in 2004, but far too late and on too small a scale to make much of a difference.[19]

An important obstacle that Obama had to overcome to connect to this traditionally-conservative voting group was his actual beliefs on abortion, stem cell research, gay rights and a host of other issues at which liberals and evangelicals had long been at odds. One of Obama's tactics was to shift his discussions of faith away from such theologically-grounded issues and toward "this-worldly" issues such as charity, poverty and community service. The absence of such a "social justice" discourse had long been a prominent theme of contemporary criticisms of the evangelical movement, which charged that evangelical leaders focused more on life in the hereafter, and on self-fulfillment, than on good works here on earth. Obama's eagerness to introduce such terms resonated with particular clarity among a new, younger generation of evangelicals who preferred to see their faith in terms of choices rather than age-old restrictions.[20]

Obama also softened his rhetoric on the political issues that had often kept social conservatives far way from the Democratic Party. Although his own voting record was radically pro-choice, Obama steered questions and debates away from his views on a woman's right to choose or the moment of conception, and spoke instead about the need to prevent teenage and unwanted pregnancies. He still tripped himself up sometimes, and said, on one occasion, that he wouldn't want his own daughters "punished" with a child.[21] But in moving beyond the narrow constrictions of the usual debates on abortions, he encouraged many evangelicals to give his candidacy more serious consideration than he would have otherwise. He also toned down his support for gay rights. Obama had openly supported gay marriage in 1996,[22] and had said that he would like to see the repeal of the military's pol-

161

icy of "don't ask, don't tell" with regard to homosexual soldiers.[23] Yet on the campaign trail, while retaining his hospitable attitude towards gay rights, he indicated that he—like Clinton and McCain—opposed a constitutional amendment to restrict marriage to heterosexual couples, but also opposed gay marriage itself, favoring civil unions for gays instead.

Whether Obama could sustain this posture through the campaign remained uncertain. His most important test came in late August at the Saddleback Forum, hosted by Pastor Rick Warren. It was to be Obama's first major public appearance since returning from his vacation in Hawaii earlier that month, and the first time both candidates would share the same stage. They would not appear together, save for a brief moment at the end. Instead, they would each address questions for an hour in turn, with the same questions given to both. Obama, who went first, looked well rested, but became more and more uncomfortable throughout the exchange and gave answers that the restive audience found unsatisfactory. When asked to define the moment that life begins, for example, Obama replied: "That's above my pay grade."[24] He dodged other difficult questions, such as whether evil existed and what to do about it:

> WARREN: OK, we've got one last time—I've got a bunch more, but let me ask you one about evil. Does evil exist? And if it does, do we ignore it? Do we negotiate with it? Do we contain it? Do we defeat it?
>
> OBAMA: Evil does exist. I mean, I think we see evil all the time. We see evil in Darfur. We see evil, sadly, on the streets of our cities. We see evil in parents who viciously abuse their children. I think it has to be confronted. It has to be confronted squarely, and one of the things that I strongly believe is that, now, we are not going to, as individuals, be able to erase evil from the world. That is God's task, but we can be soldiers in that process, and we can confront it when we see it.
>
> Now, the one thing that I think is very important is for to us have some humility in how we approach the issue of confronting evil, because a lot of evil's been perpetrated based on the claim that we were trying to confront evil.

REV. RICK WARREN, SADDLEBACK CHURCH: In the name of good.

OBAMA: In the name of good, and I think, you know, one thing that's very important is having some humility in recognizing that just because we think that our intentions are good, doesn't always mean that we're going to be doing good.

As Obama rambled to a close, Warren hurried Obama along to the next question. McCain's answer to the same query an hour later was far more decisive, and he used it to build up to a strong argument on foreign policy:

WARREN: How about the issue of evil. I asked this of your rival, in the previous debate. Does evil exist and, if so, should ignore it, negotiate it with it, contain it or defeat it?

MCCAIN: Defeat it. A couple of points. One, if I'm president of the United States, my friends, if I have to follow him to the gates of hell, I will get bin Laden and bring him to justice. I will do that. And I know how to do that. I will get that done. (APPLAUSE). No one, no one should be allowed to take thousands of American—innocent American lives.

Of course, evil must be defeated. My friends, we are facing the transcendent challenge of the 21st century—radical Islamic extremism.

Not long ago in Baghdad, al Qaeda took two young women who were mentally disabled, and put suicide vests on them, sent them into a marketplace and, by remote control, detonated those suicide vests. If that isn't evil, you have to tell me what is. And we're going to defeat this evil. And the central battleground according to David Petraeus and Osama bin Laden is the battle, is Baghdad, Mosul, Basra and Iraq and we are winning and succeeding and our troops will come home with honor and with victory and not in defeat. And that's what's happening.

And we have—and we face this threat throughout the world. It's not just in Iraq. It's not just in Afghanistan. Our intelligence people tell us al Qaeda continues to try to establish cells here in the United States of America. My friends, we must face this challenge. We can face this challenge. And we must totally defeat it, and we're in a long struggle. But when I'm around, the young

163

men and women who are serving this nation in uniform, I have no doubt, none.[25]

As he eased into the question-and-answer session, McCain looked more and more confident. The audience was pleased—and perhaps surprised—by his straightforward answers. He was even self-deprecating and candid about his personal failings and religious convictions. After being held in suspicion for so long by conservatives, McCain—in a single performance—seemed to dispel many doubts, and the audience rose to its feet in a standing ovation.

The media realized that Obama had done poorly, and attempted to spin his loss as a victory. They cast his waffling responses as more "nuanced" than McCain's forthright answers.[26] When that defense crumbled, the story became that McCain must have cheated because while Obama was onstage McCain was not *literally* in a "cone of silence," the term half-jokingly used by Warren to describe McCain's sequestration. Instead, McCain was on his way to the forum when the debate began. The accusation was featured prominently in a story by the *New York Times*, which seemed determined to rewrite Obama's loss as a win.[27] Though journalists did their best to bury evidence of McCain's solid showing, his victory resonated with the voters—at least, with that portion of the electorate that Republicans had depended on most heavily in recent elections and that McCain, until 2008, had struggled to reach.

By the time the Democratic National Convention was held in Denver at the end of August, McCain had succeeded in closing the gap in the polls substantially. Just before the convention started, Barack Obama announced his running mate. A promotional effort by the campaign to send the name of the vice-presidential nominee via text message to campaign supporters' cell phones garnered millions of new contacts for the campaign but was undermined when a leak to the media resulted in the public finding out first (one of the few failures of Obama's technological team).[28] The choice—Senator Joe Biden of Delaware—was not the best

Obama could have made, though many sympathetic commentators argued it was the best Obama could have made under the circumstances. Biden was the chair of the Senate Foreign Relations Committee, and regarded as something of a foreign affairs expert. Curiously, he had been "wrong" on a number of prior foreign policy issues: opposing the Gulf War but supporting the Iraq War; supporting ineffective UN intervention in Bosnia rather than an active American role;[29] proposing the partition of Iraq into separate ethnic zones and then denying he had ever done so.[30] In choosing him, Obama was tacitly admitting his own lack of foreign policy experience; the campaign admitted as much, reassuring voters that Biden would be there to help Obama govern.[31]

It was an ironic choice, given that Biden had mocked Obama's inexperience when the two were still running against each other ahead of the Iowa primary. Biden had also referred explicitly to Obama's race when describing Obama's appeal in 2007: "I mean, you got the first mainstream African-American who is articulate and bright and clean and a nice-looking guy."[32] That was not the first of Biden's racial comments; he had a penchant for such gaffes. And worst of all, from a short-term political point of view, was that Obama's choice was seen a snub to Hillary Clinton and her supporters. It became clear that Clinton had not even been considered for the job. Many of her backers had expected Obama to at least choose a woman, out of respect for Clinton's achievement in the primaries. But in choosing an older, white male—one of the few people who had been in Washington longer than McCain—Obama had confirmed the worst fears of the PUMAs and left an opening for McCain to win their support.

The convention was a huge success in terms of ratings and reviews. Both Hillary and Bill Clinton gave gracious speeches that signaled to the Clinton camp that they had not only accepted their defeat, but that they also fully endorsed the Obama candidacy. A few grumblings aside, most of the Clinton delegates accepted their leader's decision to concede without a floor fight. For the convention's final evening, the Obama campaign adjourned the convention to Denver's Invesco Field for Obama's acceptance speech. In yet another conscious emulation of JFK, who had given his famous "New Frontier" speech in the Rose Bowl in Pasadena at the end of the Democratic National Convention in 1960, Obama sought to address a large stadium crowd. The campaign explained that he wanted to open the doors of the convention to ordinary Americans, but in reality the only tickets available were to those who had pledged labor hours or money to the campaign.[33] Still, the gesture was a grand one, but the Obama campaign again nearly ruined it by taking on too much of the grandiose persona of the candidate. In the center of the stadium, the campaign built a strange temple-like structure of Greco-Roman columns (conservative bloggers dubbed it "the Barackopolis"), making the entire spectacle appear like some ancient worship ceremony. And indeed, this was the Dionysian moment for the Democrats, though the speech was rather flat and few of the lines were remembered the morning after. Obama was rewarded by a huge boost in the polls, putting him far ahead of his rival by a wide margin.

The Palin Surprise

But the Democrats' bounce was deflated immediately the next day when McCain announced his choice for vice president: Governor Sarah Palin of Alaska, well-loved in her home state but virtually unknown to the rest of the country. Her nomination stunned the media and set off a frenzied search for information about her. Palin, the first female Republican nominee for vice president, complemented McCain well. She was a fellow "maverick" and reputed reformer who had fought corruption in her own party as well as on the other side of the aisle. Born in Idaho, she had been a high school basketball star and beauty queen before attending college in Hawaii. She transferred between a number of different colleges before completing her degree in journalism and returning to Alaska. Married to her high school sweetheart, Todd Palin, who was a commercial fisherman, oilman and world snowmachine champion, she was also the mother of five children. The youngest, Trig, was less than one year old, having been born with Down's Syndrome in the middle of Palin's gubernatorial term. After her early involvement with her school's parent-teacher association, Palin became a city councilor and then mayor of her small home town of Wasilla in southcentral Alaska. She was nominated to the State Oil & Gas Commission and then became a local heroine as she blew the whistle on corruption that persisted in the tight circle between the big oil companies and the state's political parties. When state regulators refused to investigate her allegations of corruption openly, she resigned.[34] That only added to her popularity, and she finally ran for governor in 2006, winning despite opposition from her own party.

Once elected, she immediately got to work, getting rid of waste and corruption in the state government, offering the gubernatorial airplane for sale on eBay and signing ethics reform legislation. Her husband also resigned from his oil job so as to avoid any impression of conflicts of interest. Palin then went about restructuring the state's oil and gas industry, opening the doors of state bidding processes and negotiating a deal to build a natural gas pipeline from Alaska to the "lower 48" that would be one of the most ambitious infrastructure projects in the history of the country. Her predecessors, with years to work on the project, had failed to secure a deal, but Palin accomplished it in a matter of months. She also governed in a spirit of bipartisanship and tolerance, including Democrats in her administration and continuing to oppose the Republican establishment on occasion, as she did in endorsing Lieutenant Governor Sean Parnell's unsuccessful bid to unseat incumbent congressman Don Young in 2008. While she herself had strong social conservative views—she opposed abortion in all cases, even in rape and incest, and supported constitutional amendments to restrict marriage to heterosexuals—she was reluctant to foist them on

167

others. In one instance she vetoed a bill that would have denied homosexual couples benefits such as health insurance.[35] And she could practice the values she preached, having recently given birth to a Down syndrome child. Shortly after she was announced as the vice-presidential nominee, it was revealed that her eldest daughter, Bristol, was pregnant. That revelation could have have been a public relations disaster, but when Palin announced that her daughter had chosen to keep the child, it set off a groundswell of support among social conservatives.

The Democrats were completely caught off guard. If they had heard of Palin at all, they had not even considered her a likely pick. In retrospect, however, her selection became more likely the moment Obama picked Biden. McCain needed a pro-life running mate to satisfy the conservative party base. But once Obama left Hillary Clinton's voters grasping at straws, McCain also had to make the most of the opportunity to steal away female Democratic voters—and to give voters who wanted to cast their ballots for an historic "first" another way to do so.

Palin was much more than a symbol, of course. As a former broadcast sports journalist, she was an excellent speaker, and connected easily with crowds across the country. And unlike Biden, whose false attempts to sound working-class simply sounded drunk, Palin was a real middle-class working mother—the kind Democrats liked to claim they were fighting for. She became immediately popular—and controversial. People could not stop talking about her, whether they loved or hated her. The conservative base of the Republican Party felt it had finally found a good reason to support the McCain ticket. And the liberal base of the Democratic Party—including the media—finally had a reason to fear it. Money began pouring into McCain's coffers just before the public financing limits would kick in; similarly, money continued flowing into Obama's coffers after every major Palin speech. As Obama's campaign manager, David Plouffe, would later say: "She was our best fundraiser and organizer in the fall."[36]

And Obama's activists, together with left-wing bloggers and even mainstream journalists, began a concerted—if somewhat crazed—effort to smear her by any means necessary. Obama led the way himself. His spokesperson welcomed her appointment not by congratulating her, but by belittling her and small-town America: "Today, John McCain put the former mayor of a town of 9,000 with zero foreign policy experience a heartbeat away from the presidency."[37] Journalists, lawyers and investigators flocked to Alaska to begin digging up dirt—real and imagined—to tarnish Palin's ascendant image.

Part of the enthusiasm—and fear—surrounding Palin was evoked not just by the fact that she is a woman, a governor and a social conservative, but simply because she was unfamiliar and unexpected. She was a new face—and a symbol of all those Americans whose lives had refused to follow the dominant media narrative of failure and frustration, who had enjoyed the fruits of progress during the Bush administration and had not come out the other end of it with feelings of resentment. Her character, and what she represented, were exciting because they were fresh. And nothing is more exciting in America's culture of novelty than new ideas and new leadership, no matter how controversial. Most of all, she spoke directly to the American people, in the language and idiom shunned by the country's elite but shared by the majority. More than any other leader in 2008, she was able to articulate a clear and coherent alternative vision for America in the midst of crisis. She fumbled, to be sure, when probed for detail, but there was no politician—not even Obama—that could match her ability to communicate to ordinary people.

For the first few days after her nomination, Palin was riding high, and McCain enjoyed a massive surge in the polls. With just two months to go before voting, he suddenly had his first lead of the general election. He and Palin toured the country together, greeting ecstatic crowds who wanted a glimpse of their new heroine. Mothers and fathers brought their daughters to see her; parents of disabled children in particular came to her rallies, moved by her example as a mother of a "special needs" child. Best of all, she defined the issues of the campaign in clear terms—often clearer than McCain himself—and delivered a speech at the Republican National Convention that seemed, for the moment at least, to dispel any doubts about her. One of her best lines was a retort to the Obama campaign's jab at small towns: "I guess a small-town mayor is sort of like a 'community organizer,' except that you have actual responsibilities," she joked.[38] (That line was used by the Obama campaign to drum up horror among his supporters, which resulted in his single best day of fund-raising as he raked in $10 million.) She also came up with the ad-lib of the campaign: "What's the difference between a pit bull and a hockey mom?" she asked the crowd. "Lipstick!" The headline the next day in the tabloid press was: "Lipstick on a pit bull."[39] The country was obsessed with her.

One of Palin's greatest strengths was the positive influence she seemed to have on McCain. When they shared the stage, he smiled and seemed more relaxed. She brought the campaign more attention, which also helped him reach more voters. The night after she gave her successful convention speech, McCain delivered his nomination address, and actually drew more viewers than Obama's acceptance speech the week before—38.9 million as opposed to 38.4 million—even though McCain had merely given his inside the convention hall, without the Greek columns and mass audience.[40] It was the first time many Americans would listen closely to McCain and hear his compelling biography, as well as what he really stood for, and his famous refrain that he would use again and again in the weeks to come:

> Fight with me. Fight with me. Fight for what's right for our country. Fight for the ideals and character of a free people. Fight for our children's future. Fight for justice and opportunity for all. Stand up to defend our country from its enemies. Stand up for each other, for beautiful, blessed, bountiful America. Stand up, stand up, stand up, and fight. Nothing is inevitable here. We're Americans, and we never give up. We never quit. We never hide from history. We make history. Thank you, and God bless you, and God bless America.

The speech was one of the best McCain had given in the entire campaign. But Palin had much to do with the new enthusiasm surrounding McCain. She was, in the words of many observers, sympathetic and otherwise, a "game-changer."

Liberal journalists and Obama supporters flew into a panic. Some reported having nightmares about Palin. When the left-leaning online magazine *Slate* asked readers to submit their dreams about Palin, there were five hundred responses, most of them from opponents of the Republican ticket. The magazine reported:

> It's hard to generalize about such a large group of dreams, but there were a few persistent themes: Palin as a gun-toting animal killer, pregnancies and denied abortions, baby Trig, and the landscape of Alaska. Many of you reported dreaming about John McCain dying and Palin taking over the Oval Office. Both men and straight women reported sexual fantasies involving the Alaska governor.[41]

Not content with searching through her background for any defect they could find, journalists began attacking the way the campaign had handled the Alaska governor. She had done well on the campaign trail, repeating her stump speech across the country, but was not made available to the press for open question-and-answer sessions. That was fair criticism—or would have been, except that Obama had also avoided journalists for long stretches of the campaign, and that Palin's opponent, Joe Biden, hadn't been allowed to speak to the media for weeks. Other journalists, alarmed at the bounce the McCain-Palin ticket was enjoying, and particularly at Palin's ability to connect to ordinary Americans, urged Obama to begin attacking, to show more enthusiasm and even anger in his campaign. Instead of the usual, confident swagger, Obama sounded nervous on the campaign trail in early September, his voice rising into a higher register, weak and almost plaintive. Thomas Friedman of the *New York Times* urged:

> Whoever slipped that Valium into Barack Obama's coffee needs to be found and arrested by the Democrats because Obama has gone from cool to cold.

> Somebody needs to tell Obama that if he wants the chance to calmly answer the phone at 3 a.m. in the White House, he is going to need to start slamming down some phones at 3 p.m. along the campaign trail.[42]

The Obama campaign took the advice to heart, launching a massive media campaign that not only played up their candidate's strengths, but also ruthlessly attacked McCain and his new running mate.

There were to be no limits to the harshness and scope of the attacks. Obama, in an apparent gesture of maturity and grace, said he did not want to criticize Palin's daughter for having a child out of wedlock.[43] After all, he, too, had been conceived by his mother when she was just a teenager and not yet married. But other Obama enthusiasts would not be so restrained. Blogger Andrew Sullivan of *The Atlantic* became obsessed with the theory that Palin's fifth child, Trig, had really been conceived by her daughter Bristol and that Palin had faked her pregnancy as a cover-up. Other groups, some more closely connected to the Obama campaign than others, made fun of McCain's age; they attacked his past history of skin cancer, suggesting he would not survive through the end of his term;[44] and they played endlessly on the caricature of McCain as a "warmonger." One ad, by the far-left Internet activist group MoveOn.org, featured a young mother clutching her baby and warning McCain that she would not let him take her baby away to fight a war.[45] Another, released by the Obama campaign itself, made fun of the fact that McCain did not use a computer or a handheld device such as the Black-Berry. The aim was to portray McCain as hopelessly out of touch. But the reality was that McCain's war injuries and his disability made typing excruciating for him—a fact the Obama campaign did not care to discover or reveal. Even Biden publicly objected to the ad, calling it "terrible," but the campaign continued, relentless.[46] And Obama, in an unguarded moment, made a comment that most observers took as a direct reference to Palin, and which revived memories of his digs at Clinton during the Democratic primary: "You can put lipstick on a pig," Obama said, "it's still a pig."[47]

The media followed on, calling McCain a "liar" when he ran negative ads of his own. Many journalists echoed the Obama camp's claim that McCain was running the most negative campaign in history[48] (a charge that the McCain camp would fire back at the Obama campaign[49]). Joe Klein of *Time*, one of the media's most relentless supporters of the Obama cause, agreed with Obama and noted that much of the media felt the same way:

> John McCain has allowed his campaign to slip the normal bounds of political propriety. The situation has gotten so intense that we in the media have slipped our normal rules as well. Usually when a candidate tells something less than the truth, we mince words. We use euphemisms like mendacity and inaccuracy ... or, as the Associated Press put it, "McCain's claims skirt facts." But increasing numbers of otherwise sober observers, even such august institutions as the New York Times editorial board, are calling John McCain a liar.[50]

One of the examples Klein cited was an ad run by the McCain campaign claiming that Obama had supported a bill providing sex education for kindergartners. The larger point of the ad was that Obama had pledged to lead the way on school reform but had never done anything about it; the point about kindergartners was superfluous and probably should have been dropped. But as Byron York of the *National Review* noted, McCain's claim was actually correct:

> The fact is, the bill's intention was to mandate that issues like contraception and the prevention of sexually-transmitted diseases be included in sex-education classes for children before the sixth grade, and as early as kindergarten. Obama's defenders may howl, but the bill is what it is.[51]

Independent observers also contested the argument that the 2008 campaign was the most negative the country had seen.[52] And voters—surely an important jury in such matters—did not feel the campaign had been especially negative: polls showed that most agreed it was par for the course, with only 1 in 4 reporting that it was more negative than in most election years.[53] Nearly 7 in 10, by contrast, said they believed that reporters were trying to help the candidate they wanted to win.[54]

In any event, the worst attacks of the 2008 campaign were not aimed at Obama, or McCain, but rather at Sarah Palin. Rumors were circulated on the Internet that she had variously: ordered a school library in her town to ban books (though some books on the list she had supposedly banned had not even been printed yet when she was the mayor); forced rape victims to pay for their own "rape kit" examinations (which she had not done, and which had been a problem throughout rural Alaska but not specifically in Wasilla); improperly tried to fire a state trooper, who was also her sister's ex-husband, from the state police force (the trooper had used a Taser stun gun on his own stepson, and Palin was cleared of any wrongdoing by an independent investigation on the eve of the election). One Democrat in Congress, Steve Cohen, even repeated a line that had been promoted on left-wing blogs: "Jesus was a community organizer; Pontius Pilate was a governor."[55] Ironically, Cohen—who is Jewish—had been the target of a vicious antisemitic campaign in the primary race in his district.[56] But he saw no problem with attacking Palin with an absurd religious slur. The media quickly spread and amplified rumors that painted Palin as an extremist firebrand, such as the claim that someone at a rally had shouted "Kill him!" when Palin referred to Obama. When the Secret Service later reported that no such incident had happened, there was little coverage.[57] Another Palin myth had entered the imagination of millions of Americans as fact.

Obama's campaign had repeatedly complained about "smears," such as the claim that he was a Muslim. The media and even civic organizations such as the Anti-Defamation League and other Jewish community groups, rushed to his defense.[58] But they did not respond with similar urgency or enthusiasm to the attacks against Palin. The mechanism through which the lies about Palin spread was murky. To some extent they simply had a life of their own. But one intrepid blogger put together an investigation that revealed that many of the worst smears had been posted on the Internet by an employee at a public relations company, Winner & Associates, using false aliases or "sockpuppets."[59] It was a technique known as "astroturfing"—staging the appearance of a grassroots campaign. Worse yet, the firm had ties to Obama's chief strategist David Axelrod—considered the father of astroturfing techniques—and may have used the same voice-over artist in its videos that Axelrod's own company employed in its productions. It seemed likely that the Obama campaign itself had been the source of many of the anti-Palin smears, using Axelrod's tried-and-tested techniques.

At least some of the allegations of astroturfing were proven true when the individual who posted the videos confessed his involvement. But there was never any follow-up on the story by the mainstream media. Instead, journalists remained determined to expose Palin's weaknesses. They finally had their chance when the McCain campaign—foolishly, in the view of many sympathetic observers—granted Palin's first exclusive interviews to ABC's Charlie Gibson and CBS's Katie Couric. Both exuded condescension in their conversations with Palin. Gibson grilled Palin, asking several times if she really felt "ready" for the job of vice president.[60] He also asked her about her feelings on the "Bush Doctrine," and when she asked him to clarify his question, he defined it for her—completely incorrectly. As Charles Krauthammer—inventor of the term "Bush Doctrine," later wrote:

> There is no single meaning of the Bush doctrine. In fact, there have been four distinct meanings, each one succeeding another over the eight years of this administration—and the one Charlie Gibson cited is not the one in common usage today. It is utterly different.
>
> He asked Palin, "Do you agree with the Bush doctrine?"

She responded, quite sensibly to a question that is ambiguous, "In what respect, Charlie?"

Sensing his "gotcha" moment, Gibson refused to tell her. After making her fish for the answer, Gibson grudgingly explained to the moose-hunting rube that the Bush doctrine "is that we have the right of anticipatory self-defense."

Wrong.

Yes, Sarah Palin didn't know what it is. But neither does Charlie Gibson. And at least she didn't pretend to know—while he looked down his nose and over his glasses with weary disdain, sighing and "sounding like an impatient teacher," as the Times noted. In doing so, he captured perfectly the establishment snobbery and intellectual condescension that has characterized the chattering classes' reaction to the mother of five who presumes to play on their stage.[61]

Moreover, Gibson's interview had been edited, critics charged, to reflect Palin in as poor a light as possible. Gibson's confrontational, condescending approach to Palin contrasted sharply with the sycophantic approach he had taken with Barack Obama in their first interview, in which he had asked such questions as "Senator, I'm curious about your feelings last night. It was an historic moment. Has it sunk in yet?" and "[D]o you say to yourself: 'Son of a gun, I've done this?'"[62]

Couric's interview with Palin was even worse—partly because Palin, nervous from her previous encounter, was both defensive and clumsy. Nothing she said was false or misleading, but she failed to answer a simple (if asinine) question about what news sources she read, and offered this in response to a question about whether she had been involved in negotiations with Russia:

We have trade missions back and forth, we do. It's very important when you consider even national security issues with Russia. As Putin rears his head and comes into the air space of the United States of America, where do they go? It's Alaska. It's just right over the border. It is from Alaska that we send those out to make sure that an eye is being kept on this very powerful nation,

Russia, because they are right there, they are right next to our state.[63]

Though the germ of an idea was there, it was a rambling, incoherent response, and was mocked relentlessly for weeks by late-night comedians. The most famous joke at her expense was that of *Saturday Night Live*'s Tina Fey, who performed an impression of Palin as a gun-toting bimbo. When Fey, playing Palin announced, "I can see Russia from my house!"[64] the line entered the public imagination as something Palin had *actually* said. Election Day polling of Obama voters revealed that 87 percent thought Palin herself, not Tina Fey, had said those words.[65]

In truth, Palin had been out of her depth in these interviews. But she had done no worse than Joe Biden, and even Barack Obama had also had his share of disastrous interviews and press conferences, though he was punished far less severely. Still, in the heat of a close race, and with the press corps waiting to pounce for weeks, Palin's performance was damaging. It did not matter that Palin had passed every other test that had been set for her; the media had already been disparaging her as a mere "bimbo" (in the words of Bill Maher[66]) before her convention speech. But her interviews gave some wavering moderates a reason to believe the smears about her and to abandon McCain. So, too, did a late-breaking story in October about the $150,000 that the RNC had used to purchase a new wardrobe for the dressed-down Alaska governor.[67] Few thought to ask how much Barack Obama or Joe Biden spent on their clothes. Palin was the target, and would continue to be so long after the campaign was over.

The Moment of Truth

Nonetheless, for the moment, the McCain-Palin ticket maintained its lead. It might have continued to do so, even in the face of the campaign's own stumbles and Obama's relentless attacks, had it not been for the financial crisis that struck in mid-September. For months, Obama had been talking about the weak state of the economy, describing its condition as "recession" even though the U.S. had not yet experienced two consecutive quarters of economic contraction, the standard definition of the term. In fact, in the second quarter of 2008, the economy grew by nearly three percent—a healthy rate—due largely to surging exports. The rhetoric of the two candidates mirrored their respective offers of change. McCain had acknowledged the economic challenges facing the economy, but focused on making the most of the country's enduring strengths. Obama projected an image of a nation whose economy was actually broken and on the edge of despair, but which could be rescued with bold new leadership. The version of America Obama offered seemed a far cry from reality; it was arguably the same election-year rhetoric of every four-year cycle. But the idea of an economic "crisis" became a central theme of media reports, especially with fuel prices skyrocketing by midsummer. Consumer confidence, meanwhile, fell steadily despite successful interventions by the Federal Reserve that had steadied the markets in the summer of 2008.

And then, suddenly, reality caught up to Obama's image of despair. Financial markets had been behaving strangely for months, and credit had been growing steadily more scarce, by the time panic struck in September 2008. On September 15, investment bank Merrill Lynch announced that it was selling itself to Bank of America for $50 billion.[68] Another investment bank, Lehman Brothers, which had been even more exposed to sub-prime loans in the housing market, failed to find a private buyer. When the government refused to intervene, the firm—which had been a Wall Street institution for a century and a half—collapsed, sparking a worldwide financial panic. By then, McCain's campaign had long since abandoned trying to color the economy in rosier terms than the Obama camp: it had adopted the use of the terms "crisis" and "recession." But at a town hall meeting in Jacksonville, Florida, on September 15, as news of Lehman's collapse was breaking, McCain insisted: "the fundamentals of our economy are strong." It was a catastrophic mistake. In fairness, McCain

178

had gone on to describe the country's economic challenges. Moreover, as more than one commentator pointed out, many of the economic "fundamentals" of the economy—worker productivity, for example—were indeed strong.[69] But McCain had once again offered the Obama campaign the opportunity to lift a damaging quote from his remarks and use it against him in speeches and sound bites, which it did to maximum effect.

All was not yet lost. The crisis benefited Obama, but it could just as easily have hurt him. As the less experienced candidate, he had yet to convince voters he was the right person to lead the country in times of crisis. His previous attempt, during the Russian invasion of Georgia a month before, had been a flop. McCain also had to prove himself: the country trusted his leadership on foreign policy and the fight against terror, but not on the economy. That had partly been the result of effective campaigning by Obama. Though McCain had served as chairman of the Senate commerce committee, Obama (and before him, Mitt Romney in the Republican primary) had taunted McCain with a quote from a 2005 interview with the *Wall Street Journal* in which he had said, with astonishing—and perhaps unwise—candor: "I'm going to be honest: I know a lot less about economics than I do about military and foreign policy issues. I still need to be educated."[70] The financial crisis was an opportunity for McCain to show that he could lead on the economy—not just by proposing policy interventions, but by presenting a coherent alternative to what the Bush administration had done and what the Obama campaign was promising to do.

It was a moment of truth for McCain. And it involved the $700 billion Troubled Assets Relief Program (TARP)—known to most Americans as "the bailout"—that Secretary of the Treasury Hank Paulson had proposed, and which Bush had appealed to the nation to support. McCain had already looked unsteady on the topic of financial bailouts. He had criticized the idea of a government rescue for the giant American Insurance Group (AIG), telling an interviewer on

September 16, "I do not believe that the American taxpayer should be on the hook for AIG."[71] But the next day, McCain backed away from his initial opposition, saying, "I didn't want to do that. And I don't think anybody I know wanted to do that. But there are literally millions of people whose retirement, whose investment, whose insurance were at risk."[72] Obama, too, had been noncommittal, calling AIG's troubles "the final verdict on the failed economic philosophy of the last eight years" and opposing a bailout for "the shareholders or management of AIG" without specifically opposing a rescue of its bad debts.[73] But there was not much Obama needed to say. This was the crisis he had been waiting for. He endorsed the $700 billion bailout, and would later take credit for various features of the TARP proposal as evidence that the country's leaders had been guided by his advice. But there was little he was expected to do other than point the finger of blame at the president and stay out of the way of a crisis that few economists had any real idea how to resolve.

It was McCain's decision to make. With so many economic arguments to choose from, all disagreeing with each other or simply giving up in confusion, McCain ought to have considered the political arguments. Bush had proposed the bailout; Obama had supported it; but it was not entirely clear what it was meant to do, nor where the figure of $700 billion had come from. There were also the taxpayers' interests to consider, as well as McCain's consistent arguments against runaway government spending, and the conservative preference for free markets and antipathy towards big government. The Republican base was deeply suspicious of the bailout and it lacked the full support of the Republican caucus in Congress. No one, though, emerged to articulate a clear philosophical basis for opposing it other than concern for the taxpayers. That alone was not sufficient as a basis for opposition, because many of those taxpayers stood to lose their jobs anyway if the economy collapsed. Yet someone had to transcend the economic deadlock and offer a political basis for opposition. One of the few who realized this was conservative *New York Times* columnist and *Weekly Standard* publisher William Kristol. He hoped McCain might have the courage to use the bailout debate as an opportunity to triangulate against both Bush and Obama, and state his own, clear, conservative economic proposals as the alternative to the bailout.[74] It was a unique opportunity for "Straight Talk" from the "Maverick" himself, a chance to prove who he was to the American people.

Instead, McCain chose a different sort of political tactic. On September 24, he announced that he was suspending his campaign and returning to Washington to press for Republican support for the bailout. He also asked that the first presidential debate, scheduled for the 26th—just two days later—be postponed.[75] The move took the entire political world by surprise—not least Obama, who had apparently spoken to McCain earlier that day about issuing a joint statement of support for the bailout. According to reports from the Obama camp, McCain had given Obama no indication about his impending announcement.[76] It was an unanticipated, unprecedented maneuver.

It was also a gimmick—but a potentially brilliant one, if McCain had been able to convince Congress to pass the bailout quickly. Unfortunately, his arrival in Washington gave Democrats a strong political incentive to stall progress in the bailout talks. There was resistance from Republicans, too, but many were willing to fall into line. The Democrats, as the majority party, held all the cards and were able to deny McCain the victory he sought. For his part, Obama stuck to supporting the bailout in the most general terms; he did not press his Democratic colleagues to pass it. For all his talk of economic crisis, he was opposed to treating the situation like one. The public, evidently, agreed: opinion polls showed that a wide majority of Americans opposed postponing the presidential debate, even given the grim economic circumstances.[77] Eventually Obama was summoned to Washington by President Bush, and briefed on the bailout proposal along with McCain. But he was not a major figure in the legislative fight—just as he had not been a major figure in any legislative struggle before. This was McCain's battle, and the message he sought to project was that he had once again put country first, national priorities ahead of political ambitions.

But the bailout bill stalled, and McCain lost both ways: not only had he failed to help pass the bailout, but he had publicly staked his claim to a drastic policy initiative that grew more and more unpopular with the Republican base and the electorate in general with each passing day. On the following Monday, September 29, the bailout failed in the House of Representatives. Republicans were blamed for opposing it (or, alternatively, hailed by conservative commentators) even though there had been plenty of Democrats who had defected from the pro-bailout line taken by their leadership. House Speaker Nancy Pelosi made things worse by lashing out against the economic policies of the Bush administration on the floor of the House of Representatives just when she needed the cooperation of House Republicans.[78] A revised version of the bailout package passed a few days later, but the damage to McCain was already done. He had not only bound himself to the Bush administration's policy more publicly and energetically than Obama, but he had also looked both uncertain and ineffective in the process. His poll numbers reversed dramatically, never to recover.

Yet McCain should not bear most of the blame. In fairness, there had been a conservative collapse across the board. Many of the people and institutions that might have been expected to oppose such a sudden expansion in federal spending—especially one rushed through Congress with little or no debate—either supported it or fell silent. Chief among these were the members of the Bush administration itself. In mid-November, with both the bailout and the election long behind him, Bush stood up for the free market:

> While reforms in the financial sector are essential, the long-term solution to today's problems is sustained economic growth. And the surest path to that growth is free markets and free people... This is a decisive moment for the global economy. In the wake

of the financial crisis, voices from the left and right are equating the free enterprise system with greed and exploitation and failure. It's true this crisis included failures—by lenders and borrowers and by financial firms and by governments and independent regulators. But the crisis was not a failure of the free market system. And the answer is not to try to reinvent that system. It is to fix the problems we face, make the reforms we need, and move forward with the free market principles that have delivered prosperity and hope to people all across the globe.[79]

It was an eloquent defense, but one that came two months too late. Instead of standing up for the free market, Bush and his cabinet seemed to have skewered a few of the last remaining conservative principles left standing.

Even the conservative Heritage Foundation had tentatively supported the bailout. Other conservative economists did, too—albeit reluctantly—on the basis of the theory that a sudden, temporary infusion of liquidity into the capital markets would restore investor confidence, free up scarce cash and slow the ongoing panic. Martin Feldstein of Harvard, one of Reagan's former economic advisers, suggested a proposal to use federal spending to help prop up home prices, an idea McCain took up eagerly.[80] The conservative talk show hosts slammed such bailouts as a waste of taxpayer money, but the experts seemed evenly divided. What no one seemed to be saying loudly enough was that while some conservatives were in favor of *temporary* expansions of government spending, the Democratic Party would seize the opportunity to make such spending *permanent*—until rising debt finally made the entire financial system unsustainable without huge tax increases.

What was lacking was any sort of coherent political opposition—even a political *alternative*—to the bailout. An opposing view needed to be expressed not just for its own sake, but also to ensure that if a bailout did in fact pass, it would be closely scrutinized en route to enactment and execution. Instead, bills were rushed through Congress on the basis of the understanding that they were urgently needed. But the day after the first bailout bill failed, the stock market rose dramatically, offsetting many of its losses from the day before (though the media credited talk of a renewed bailout bill for the recovery).[81] When the bill finally passed, the market fell again.[82] Meanwhile, the funds allocated to the TARP package were not actually released for distribution, and half were being held in reserve for the new administration to distribute. The authors of the bailout believed that their action—even if it had simply been a commitment to spend money in the future—had saved the world financial markets from collapse. But disaffection with the bailout grew as Americans began to suspect they had been sold a false bill of goods.

McCain may have believed at the time that he had been doing the right thing for the country. However, what the country really needed him to do was provide an alternative—one that could ensure a better response to the financial crisis in the short term, and provide a principled basis for opposition to big government policies in the future, once the election and the crisis had passed. Instead of following his own principles—the simple verities that had sustained the Reagan revolution—McCain opted for a short-term political calculation that backfired and left him without a real foundation for opposition to the Democrats' big-government agenda. His great character strength, and his strongest selling point to the electorate, was that he could be trusted to do the right thing even if it was unpopular. Just as he declared he would have been willing to lose an election to win a war, he ought to have been willing to risk the election to save the principles of a free-market economy. In the moment of truth, he failed to be true to himself.

Obama, meanwhile, reaped the benefits. Never good at coping under strain, Obama had been rescued by the financial crisis, which fit his vision of America better than McCain's. The tide of the election suddenly swung his way, and Obama's old confidence returned. It was for that reason that he appeared calm during the economic storm—not his innate "cool demeanor," which soon acquired mythological dimensions, but the fact that he was on a winning streak while the country was in turmoil. He did not do much to intervene in the crisis; he did not offer any big solutions. What he offered instead was the abstract concept of hope—hope that a solution would arrive if a new leader from a different party was given the chance to make the country's most important decisions.

Slowly Slipping Away

In the weeks following the financial crisis, McCain's lead in the polls became a distant memory and the prospects of regaining it slipped steadily away. He decided, after all, to attend the first presidential debate, despite Congress's failure to pass a bailout. But by the time he turned up, there was little left to debate on the economy except relatively small issues such as earmarks. In endorsing the bailout, McCain—and Bush—had effectively given up the core difference between the two parties, and the key appeal of the Republican alternative for conservative voters. McCain seemed to have "won" that debate, which focused on national security, but did very poorly in the first half-hour, which was devoted to the economic crisis. Once the questions dealt with foreign policy, he trumped Obama, who doggedly refused to admit the Iraq surge had worked and struggled to explain his curious position on meeting unconditionally with foreign autocrats. Still, McCain seemed to lack much of Obama's charisma. He was not as physically impressive as his opponent, who seemed to have had more rest and was dressed in what looked like a suit one size too large that added bulk to his normally lanky frame. That physical advantage proved critical in the second presidential debate, which was held in a more informal town hall setting. It was a format that played to McCain's "Straight Talk" style, but his gait and gestures looked jerky and uneven next to the smooth strides of the younger, larger Obama. The only debate in which everything seemed to go right for McCain was the third, in which both men were sitting down. With the physical differences more or less eliminated, viewers could focus more on the substance of the two men's remarks. Despite Obama's supposed economic prowess, his defenses of his policies were patchy. In defending his opposition to a free trade deal with Columbia during the third debate, for instance, he referred to a left-wing canard about union members being killed there, whereas such murders had been successfully prosecuted by the Columbian government and were falling rapidly.[83]

In general, voters who had watched the debates on television thought Obama had won all three, according to opinion polls. McCain may have suffered from the same handicap that allegedly hurt Richard M. Nixon in his debates with JFK in 1960, the first-ever televised debates. According to (perhaps mythical) political lore those listening on the radio thought Nixon had won, but the more handsome and affable Kennedy won among television viewers. Obama carried himself with greater poise; his answers were more confident, even if McCain's hurried responses were more competent. But another factor may have accounted for Obama's success: voters may have been asking themselves different questions about each candidate. With Obama in the lead, voters may have been seeking confirmation that he could be their president; with McCain losing, voters may have needed him to do something to prove they ought to give him a second chance. So while Obama's confident style reassured voters, McCain's reluctance to attack his rival aggressively amounted to wasting each debate opportunity. Critics—and apparently Obama himself—had widely expected McCain to bring up Obama's association with William Ayers during the second debate; when he didn't, Obama speculated that McCain had been afraid to stand up to him. Obama also frequently bent the rules, speaking past his time limit and demanding the right to rebut arguments he did not like when his chances for rebuttals had been exhausted. Instead of pointing out Obama's numerous violations, McCain simply allowed him to dominate the discussions.

The vice-presidential debate was watched by many more people than any of the three presidential contests.[84] Palin was the main draw: the country was still in doubt as to whether she was up to the job. Left-wing attacks and the media's relentless campaign against her had so lowered expectations that half the country expected her to suffer a breakdown on national television—one that many Democrats eagerly anticipated. But Palin delivered Biden a stunning defeat. Though the post-debate spin softened the blow and gave the impression that Biden had won—just as political analysts spun the debates in favor of Obama in all three presidential debates—Palin came through with flying colors. She did so against the challenge posed by the unanticipated problem that the moderator, Gwen Ifill of PBS, had written a book about Obama's campaign for president that was due to come out on January 20, 2009. That gave her a pecuniary interest in the outcome of the election that she had not previously disclosed and which the McCain campaign, at least, had not been aware of.[85] Palin handled Ifill deftly, insisting that she was going to use the debate as an opportunity to speak directly to the American people rather than through the filter of the moderator and the media that had so abused her. This tactic was later spun by the left as an attempt to evade questions or merely speak from talking points, but it was very effective in helping her connect to her national audience.

Biden seemed surprised by Palin's feisty resistance; he seemed flummoxed from their very first meeting onstage, in which she had disarmed him by asking: "Mind if I call you Joe?". He also failed to get the better of her in their exchanges and looked almost defensive in many of his responses to questions. But he used a ruse that he had relied on for much of his political career: using confidence to create the impression of great knowledge and worldly expertise where very little of either actually existed. He gave several dozen answers to questions that were false to varying extents, from jarring inaccuracies to outright lies. But like Obama, it was not the substance of Biden's words but his style that mattered. Biden *sounded* like he knew what he was talking about; Palin was ridiculed for "not answering the questions," a highly mendacious twisting of her warning that she was not going to yield to her opponent: "I may not answer the questions that either the moderator or you want to hear, but I'm going to talk straight to the American people and let them know my track record also."[86] The analysts and journalists could not be bothered to check Biden's facts, and the majority declared him the winner, a "fact" later reflected in opinion polls. But Palin had reached the American people. For a brief moment, she had won back the respect that had been lost over the previous several weeks.

Meanwhile, the polls continued to show Obama with a commanding lead. States that had looked likely to swing towards McCain in early September—even traditionally "blue" states—were now firmly back in the Democratic column, while many traditionally "red" states suddenly looked vulnerable. It wasn't just that Obama was winning over undecided and independent or moderate voters; he had begun winning Republicans as well. At the very least, he was consolidating support among Democrats while McCain lost support in his own party. McCain's rallies were still drawing large and enthusiastic audiences; Palin's crowds were even larger, typically well over capacity with hundreds of supporters lined up outside the door. Some of her rallies competed with Obama's for sheer numbers in attendance. But Obama had the organization and the money consistently to stage enormous rallies that neither McCain nor Palin could match. And—critically—he had the money to run many more ads on television and radio.

Obama also had keen political instincts, especially for the way in which the media shaped public opinion. If he had projected an air of frustration and anger prior to the financial crisis, in its aftermath he exuded calm and stability. His supposed "cool demeanor" was at least partly the result of the fact that events were going his way: in early September, when he was losing in the polls, he lashed out almost desperately at his opponents, his voice nearly cracking as he exhorted voters: "I mean come on, they must think you're stupid!"[87] But none of that mattered after the financial crisis struck. Obama had promised "change," but it was in fact McCain who had changed his position on the bailout. Obama's vague stance, while hardly the stuff of great leadership, was at least a stable position. McCain's decision to abandon the rock of conservative principles cast him adrift in stormy political waters.

Even in the traditionally conservative state of New Hampshire, McCain's long-time stronghold, a new mood had swept the voters. On the one hand, voters were still worried about Obama, whose policies, inexperience and past associations provoked mistrust. On the other, residents of the Granite State were angry at the Bush administration and seemed to resist the idea that McCain—or any Republican—would be different. These two feelings defined the battling impulses of swing voters in traditionally conservative parts of the country. While the Democratic base might have convinced itself that the country was voting for "hope," in many ways the contest was a choice between caution about the future and retribution for the past.

In the final days of the 2008 campaign, McCain was trailing badly. Though some polls showed the race to be within a few percentage points, others suggested that Obama's lead could reach double digits. Nevertheless, McCain pressed onward with renewed energy, even as many sympathetic observers began to conclude that the race was over. He also began—perhaps too late to make much difference—to find a core to his political message in the aftermath of the bailout. One theme was to link Obama to the mortgage giants Fannie Mae and Freddie Mac. These two former government-run companies had invested heavily in sub-prime mortgages and had lobbied Congress to resist regulation of the sub-prime market, providing generous contributions to their (mostly Democratic) congressional allies. Several of Obama's advisers—including housing adviser Franklin Raines, former vice presidential search leader Jim Johnson, and political fixer Rahm Emanuel—were closely tied to the sub-prime companies. McCain began to find traction among the electorate when he laid the blame for the financial crisis at the feet of the Democrats in Congress who had blocked his attempts to regulate the industry—as well as those, like Obama, who had done nothing to help press the issue.

McCain had help from another, unanticipated source. On October 12, Obama decided to walk around a neighborhood in Oregon, Ohio, joining canvassers in door-to-door campaigning. One man—Samuel J. "Joe" Wurzelbacher—approached Obama and asked how his proposals for tax increases on individuals making more than $250,000 per year would affect him. He was a plumber by trade, he said, who wanted to buy the business he was working for but was afraid that doing so would put him in a higher tax bracket. Obama did his best to respond, giving a detailed account of how his tax policies would be different from George W. Bush's in that they would give greater opportunities to those earning less. But after going over the issue back and forth, Obama hadn't quite answered Wurzelbacher's question, which had more to do with the effective marginal tax rate—the taxes paid by people as they moved to higher levels of income. In the end, Obama had to admit that his tax policy was motivated by egalitarian ideas:

> My attitude is that if the economy's good for folks from the bottom up, it's gonna be good for everybody. If you've got a plumbing business, you're gonna be better off if you're gonna be better off if you've got a whole bunch of customers who can afford to hire you, and right now everybody's so pinched that business is bad for everybody and I think when you spread the wealth around, it's good for everybody.[88]

That single phrase—"spread the wealth around"—crystallized everything that McCain had been struggling to highlight about Obama for months: that he was fundamentally a left-wing politician whose redistributionist sentiments and policies were dictated by ideology, not economic sense. "Joe the Plumber," as he became known, was an instant celebrity on conservative talk shows and television. He opined

190

that Obama's proposal sounded like "socialism," and many Republicans seemed to agree. McCain was quick to quote Joe the Plumber's exchange with Obama, and soon invited him on the campaign trail. One man from a Toledo suburb had managed to do what McCain's entire staff, and the whole of the Republican Party, had not: find a coherent message to run with against Obama.

The Democrats, immediately seeing the danger of Obama's remark, began an all-out smear campaign against Joe the Plumber. With the help of state officials who were Obama supporters and fundraisers (and who were subsequently punished), the left seized on embarrassing details in an attempt to humiliate Joe the Plumber: his real name was not "Joe"; he was not a licensed plumber; he owed tax liens to the government. Obama himself mocked Wurzelbacher: "A *plumber* is the guy he's fightin' for!" he jeered, before a cheering crowd in Londonderry, New Hampshire.[89] These attacks evaded the real strength of Joe the Plumber and failed to defuse his argument: the point was not Joe the Plumber's questions but Obama's answer. Joe the Plumber became a symbol for the American everyman, and gave McCain and Palin a theme for their final weeks on the trail.

As Election Day drew nearer, it seemed clear that Obama would win several states that Bush had won in 2004. But McCain could still win—if not the popular vote, then in the Electoral College. He had to secure wins in Ohio and Florida—both of which seemed within reach—as well as Pennsylvania and some combination of New Hampshire, Virginia and Nevada. It could be done—and McCain and Palin spent the little time and money they had left in those states.

Yet Obama's operation in the closing days was simply overwhelming. He already had thousands of volunteers on the ground throughout the nation, pulling them out of states he was likely to lose, like North Dakota, and reinserting them in states where they were needed, such as Ohio and Pennsylvania. His online campaign allowed people to canvas from their own homes; it even developed an iPhone application

191

designed to re-organize a cell phone's list of contacts in order of swing states so that users could call and remind their friends to vote.

The McCain campaign and the RNC had managed to close the technological gap in the last months of the campaign. Even Obama's technical team expressed admiration for the way the RNC had used "crowd-sourcing" to solicit video submissions from the public at large about what the party should include in its election platform, as well as how the McCain campaign sent voter call sheets directly to supporters' inboxes to enlist their help in getting out the vote. The new web-messaging service Twitter also became a potent political tool for Republicans. In August, when the fuel crisis was at its worst and House Speaker Nancy Pelosi dismissed Congress without reaching an agreement on offshore drilling, Republicans decided to continue speaking on the House floor. The Capitol staff was instructed to turn off the microphones and the lights, but a few representatives remained, determined not to leave when the nation's energy needs were so urgent. Enthusiastic staffers began sending out updates over Twitter, using "#dontgo"—a "hashtag" that allowed anyone who was interested to follow what was happening and share ideas. Soon the protest took on a carnival-like atmosphere, with tour groups, ordinarily excluded from the Senate floor, milling about with legislators and applauding their speeches from the benches.[90] After the election, Twitter continued to be an important meeting place for conservatives, and an initiative called Top Conservatives On Twitter—#tcot—brought many of the leading conservative thinkers and critics in touch online for the first time. It was a reminder of the power of words, when combined with new technology and bold leadership.

It was ironic that conservatives found themselves catching up to the Democrats on technology, when the first and most successful bloggers were conservative critics of the left-leaning media who could find no other outlet for their views. Independent journalist Matthew Drudge, one of the first true bloggers, broke the Monica Lewinsky scandal on his website in 1998. Charles Johnson, owner and moderator of the blog *Little Green Footballs*, revealed in 2004 that documents used by veteran CBS News journalist Dan Rather to smear George W. Bush before Election Day that year were forgeries, costing Rather his job. In the early days of technology-driven politics, conservatives made the best use of new media because it gave them what little else could: independence from mainstream media bias.

Yet instead of capitalizing on that independence—even when a maverick campaign like McCain's came along—Republicans still applied old, hierarchical organizational models to managing new media. They used technology to broadcast messages to supporters, and to contact donors, but were reluctant to give their activists any control over the message themselves. It was a centralized model, more appropriate to a media age long since gone by—and to a centralized hierarchy benefiting an old-style left-wing political movement rather than a party based on ideals of freedom and the devolution of power. Ironically, it was the Democratic campaign of Barack Obama that adopted the conservative idea of putting the tools in the hands of the grass roots, giving ordinary people maximum power and autonomy rather than dictating every fine point in a top-down fashion. Though it clouded Obama's message and created contradictory expectations of the Democratic nominee, that difference in philosophy was to prove decisive in helping him motivate the "netroots" to get out the vote.

Obama also had television ads running in all of the swing states, outspending McCain several times over. With a few weeks left in the campaign, Obama booked all of the remaining television time, plus half an hour of prime time television on most major networks to run an "infomercial" that was seen by one in five American households.[91] It did not actually offer voters any new information, but was a potent reminder to the electorate of just how much Obama wanted to be president—and just how well his campaign had been run.

The newspaper endorsements came in; the celebrity endorsements went out; and while there were a few surprises—like Aerosmith guitarist Joe Perry—for McCain, the bulk of them went Obama's way. One endorsement that was particularly important was that of Colin Powell—a Republican, former chairman of the Joint Chiefs of Staff, former Secretary of State during Bush's first term, and a good friend of McCain besides. Obama simply looked unstoppable.

Election Day

The long-awaited day finally arrived. The weather was clear and calm across the country and unseasonably warm, portending a strong voter turnout. People gathered early at polling stations and stood in long lines at schools and community centers converted for the purpose. Inside, the atmosphere was typically solemn, but festive. There were a few problems. Polling places struggled with the high number of absentee votes, and there were a handful of bizarre events as well, such as Republican observers being unlawfully excluded from a few polling places and Black Panthers "guarding" a Philadelphia voting station.

But for the most part, it was a smooth, exemplary election. A carnivalesque atmosphere surrounded some voting stations; in Portsmouth, New Hampshire, a marching band entertained voters at each voting station in town. Children walked into voting booths hand-in-hand with their parents; old couples helped each other sign in together at the welcome tables. By mid-morning, turnout had leveled off in most areas of the country; unlike the Democratic primary, when many voting stations had run out of ballots, there were few such problems. By day's end, it was clear that turnout would exceed that of 2004 by a small margin. It was the composition of that turnout, not the sheer numbers, that would count most.

At polling places in urban centers, Obama's volunteers swamped McCain's—by a factor of ten to one in some places. They were not only monitoring the voting and counting of ballots; they were also checking off lists of registered voters and contacting those who had not yet shown up, arranging transportation for them if they needed it. The goal was to run up the score in urban and heavily Democratic areas to ensure overall victory.

The results began to trickle in just after the first polls closed. McCain, watching from the Biltmore Hotel in Phoenix, took heart from his win in West Virginia—a state few Democrats had lost and still won the White House. But one by one, the dominoes McCain needed refused to fall. And Obama's supporters gathered by the hundreds of thousands in Grant Park, Chicago, forty years after radical activists had gathered there to battle police outside the Democratic National Convention in riots that would divide the party and the country for decades. They cheered each victory in turn—in New Hampshire, Pennsylvania, Ohio, Florida, Virginia, and—almost unthinkably—North Carolina, a traditionally deep "red" state. And finally, well before midnight, the television networks flashed their projection: Obama would be the nation's 44th President. He had won. It was over.

The damage would not be limited to McCain's presidential run. Across the country, Republicans lost good representatives and senators to the Obama onslaught—none better, perhaps, than John Sununu of New Hampshire. Sununu, a first-term senator and the youngest man in the Senate, had led the way in trying to stop the financial crisis from happening and dealing with its aftermath. He was considered a promising future Republican leader. But for now, he was gone, along with many others, and the party's future as a whole looked bleak.

McCain offered a gracious concession speech. It was not too different from the stump speeches he had offered day in, day out on the campaign trail. This time, however, the country was actually listening. Democrats, especially, listened for the first time in months: this was McCain once again as they

195

knew him, the fallen hero, the nice guy in second place. He acknowledged the historic nature of Obama's win:

> This is an historic election, and I recognize the special signifi-
> cance it has for African-Americans and for the special pride that
> must be theirs tonight...I've always believed that America offers
> opportunities to all who have the industry and will to seize it.
> Sen. Obama believes that, too...Let there be no reason now for
> any American to fail to cherish their citizenship in this, the
> greatest nation on Earth.[92]

In perhaps the most moving passage, McCain accepted full responsibility for his defeat: "We fought—we fought as hard as we could. And though we fell short, the failure is mine, not yours." A chorus of voices on the lawn of the Biltmore cried out—some in anguish: "No!" And interjections continued throughout the speech—some rudely so, at moments when McCain praised his opponent. He paused and stretched out his hands to his disappointed supporters, asking them to remain calm. It was then that the world saw the essential decency of the man, and the scattered and undisciplined nature of the party that in many ways had let him down. For a moment, he towered above them, and above the whole country save the man that had bested him. And he concluded with his customary war cry, this time in defeat: "Americans never quit. We never surrender. We never hide from history. We make history. Thank you, and God bless you, and God bless America. Thank you all very much."

But this was Obama's moment. Across the country, to the soaring music of a Hollywood composer, Obama emerged to a cheering, tearful crowd and congratulated America for electing him: "If there is anyone out there who still doubts that America is a place where all things are possible; who still wonders if the dream of our founders is alive in our time; who still questions the power of our democracy, tonight is your answer."[93] It was one of the best speeches of his political life thus far, made so by the unique circumstances of a victory that had once seemed almost beyond the realm of possibility. He acknowledged those who had made his win possible, with earnest humility:

> I was never the likeliest candidate for this office. We didn't start with much money or many endorsements. Our campaign was not hatched in the halls of Washington - it began in the back-yards of Des Moines and the living rooms of Concord and the front porches of Charleston.
>
> It was built by working men and women who dug into what little savings they had to give five dollars and ten dollars and twenty dollars to this cause. It grew strength from the young people who rejected the myth of their generation's apathy; who left their homes and their families for jobs that offered little pay and less sleep; from the not-so-young people who braved the bitter cold and scorching heat to knock on the doors of perfect strangers; from the millions of Americans who volunteered, and organized, and proved that more than two centuries later, a government of the people, by the people and for the people has not perished from this Earth. This is your victory.

He continued: "The road ahead will be long. Our climb will be steep." And then, as if he could not resist the urge, he focused again on his own political ambitions, effectively announcing his 2012 re-election bid: "We may not get there in one year or even one term, but America—I have never been more hopeful than I am tonight that we will get there." Even in celebrating victory with the nation, he could not resist hinting at a second term in office.

Throughout the rest of his address, there were gracious nods to his critics, and an acknowledgment that the greatest Illinois president, Abraham Lincoln, had been a Republican. It was an emotional speech, even for his opponents, even for those who had campaigned against him for so long.

But would his words—all of his words—matter? The test was yet to come. And though Obama closed his speech with the same refrain he had used for months on the campaign trail, the same slogan he had used in his 2004 Senate run—"Yes We Can"—mere slogans would not suffice to lead a nation founded by men and women who put their faith in more than words alone.

6

Obama's America

Looking Back

Words mattered more in the 2008 American presidential election than in any other. Americans chose a president with little experience and few convictions, solely on the strength of his speeches. Barack Obama, great speaker that he is, had achieved little in his short and largely obscure political and legal career before running for president. He stood for no great cause or idea, beyond the symbolic achievement of electing the nation's first black president. When he did take a stand on an issue, Obama tended towards vaguely articulated but definitively radical views, long since relegated to the margins of American politics. In an hour of military danger and economic crisis, he offered few new ideas, merely a retreat to the failed policies of a much-romanticized, liberal past.

And yet American voters went to their polling places on November 4, 2008 and entrusted Obama with the vast and expanded executive powers bequeathed to him by his predecessor. He won us over with his words—and it was not what he said, which few seemed able to remember, but *how* he had said it that left a lasting impression of strength, confidence and will. His speeches were more than "just words" to millions of Americans: they were a renewed covenant between the would-be president and the people. Yet few had bothered to examine his words in any great detail, nor to inquire about the ideas inspiring them, nor to examine their sincerity. Few scrutinized his ability to honor the commitments he was making, or to hold them up to his past political record. As a nation, as a whole, almost all of us (at one time or another, even his opponents) simply trusted Obama's magnificent-sounding words, and believed in the larger-than-life man who had spoken them, with a blind hope that was both admirable and frightening.

Perhaps Americans had been eager to escape the legacy of Obama's predecessor, for whom words seemed to present a unique and insurmountable challenge. George W. Bush became famous for his malapropisms even before he became president, spawning a cottage industry of books and websites devoted to keeping track of his many stumbles and bumbles. He even struggled with prepared texts—right down to his farewell address to the nation in January 2009, an eloquent address that still featured its share of trip-ups. And in extemporary remarks, Bush's eyes shone with conviction but his tongue seemed unable to avoid extraordinary gaffes.

Moreover, Bush's rhetoric could be sharply divisive; it certainly sounded so to many Americans, and to much of the rest of the world as well. In the aftermath of the terror attacks of September 11, 2001, for example, Bush cast the struggle against Islamic extremism in starkly moral—some would even say Manichean—terms. "You're either with us or against us in the fight against terror," he said in a joint news conference with French President Jacques Chirac in November 2001.[1] In his first State of the Union address to both houses of Congress early the next year, he called on Americans to confront an "axis of evil." He also frequently cast America's struggle in the colloquial black-versus-white terms of the Western genre, using phrases such as "smoke 'em out," "dead or alive," and "bring 'em on"[2]—language he would later regret.

Bush did make some bold and memorable speeches. In November 2003, long after the U.S. and its allies had failed to find weapons of mass destruction in post-Saddam Hussein Iraq, Bush delivered a stirring call for democracy in the Middle East at Washington's National Endowment for Democracy.[3] In the waning months of his tenure, speaking to the Knesset on the occasion of Israel's 60th anniversary, Bush warned sharply against the politics of "appeasement" in the western world's approach to terror.[4] These were grand orations, expressing the great values America stands for, and the will of Americans to pursue them. But by then, most Americans had simply stopped listening to Bush. His words had lost whatever power they once possessed, and the people's trust as well.

Worst of all, perhaps, was the way in which Bush had seemed to betray his own words: his "Mission Accomplished" banner on the flight deck of the U.S.S. *Abraham Lincoln,* for example, when the worst of the Iraq adventure was yet to come, and his promise of "compassionate conservatism" in the 2000 campaign, which preceded the greatest increase in the size and cost of government since the Great Society of Lyndon Baines Johnson. By the end of his presidency, Bush could point to a few critical achievements. He had kept the country safe from an additional terror attack, for one. But he had emptied "conservatism" of its practical meaning in Americans politics. It was no longer a word that meant much—or at least much good—to many Americans.

What the American public hungered for in the twilight of the Bush presidency was more than "just words." Americans wanted authenticity—not just an honest attempt at truth, but a truth whose beginning and end were knowable and known. They wanted leaders who could promise to do more than be faithful to their own convictions; who could offer something entirely new to believe in. In a sense, Americans had despaired of the political process, with all of its cant, fraud and disappointment. The ironic detachment with which much of the media had greeted Bush's controversial victory in 2000 had consumed itself, and spawned a kind of bitter cynicism that only a deluge could wash away.

Plain speech would not do. Americans had tired of plain speech already—it seemed all that the incumbent president was capable of providing to the public at moments when not only courage but wisdom and sensitivity had been desperately needed, and perhaps in short supply. No—Americans wanted a leader who could not only speak clearly, to us and for us, but who could transcend the depressing reality of politics at present. Voters were willing to suspend, for the moment at least, their innate and well-rehearsed skepticism about *any* politician's claims to truth, and to trust the seemingly prophetic words of one politician in particular. Having convinced ourselves that the country's problems were largely the fault of one inarticulate man, we quickly concluded that the solutions, too, lay in the hands of one extraordinary individual. It was a millenarian moment, one in which "just words" would be infused with power far beyond their simple meaning—and power perhaps beyond the healthy restraints of democracy.

There was another alternative on offer, one personified by John McCain, the Vietnam War hero and twenty-five year Senate iconoclast. McCain made a particular style of words—"straight talk"—the motto of his presidential campaign in 2000, and revived it for a second try in 2008. McCain promised to deliver the candid truth, both about himself and about America, unvarnished and unembellished, as he toured across the country in his aptly named bus, the "Straight Talk Express." His words were blunt, gruff, and controversial. Perhaps the model for McCain's persona as a presidential candidate was Warren Beatty's character in *Bulworth*, a 1998 film about a morose left-wing senator who has hired a hit man to kill him. Thus liberated from the political consequences, the senator begins to tell the truth to the American public, which reacts with adoration. That idea, and the form of rhetoric it embraced, was the antidote to an era of bloodthirsty partisan bickering set against the ironic backdrop of ideological convergence between the country's two political parties. McCain, whose "straight talk" had made him plenty of enemies among his fellow Republicans, had a similarly self-sacrificial—or self-destructive—quality in his truth-telling. Yet what he offered in style he frequently backed up in substance, taking on issues such as campaign finance reform even though reducing the power of money in politics stood to hurt his own political fortunes. He was a man who would say and do what he thought was right, regardless of whether it was popular.

By 2008, the appeal of "straight talk" had faded. If irony had once been the great obstacle to broad political participation, now that obstacle was belief. The conformity that had briefly descended upon America in the wake of 9/11 and calls to "national security" had been transformed into the polar opposite: a steadfast conviction, among a loud, large and educated minority, that George W. Bush had been the worst president in the history of the country. For these Americans, it was not enough that his term of office would expire as it reached the constitutional limits; it had to be expunged from memory, or else demonized beyond reason. For many others, who did not share the same fervor but harbored many of the same doubts about the eight years of the Bush presidency, only something new and transcendent could rescue America from what it had become.

Ordinary speech did not seem equal to the task. And whatever appeal McCain's approach had at the close of the scandal-tainted Clinton era, it had faded in the face of the tempest—real and rhetorical—lashing the Bush White House in the final days of his presidency. If anything, many Americans were downright hostile to plain talk: they wanted precisely the mixture of inspiration and intellect that Obama seemed to offer. When McCain nominated the reform-minded governor of Alaska, Sarah Palin, as his running mate, her own brand of plain speaking thrilled millions of ordinary Americans but horrified the nation's urban elite—both Republican and Democrat. They would not, could not see her achievements, or her potential; they could not listen past the inflammatory rumors about her beliefs to what she actually said about her convictions; they generally refused to see her authenticity as more than a cheap political gimmick. Her words simply sounded like more of the same—and worse.

Ultimately, it was not Palin but McCain himself who lost the 2008 race. When financial crisis hit in September 2008, he could not find the words he needed—or perhaps even the courage to use them. He opposed a government bailout, then supported one, then suspended his campaign to make sure

Congress passed one. Only many months later, back in the Senate, would he find the words he had lacked and emerge to lead Republican opposition to Obama's brazenly wasteful, trillion-dollar "stimulus" package.[5] For that moment, it was Obama's words—empty, but calm—that won Americans' trust and carried him to his historic victory several weeks later.

The Meaning of the 2008 Elections

As the Obama transition began in November 2008, building towards the anticipated ecstasy of the inauguration in January 2009, observers grappled with the meaning of the Obama victory. Did it, by itself, represent "real change" in America? Or was that change yet to come, after Obama had taken office? Some of his most enthusiastic supporters in the media urged that he be sworn in early—that January 20th was too long to wait. "If I had my druthers right now," wrote *New York Times* columnist Thomas Friedman less than three weeks after the election, "we would convene a special session of Congress, amend the Constitution and move up the inauguration from Jan. 20 to Thanksgiving Day."[6] The need for change was too great, Friedman and others argued, and the desire to get rid of Bush to be too strong, to worry about the constitutional change (or suspension) that would have been required to allow such a move. But would Obama truly bring the kind of salvation that he had promised to the country—or would he turn out to be a failed messiah? Did his election absolve the United States of its racial sins—or did it mean race would be more important than ever? Could he turn the economy around—or would he make it worse? Was he just another politician—or had he changed politics in America, in the world, forever? We could not know at the time. All we had to go on were his speeches, his approximately 510 promises (according to one newspaper)[7], his rhetoric—his words.

Amidst the many feverish post-election speculations, it soon became apparent what Obama's election did *not* mean.

It was certainly a decisive victory—growing ever more decisive as the absentee ballots were counted—but it was not a victory by acclimation. Nearly half the country had voted against him. True, Obama would have almost total control of the government. The Democratic Party ran both houses of Congress, and Obama towered above his party. New Supreme Court vacancies were anticipated, as well as many more federal judgeships in the lower courts, and Obama likely would lose no time in leaving his mark. Yet his control would not quite be complete. The Republicans preserved the filibuster in the Senate by a slender margin of one vote (lost in April 2009 with a defection to the Democrats). That procedural power to prevent closing the debate on bills that would otherwise move immediately to a vote could be the only effective tool of opposition in Washington. It was a weak force, but it was a real one, for a while.

Moreover, though Obama would bring a new cohort of young, left-wing Obama activists to Washington, his victory did not herald a victory for everything they stood for, or for the left in general. The narrow victory of Proposition 8 in California, which banned gay marriage and overturned the state supreme court decision in May 2008 that had allowed it, was evidence that even in one of the most liberal states in the nation there was substantial support for conservative values, as well as the political organization to back them up. Immediately the left flew into paroxysms of rage over the measure; Mormons, who were blamed for organizing much of the support for the ballot Proposition 8 asure, were targeted by marches and boycotts.[8] Black voters and Latinos, too, had voted overwhelmingly for the measure, even though they had also backed Obama by enormous margins[9]; this, too, created tensions with the more radical fringes of the gay rights movement.[10] Governor Arnold Schwarzenegger—a Republican with liberal social views—vowed to find some way around the ban.[11] But there was no denying what it stood for: Republicans might have lost, but conservatism as a political and social movement was far from finished.

The results of three late elections, each of them after November 4th, were further proof that the GOP had not been destroyed, as some left-wing commentators had hoped. One was the victory of Saxby Chambliss in a runoff election for the U.S. Senate in Georgia. Sarah Palin—denying herself a much-needed rest after the intensity of the fall election contest—came to the state to campaign for Chambliss.[12] Democrats, surprisingly, mounted a rather lackluster effort—so weak, in fact, that at least one observer at a conservative blog wondered whether Obama's party had wanted to lose, the better to avoid the total responsibility that governing without fear of a filibuster would have conferred on them.[13]

Another two victories came in congressional races in Louisiana, which had been postponed due to the effects of Hurricane Gustav in September. At the time, the storm had also encouraged Republicans to postpone the Republican National Convention for a day, the better to avoid appearing insensitive to the effects of the storm and reminding voters of the failures of Hurricane Katrina. New Republican Governor Bobby Jindal—the first Indian-American governor of any state—led the emergency and evacuation efforts. This time, the levees held, and the city of New Orleans was spared the suffering of three years before. Now, with the November election fading into memory, Republicans won a close race in western Louisiana to replace a retiring Republican incumbent. Even more important was the GOP victory in a predominantly African-American district in northern Louisiana that had not elected a Republican since 1891. The winner, lawyer Anh "Joseph" Cao, was a former Vietnamese refugee. He had taken on Democrat William "Dollar Bill" Jefferson, who had been indicted on bribery charges after large amounts of cash were found in his freezer. Cao sparked new hope that the GOP was making inroads into immigrant communities, and that it could still win in the unlikeliest of places. The party took heart; all was not lost.

Despite all that was at stake—especially in the Georgia senate race, which could have given the Democrats the unfet-

tered power to implement their agenda—Obama did not in-
volve himself in any of these races in any significant way.[14] He
did not travel to the region to lend his charisma to close-run
Democratic campaigns, nor did he offer any of the $30 mil-
lion in unspent campaign funds as assistance to his party colleagues.[15] Obama's reticence evoked the ire of some Democrats, who expected him to lead with more than "just words."
Whatever the reason for his absence, it was clear that Democrats struggled to win without his name on the ballot.

Still a Center-Right Nation

It seemed, likewise, that despite his eloquent appeals to
bipartisanship and national unity, Obama had failed to con-
vert the electorate to his left-wing worldview—largely because he had kept it hidden behind his centrist rhetoric as far
as possible. America was, as many pundits pointed out after
the election, still a center-right country. Americans seemed—
momentarily, at least—to have lost confidence in the ideal of
the free market and in the efficacy of a strong foreign policy,
but they remained suspicious of government power and jeal-
ous of their hard-fought, long-cherished rights and freedoms.

It was clear that many of the people who had voted for
Obama had done so simply because they wanted "change"—
not because they were intimately familiar with his policies,
not because they agreed with him, and not even because they
disagreed sharply with the McCain and the Republicans.
Some conservatives, for example, had voted for Obama (or
stayed home) out of disgust for the way that their movement
had seemed to lose its way after eight years of the Bush administration. There were others who were wooed by Obama's
apparent grasp of conservative principles—even if he had not
actually embraced them; others simply admired the leadership
he seemed to exude at the podium and on the trail. And there
were many conservative Americans who had simply gone
along with the flow and the intellectual fashion of the moment—those among the "wishful thinking" crowd who

hoped Obama would do the right thing once elected. For these voters especially, Obama's words were critical: they had crossed party lines based almost entirely on what Obama had said to them, or what they thought they had heard him say.

And some Americans, it was painfully clear, did not understand what Obama had stood for at all. Just hours before Americans headed to the polls, one excited Obama supporter, Peggy Joseph, gushed: "I won't have to work on puttin' gas in my car. I won't have to work at payin' my mortgage. You know. If I help him [Obama], he's gonna help me."[16] Surveys of Obama voters on Election Day sponsored by documentary filmmaker John Ziegler and conducted by Zogby International revealed that many were familiar with McCain's and Palin's weaknesses, but few had heard of Obama's and Biden's flaws. According to the poll, 57.4% of Obama voters did not even know which party controlled Congress; 82.6% did not know that Obama had won his first election by removing his rivals from the ballot; and 86.9% thought that Palin had said she could see Russia from her house.[17] (If any words changed the outcome of the election, they were Tina Fey's lines, spoken in jest but taken by millions as the truth of Sarah Palin's beliefs.) Left-leaning undergraduates at Harvard College continued to argue against policies such as affirmative action or the government-mandated redistribution of wealth, even as they cheerfully lined up to vote or volunteer for Obama. They had been convinced to join Obama's movement for "change," but they had been swayed by his words and personality, not by his principles or policies.

Conservatives, in short, were still the winners in the battle for ideas; the hard-fought intellectual victories of the 1970s, and the political victories of the 1980s, had not yet been undone. But the ground was slowly shifting. If Obama managed to pass his massive health care reforms and public works programs, they could fundamentally alter the nature of the relationship between the citizen and the state. As Peter Wehner and Paul Ryan warned in the *Wall Street Journal*:

Nationalizing health care will be profoundly detrimental to the quality of American medicine…

It will also put America on a glide path toward European-style socialism. We need only look to Great Britain and elsewhere to see the effects of socialized health care on the broader economy. Once a large number of citizens get their health care from the state, it dramatically alters their attachment to government. Every time a tax cut is proposed, the guardians of the new medical-welfare state will argue that tax cuts would come at the expense of health care—an argument that would resonate with middle-class families entirely dependent on the government for access to doctors and hospitals.

Of course, this health-care plan is occurring against our particular fiscal backdrop: Without major reform, our federal entitlement programs will soon double the size of government. The result will be a crushing burden of debt and taxes.

In short, we may be approaching a tipping point for democratic capitalism.[18]

Once nationalized health care and other new entitlement programs were created, conservatives could no longer take comfort in the knowledge that they could win debates about the necessity of these programs. The argument would no longer be whether they should be created; it would henceforth be whether they should be dismantled. And every time Republicans had tried that tack before—with the bloated, ineffective federal Department of Education, for example—they had failed.

It was also clear that changes in foreign policy and defense strategy under Obama could have far-reaching effects. If the United States withdrew precipitously from Iraq, or allowed Iran to develop nuclear weapons, its deterrent capability might be permanently damaged. Similarly, if it backed off its support for Israel, or tried to push Israel into making damaging concessions, the conflict could shift decisively against the Jewish state, or inadvertently prompt it to take drastic, unilateral actions to defend itself. Obama had also promised to close the facility at Guantánamo Bay, and to change the

CIA's methods of interrogating terror subjects—all worthy objectives—but without proposing alternative methods of prosecuting the war against terror. If his words during the campaign meant anything at all, he would be prepared to take huge risks with American security. If he tried to compromise between his left-wing idealism and the grim reality of the threat facing the United States, he might end up dismantling the most effective parts of the war on terror, such as the new post-9/11 intelligence network, while leaving its worst and most offensive features, such as renditions, in place. Words alone—no matter how tough "tough diplomacy" sounded—would not be enough to maintain America's deterrent force. The opposition could win that argument—had won, in fact, since voters who cared most about terrorism had preferred McCain over Obama by huge margins.[19] But the terrain of debate over foreign policy and national security could shift rapidly with changing world events—and Obama seemed determined to bring about "change" of some sort, for better or for worse.

The Republican Party was, in a sense, a victim of its own success. Though conservative ideas still reigned, they were no longer *Republican* ideas. They had been absorbed by parts of the Democratic Party under Clinton and the New Democrats; they were acknowledged, at least rhetorically, by Obama. Now that the GOP had failed to stick to them under Bush, it appeared to lack the credibility to oppose Obama without appearing obstructionist, especially when faced with Obama's charismatic leadership. And as the day of the inauguration drew nearer, Republicans in the Beltway—no doubt caught up in the myopic mood of the famously insular capital city— began to lavish praise on their opponents and ignore Obama's weaknesses. They had, in the words of conservative bloggers, caught the fever of "hopenchange." They had forgotten their true duty to the public was not to ensure they were well-liked but that their principles were well-defended. The power of Obama's words had begun, it seemed, to subdue and charm the opposition.

210

Obama The Centrist?

Once he had been elected, some of Obama's words and departures from his campaign rhetoric were notable. During the election, for example, he had argued vigorously against free trade agreements—from the North American Free Trade Agreement (NAFTA), to the Central American Free Trade Agreement (CAFTA), to a new proposed agreement with Columbia, America's strong ally in Latin America. Yet just a few days after winning the election, he announced that his choice to lead the White House Office of Management and Budget—the major policy wing of the executive—would be Peter Orszag, an outspoken champion of free trade widely viewed as a "centrist" on major policy issues.[20] (These hopes would be set back yet again when Obama and his party included several "Buy American" provisions in their trillion-dollar 'stimulus' legislation in February 2009.)

On the campaign trail, Obama had lashed out against what he perceived as the fundamentalism of the free market, which he claimed George W. Bush had championed to the detriment of the country. That was, in fact, an old and familiar theme of the left, whose partisans not only blamed Bush for the country's present economic woes but also complained bitterly about the deference shown to free-market ideas by the "New Democrat" administration of Bill Clinton before him. It was as if Obama wished to undo the legacy not only of a single predecessor but of Ronald Reagan and the generation that had governed in his wake. Yet upon winning the election, Obama nominated Larry Summers, Clinton's former treasury secretary, to head his administration's National Economic Council, signaling a possible move back towards the "New Democrat" embrace of free markets and free trade that had helped make the Clinton years a period of rapid economic growth and rising prosperity.

Summers wasn't the only former Clinton fixture to return to the White House. Though Obama had run in the Democratic primary as the party outsider who was up against the

211

Clinton machine, as president he seemed to have brought back the entire Clinton cabal. There was Emanuel, a former Clinton White House staffer; Leon Panetta, Clinton's former chief of staff and Obama's pick to head the Central Intelligence Agency (CIA); Eric Holder, Obama's choice for attorney general and a former U.S. Attorney under Clinton; and Hillary Clinton herself. The former First Lady-turned-Senator-turned-presidential rival, who had made Obama's naïvely sentimental foreign policy the chief target of negative campaign ads during the primary, humbly accepted her appointment as Obama's Secretary of State.

Was the visionary who made "change we can believe in" his campaign slogan determined to govern from the center, after all? As the first few appointments were announced, some observers concluded that many of Obama's nominees could just as easily have been chosen by his Republican rival for the presidency. As Max Boot, a former McCain adviser, put it: "As someone who was skeptical of Obama's moderate posturing during the campaign, I have to admit that I am gobsmacked by these appointments."[21] Obama had out-flanked Hillary Clinton on the left by running against the Iraq War and denouncing her for having voted for it. Yet the candidate who had styled himself as an anti-war icon announced, as president-elect, that he would retain Bush's defense secretary, Robert Gates, in his post. And his choice to lead the National Security Council, retired general Jim Jones, was not only a Republican but also a close friend, adviser and ally of John McCain.[22] As the last days of the Bush administration ticked away, Obama even seemed to edge closer to a foreign policy he had once denounced: he backed off pledges to withdraw troops immediately from Iraq; he continued a policy of extraordinary renditions for terror suspects[23]; and he seemed, according to some reports, ready to offer Israel security from Iran in the event the latter launched an attack with nuclear weapons.[24]

There were a few Cabinet appointees, however, who seemed to match Obama's leftist roots. Representative Hilda

Solis, Obama's choice for Secretary of Labor, was a far-left Democrat who had co-sponsored the "Card Check" legislation—named, in Orwellian fashion, the "Employee Free Choice Act"—that would allow unions to deny workers the protection of the secret ballot in union elections.[25] Arizona Governor Janet Napolitano, an early Obama political ally[26] with no previous experience in security, was nominated to head the Department of Homeland Security (joining CIA nominee Panetta, who had no intelligence experience, as a member of the most inexperienced national security team in American history). There were also twenty of Obama's Harvard Law School classmates working on his transition team[27]—competence to some, cronyism to others. But many of Obama's other top-level appointees were simply old hands—moderate, career civil servants and Washington insiders. It was still unclear whether Obama had really transcended old ideological differences or merely masked them.

Perhaps, then, it was true—as many conservative Republicans and moderate Democrats had hoped—that Obama was a pragmatist at heart. Perhaps he was sincerely interested in building a "team of rivals," so named after the moderately successful model of Abraham Lincoln's cabinet (even if its reputation had been somewhat romanticized by historian Doris Kearns Goodwin,[28] whose book Obama had read and endorsed). Perhaps Obama would live up to his billing by friends and former colleagues as "an independent thinker,"[29] a leader who would listen to all sides and draw on diverse and competing points of view before making important decisions. Perhaps he was the unifying leader that millions of Americans had hoped he would be, trusting his words with their votes.

But perhaps his reliance on recycled staffers from the Clinton and Bush years was a sign of something else—a lack of confidence, or even competence. After all, Obama had never run anything before, other than a political campaign and the *Harvard Law Review*; he had barely been in the U.S. Senate a full year before declaring his candidacy. Perhaps he was, as the McCain campaign commercials had warned, "not

213

ready to lead." After taunting McCain for months with the charge that the Republican would represent the third term of George W. Bush, it was Obama who was giving insiders the inside track to White House jobs, reviving the careers of deposed Minority Leader Tom Daschle (nominated, then withdrawn for the post of Secretary of Health and Human Services after the discovery of his failure to pay hundreds of thousands of dollars in income taxes) and former Clinton Enviromental Protection Agency administrator Carol Browner (who was also reputed to have ties to the Socialist International[30]) as his new "Assistant for Energy and Climate Change" or "global warming czar." President Obama's team of "czars"—an odd term to use for administrators in a democratic government—reprised the Bush approach to governing, which had offered in 2000 to surround an admittedly inexperienced leader with advisers of varying experience. And if it resembled the Bush administration in attitude and the Carter administration in ideology, in personnel it resembled Bill Clinton's third term more than Obama's first.

There was another, perhaps better explanation for Obama's behavior—an explanation more consistent with Obama's immense political talent and his intensely partisan political history. Obama was not, according to this view, abandoning his left-wing agenda by appointing centrists to some jobs and political hacks to others. Rather, he was digging in against a mid-term backlash, wary of encountering the same fate that Bill Clinton had, more than a decade before. By making sure he had political fixers in key positions, and deferring some of the policy changes he had promised, he aimed to extend his political control. Emanuel, to whom many of the newer members of the Democratic caucus owed their success in the 2006 mid-term elections, would help Obama dominate the legislature from the Oval Office and coordinate the all-important 2010 census; Panetta and Clinton would provide cover on security issues; and the moderate Democrats he had elevated to top economic positions, like Summers and his protégé Tim Geithner (now Secretary of the

Treasury, despite his own tax problems) would insulate him from criticism as he unrolled the most ambitious, risky and expensive expansion of government in the country's history. Obama's real aim, beyond the pragmatic political rhetoric, was great political power—power across two terms in office, power over three branches of government, power that could neither be resisted in Congress nor defeated at the ballot box.

The Blagojevich Scandal

If so, the Obama honeymoon had barely begun when a scandal erupted—one that would test the guarantees he had offered American voters of clean government and transparency. In early December, U.S. Attorney Patrick Fitzgerald announced in Chicago that Illinois's Democratic governor, Rod Blagojeivch, had been recorded in wiretapped conversations as he tried to "sell" Obama's vacant seat in the U.S. Senate to the highest bidder.[31] He had allegedly demanded the post of Secretary of Health and Human Services; or a plush job with the Service Employees' International Union (SEIU); or just cold, hard cash in the amount of $500,000. Whatever the price, he had apparently hoped to make the most of what he had called a "fucking valuable thing." In addition, he had allegedly threatened to withhold $8 million in state funds from a children's hospital unless he received a $50,000 campaign contribution, and vowed to deny state assistance to the ailing *Chicago Tribune* newspaper unless it removed his critics from its editorial board. These were words that mattered— words that Obama could not ignore.

Fitzgerald had made a spectacular career out of prosecuting corruption in government. He was a Bush appointee who had targeted Democratic state officials as well as city officials in Chicago under Mayor Richard M. Daley. But he had also gone after Republicans—notably Bush's deputy chief of staff in the White House, Lewis "Scooter" Libby, who was convicted of perjury charges related to the leaking to the media of the identity of a CIA agent, Valerie Plame. At the time,

215

Democrats praised Fitzgerald's dogged pursuit of wrongdoing and proclaimed him free of any political agendas or vendettas. Now, Fitzgerald had uncovered the political corruption at the root of the Democratic political machine in Chicago and Illinois in general—the same machine that had produced Barack Obama.

Fitzgerald emphasized that Obama himself was not under suspicion. But members of Obama's team, including Emanuel, had spoken to Blagojevich about the Senate seat. Obama's omnipresent political strategist, David Axelrod, had told a television station only weeks before: "I know he's talked to the governor and there are a whole range of names, many of which have surfaced, and I think he has a fondness for a lot of them."[32] The Obama transition team scrambled to assert that Axelrod had misspoken, but what they could not deny was that Obama had advised and endorsed Blagojevich in the past. And both Obama and Blagojevich had raised funds through convicted fraudster Atonin "Tony" Rezko, who had bankrolled Obama's early political campaigns and helped him buy his house.[33]

Obama's links to the shady world of Chicago politics, which had never been thoroughly probed by the media during the presidential campaign, were now exposed. Old stories from his Chicago days were suddenly—if briefly— remembered. The Blagojevich scandal looked bad for Obama—worse because he had been quick to deny any involvement and slow to offer any further information to the public. His campaign had evidently been aware of Blagojevich's behavior, yet Obama had not reported the governor to law enforcement agencies. Nor had he ever done anything else to tackle political corruption in his home state, despite the earnest pleas of reform-minded activists and editorialists.[34] He offered the weakest of excuses—"I was not aware of what was happening"—and was unduly cautious in his condemnation of the governor.[35] But Obama escaped the Blagojevich affair, as he had so often before, by casting himself as the exception to the rule. The *New York Times* even

216

showered praise on him for upholding the "tradition" of being interviewed by prosecutors—a veritable rite of passage for all presidents, it explained—before he had even taken office, as if this were evidence of his supreme commitment to transparency.[36] And Obama fed the myth of his own exceptionalism by pointing out, whenever given the opportunity, that the governor had complained—on tape—that the Obama transition team seemed unwilling to pay his price. Indeed, Blagojevich had referred to Obama as a "motherfucker," according to transcripts released by federal agents, prompting at least one commentator to declare that the scandal made Obama look "great."[37]

The media, and much of the country, accepted Obama's version of events almost immediately. It accepted that he was untarnished by Blagojevich—just as he had been untarnished by Rezko, and the inflammatory preacher Jeremiah Wright, and the former Weather Underground terrorist William Ayers, and his early communist mentor Frank Marshall Davis, and so many others he had established close links to in his short political career. When commerce secretary-designate Bill Richardson would resign weeks later over Blagojevich-like accusations of corruption surrounding his term as New Mexico's governor, Obama would escape again—despite the fact that the political donor who had allegedly given money to Richardson in exchange for a highway contract had also given to Obama as well.[38] There were a few who still complained that Obama had jealously guarded the truth about Blagojevich, but these doubters were silenced when Obama's own lawyer released a five-page report exonerating him, to shouts of approval and sighs of relief from the media.[39] Journalists even praised Obama for his skill in using the Chicago political world for his own political purposes without falling victim to its temptations: "Obama's success in keeping the machine in his corner while apparently avoiding any shady dealings is testimony to his political adroitness and to the tough, single-mindedness with which he has pursued each political prize," crowed one editorial.[40]

217

The president-elect then left for a vacation, and journalists resumed their adulation, fawning over his physique as he capered on the beaches and golf courses of a multimillion dollar resort in Hawaii.[41] Few thought it relevant that President Bush had long since given up golf for the duration of the Iraq War,[42] or that millions of Americans were facing what Obama had described as "the worst economic crisis since the Great Depression." Instead, Obama's health was celebrated: it was the ninety minutes per day in the gym that did it, they concluded breathlessly.[43] Never mind the cigarette habit, which he finally admitted he had not given up as promised.[44] Obama gave the appearance, at least, of firm, muscular health. And it seemed that in the age of Obama, it was appearance, not reality, which mattered most.

America Under an Obama Presidency

Meanwhile, a picture of Obama's administration began to take shape. The new White House would seek to sign a new $1-trillion-plus spending package, a "stimulus" ostensibly aimed at boosting the economy through investments in public works and infrastructure. The legislation, known as the American Recovery and Reinvestment Act, was to help cure the country's economic ills by boosting government spending and hence aggregate demand, according to the classic Keynesian theory. Obama hitched the fortunes of his presidency to the "stimulus," telling Americans that if they did not pass it quickly, the country faced an economic "catastrophe,"[45] one that the country might be "unable to reverse."[46] But the bill was written without much research and approved with little debate. Its cost was astronomical, dwarfing the size of spending on the Iraq War, or even the New Deal in present-day dollar terms, and larger than the Marshall Plan as a percentage of Gross Domestic Product.[47] Yet it was disconcertingly *small* to many on the left, including *New York Times* columnist (and recent Nobel laureate) Paul Krugman, who believed it did not go far enough.[48]

218

It was unclear in any case how the money could be spent, or even whether the government had the ability to spend it. Much of the information technology investment had already happened; the country was already crisscrossed with broadband cables, and the Bush administration had already prepared the way for the computerization of public medical records.[49] As for the other infrastructure projects, few were "shovel-ready," and the Congressional Budget Office indicated that little spending could actually happen before 2011,[50] by which time the economic crisis might already have passed. None of these facts mattered to Obama, who seemed to believe that any spending was good spending. Indeed, he opined in a meeting with Republican legislators that the problem with the original New Deal had been that it had been too small.[51] He seemed unaware that many of Roosevelt's interventionist, protectionist policies had actually prolonged and deepened the recession.

Increasingly, the "stimulus" seemed little more than a label, the sort of tribute that vice pays to virtue. Instead of the $175 billion that Obama told voters during the election he would use to boost the economy,[52] the "stimulus" aimed to spend nearly five times that amount on a variety of priorities of doubtful efficacy and urgency. Indeed, the bill seemed little more than a pretext for Obama and the Democrats to expand both the size and expense of government, and to dish out government contracts to favored contributors and constituencies. The *Wall Street Journal* calculated that the total proportion of spending on actual economic "stimulus" only amounted to 12 cents on the dollar, as the bill became swamped with left-wing spending priorities that had nothing to do with economic recovery.[53] A website called www.ReadTheStimulus.org led an effort to discover more pork in the stimulus, and encouraged volunteers to chip in by poring over portions of the 1500-page-plus bill and finding new examples of waste. It began to dawn on Americans that the legislation was not "change" but a massive, old-style po-

litical boondoggle, extremely vulnerable to waste, mismanagement and corruption.

Obama had already inherited a government that had
spent itself into a huge deficit—not only because of Bush's
big-government profligacy, but also because Pelosi and Reid
had refused to rein in congressional spending—and was set
to authorize even more spending. The U.S. would have to
borrow massively to cover the shortfall, inclusive of the government's recent purchases in the banking and insurance industries, its bailout of the American auto industry (stalled by
Congress but rescued by Bush), and its increasingly unafford-
able Medicare and Social Security entitlements. Moreover, the
government would have economic power on a scale not seen
since the days of Bernard Baruch and the First World War.
And Obama's promises to create millions of new jobs included up to 800,000 government jobs[54]—a rapidly-growing
bureaucratic albatross to manage and perpetuate the state's
increasingly interventionist role.

All "hopenchange" aside, Obama's policies stood a very
troubling chance of increasing the debt burden on future
generations and turning a short-term economic recession into
a long-term depression. There had been some encouraging
signs that he was beginning to rethink, or at least defer, some
of his policies from the campaign trail. The appointment of
centrists like Larry Summers, Peter Orszag and Tim Geithner
at the head of his economic team was one hopeful sign. Yet it
remained unclear what effect, if any, their advice would have
on his actual policies, or whether they would be forced to
suspend their better judgment for the privilege of wielding
power.

The early signs were not good. The stimulus broke every
rule that Summers had recommended for it several months
before: it was neither "timely," "targeted," nor "temporary."[55]
Respected economist Christina Romer, whose prior research
had shown that the economic benefit of tax cuts far out-
weighed the benefit of increased government spending,[56]
helped produce a new study for the Obama administration

that claimed the opposite.[57] As Geithner's tax problems emerged—he had failed to pay the Internal Revenue Service $34,000 in taxes for several years while accepting reimbursement for those taxes from the International Monetary Fund[58]—it began to seem that the Obama economic team might be less transparent, less independent and perhaps less effective than had been originally hoped.

The administration, together with congressional Democrats, planned to make two additional, massive interventions. One would be into health care, in the form of a new insurance plan designed to cover all Americans. The system, as proposed and championed by Secretary of Health and Human Services-designate Tom Daschle—whose tax problems dwarfed those of Geithner, and ultimately led to the demise of his candidacy—would work as a giant health maintenance organization, in which a national board decided which treatments would and would not be available.[59] Regardless of the negative consequences that centralized control of health care decisions could have on both quality and cost, Obama and his party were determined to provide a system of national coverage, an objective that the previous Democratic administration had failed to achieve in its first year in office.

The second intervention would be on the issue of climate change. Obama stood ready to impose a cap-and-trade system on American carbon emissions. While economists generally agreed on the value of revenue-neutral taxes on fuel (balanced by payroll tax cuts), Obama's proposals were not controversial. They also meant that the federal government would have the ability to interfere at every level of economic production. And yet the science on climate change, locked behind the impenetrable wall of "scientific consensus," had begun to look vulnerable. Instead of soaring ever upward, global surface temperatures showed recent evidence of cooling; moreover, data from ocean buoys failed to show the warming scientists had expected, and had in fact shown a moderate cooling of the earth's surface.[60] Whatever the conclusion about trends in temperature, there was no evidence

221

that any human intervention, no matter how costly or drastic, could reverse the effects of an accumulation in the atmosphere of carbon dioxide—a gas with a half-life of one thousand years.

The heavy hand of the state, relatively absent from American life for more than a generation, was poised to make a comeback. As *National Review* editor Rich Lowry observed:

> If Obama manages to cement an aggrandized government, his domestic political accomplishment will equal Ronald Reagan's—although, obviously, in reverse. The late sociologist Seymour Lipset wrote a brilliant book on why the U.S. didn't embrace socialism, called It Didn't Happen Here. In a few years, its conclusion might look premature.[61]

If any Democrat could undo the Reagan revolution, which had hung over the party for decades, it was Obama. Only he seemed prepared to recognize openly the enormity of Reagan's political achievement and the degree to which it haunted the party. He caused great controversy during the primary by declaring that Reagan "changed the trajectory of America in a way that Richard Nixon did not and in a way that Bill Clinton did not."[62] The Clinton campaign attacked him, but he stuck to his word—not only out of sheer obstinacy, but because he had been fighting Reagan's legacy for years. His ideological and educational pedigree had shaped him for the opportunity he now had to turn the tables. In his early life, Obama had been tutored by Frank Marshall Davis, a somewhat notorious communist[63]; in his university days and his twenties, he was trained in radical organizing techniques and reveled in the rump left-wing opposition to Reaganite ideas. It was true that his campaign had avoided the culture wars of the 1960s, but it had quietly re-ignited those of the 1980s. And a new generation of Americans who had been taught little about the evils of communism or the failures of socialism now formed the solid core of his volunteer network and his administrative staff. Faced with this challenge, the once-bold Republican Party had simply withered; the intellectual and political giants who might have been expected to hold the last line of defense had absconded. Obama's promise of "change" would be nothing less than an ambitious attempt to re-write history, to return to a path many believed and hoped America had long since abandoned.

As I write these words, from the vantage point of several weeks after Obama's inauguration, there is cause for regret—if not for the country's choice, then for the casual haste with which voters accepted the sincerity of Obama's promises on the campaign trail, now relegated to the status of "just words." Obama's pledge to run the most transparent administration in American history evaporated as he hired over a dozen lobbyists to staff senior posts in his administration, including several who had failed to pay their taxes. He also declared a speedy end to any true efforts at bipartisanship, telling Republican lawmakers, "I won," as his way of rejecting their proposals to rescue the economy.[64] He seemed determined to saddle the nation with trillions of dollars in new federal debt, rubbishing his campaign promises to pay for every new dollar of spending with additional savings as he pushed a "stimulus" bill that was little more than a giveaway to favored Democratic causes and contributors. His policy was also the product of a fervent but foolish faith—shared by some Republicans as well—that spending could be the cure-all for any economic decline.

Obama also began dismantling America's war on terror, casting his reforms as a moral mission to restore civil liberties but in fact leaving some of the worst Bush administration policies in place, for fear they might actually be the only way to keep the country safe. He suspended military trials of suspected terrorists at the naval base at Guantánamo Bay, Cuba, without charging the inmates with crimes or providing an alternative way of dealing with them. He decided an end to policies of "enhanced interrogation techniques"—what some called "torture"—without regard to the life-saving information they had yielded. Meanwhile, he continued Bush's policy of renditions, making it likely that prisoners not interrogated harshly by the CIA would be "tortured" somewhere else. Like his predecessor, Obama substituted moral certainty for reasoned consideration of the real dilemmas at hand. Meanwhile, he offered gestures of abject conciliation to many of America's most determined enemies, who seized the moment not to renew diplomacy but to press home their geopolitical advantage.

"Don't tell me words don't matter," Obama exhorted during the campaign.[65] And words *had* mattered—more than anything else—in selling his candidacy to the American people. But once in office, Obama seemed to behave as if those words really hadn't mattered. Yet he continued to think words were enough, attempting to govern through speeches alone. In pushing his stimulus plan—a plan even he acknowledged was not "perfect"[66]—he addressed the Democrats, he addressed the nation, and he even called for a special sitting of both houses of Congress so he could address them as well. He announced ambitious plans not only to rescue economy but also to transform it, by expanding taxes on the wealthy to fund vast new investments in public health care, clean energy and education. Still, he faltered, and the country with him, with the economy contracting at a rate of 6.1% in the first quarter of 2009, and with the stock market losing a quarter of its value in the first several weeks of his administration.[67] But he still enjoyed the approval of the majority of American people—for the moment.[68]

A New Constitution, A New World

Obama would also likely have the chance to appoint at least two new Supreme Court justices during his term in office. Now the composition of the court could shift decisively away from the conservative direction it had held for much of the previous thirty years, and from the originalist philosophies it had been testing under the sway of the powerful legal arguments and personality of Justice Antonin Scalia. Bush— after much controversy—had appointed two conservative judges, John Roberts and Samuel Alito, each of whom had

224

been among the most well-qualified in the history of the bench, and both of whom Obama had voted against. Yet the substance of their conservatism often expressed itself in decisions about jurisdiction: they believed that the courts ought to be reluctant to adjudicate matters better left to the legislature. In contrast, the "progressive" philosophy of Obama's appointees would likely not be confined to procedural issues alone.

As a senior lecturer—not a "professor," as he was frequently described, though he seemed reluctant to correct the error—Obama had published nothing in several years of teaching on the University of Chicago Law School faculty. (By way of comparison, his fellow senior lecturer Richard Posner is among one of the most prolific judicial writers in the history of the nation.) Yet Obama's few public statements, and what was known about his relationships with other legal scholars, left little doubt that he shared the general preference of the legal academic left for expanded federal power at the expense of state governments.

On the campaign trail, Obama had hinted at an additional, and more revolutionary, judicial philosophy. He wanted judges who would look beyond the letter of the constitution and the law, to empathize with—or represent—marginalized groups:

> We need somebody who's got the heart, the empathy, to recognize what it's like to be a young teenage mom. The empathy to understand what it's like to be poor, or African-American, or gay, or disabled, or old. And that's the criteria by which I'm going to be selecting my judges.[69]

That approach could amount to selecting judges solely on the basis of their identity. It also suggested that Obama might be prepared to consider judges who were prepared to use their courts to pursue socioeconomic objectives, not to uphold the principle of equality before the law—the only long-run guarantee of prosperity for the poor and marginalized of any society. Overall, Obama's approach seemed to echo that

225

of his professors at Harvard Law School who had fought against the "originalist" approach of Justice Antonin Scalia in favor of allowing judges more room to interpret the Constitution as a "living" document. To these left-leaning scholars, and to Obama, the words of the U.S. Constitution were not enough. To conservatives, Obama's approach seemed to treat the Constitution as "just words," and to substitute the will of a panel of unelected judges for that of the Framers of the constitution and the present-day electorate. It represented a potentially dangerous usurpation of power.

On foreign policy, Obama had already shown little resolve in the face of Russian belligerence during the campaign. He had also seemed oblivious to the threat of a nuclear Iran, referring to it as a "tiny" country compared to the Soviet Union, whose bombastic, Holocaust-denying leader he was prepared to meet without preconditions.[70] In contrast to the Bush administration's posture, which seemed to reflect classic Anglo-American exceptionalism, Obama seemed to have adopted the continental, western European view of military policy and diplomacy: that talks were the best option regardless of the circumstances, and that American power was greatly to be feared and resented, more so than totalitarian threats from beyond the democratic world. If Obama truly meant what he had said, the consequences for America and the world could be sweeping and severe.

There was also the danger that Obama would sacrifice Israel's interests—and that he would do so with little of the usual resistance from the American Jewish community. Mainstream Jewish voters and leaders had committed themselves wholeheartedly to Obama's election, despite the many warning signs—the Wright affair, his connection with former PLO spokesman Rashid Khalidi, his numerous statements against legitimate Israeli policies—about his true convictions. Obama had wowed the audience at the annual policy conference of the American Israel Public Affairs Committee (AIPAC) in June, promising to retain Jerusalem as Israel's united capital. But he reneged the next day in the face of Palestinian protests; his guarantees to AIPAC were "just words," after all. Yet Jewish support, marshaled by prominent Jewish politicians and Democratic activists, had continued to consolidate around Obama despite suggestions that some Jewish voters would back McCain.

The largely Democratic-aligned leadership of the American Jewish community had even prevailed on the organizers of a rally to protest the visit of Iranian president Mahmoud Ahmadinejad to the UN in September to "uninvite" Sarah Palin. Palin had been scheduled to share the stage with Senator Hillary Clinton, until pressure from the Obama campaign caused Clinton to withdraw. The Democratic National Committee then signaled that if Palin were to appear alone, the rally would be considered a partisan political event and that major Jewish organizations could lose their tax-exempt status after the election.[71] Faced with these threats, the organizers of the rally capitulated, denying Palin a much-needed public opportunity to showcase her nascent foreign policy credentials—and, worse, causing the rally against Ahmadinejad to flop.

From that point onward, Obama knew he could manipulate Jewish leadership virtually at will. When the Gaza War broke out during the transition period, Obama was, characteristically, on vacation. Given the opportunity to comment on the situation, he declined. Pro-Palestinian groups that had placed their hope in Obama were incensed; Jewish groups that had relied on hopes that he would be a strong supporter of Israel did not even offer a word of protest against his silence. Whatever guarantees Obama had provided with his words to American Jews, the community and its leaders were reluctant to question, lest they be revealed to be worth little more than a few pixels gliding across a TelePrompTer screen. It was telling that the vast majority of Americans living in Israel and casting absentee votes there had chosen McCain over Obama, according to one highly publicized exit poll.[72]

Some Americans hoped that Obama could help the country repair its relations with the world—if not with its allies, then at least with its enemies. But even if America could renew those ties, it would not do so as the same America that Obama had inherited. The value of freedom as a driving principle of foreign policy would decline in favor of amorphous, and often sentimental and unrealistic, goals of peace, perhaps at any price. The new policy—faithfully driven by Hillary Clinton, who dropped her objections to Obama's foreign policy philosophy (as he dropped his to her inexperience, which his campaign had once mocked)—would be a hodgepodge of ideas born of the increasingly outdated criticism of the Bush White House. Old "realist" goals of stability would unite with crusty leftist visions of revolution and world peace, leaving little hope for the concrete goals of human rights and democracy that the Bush administration had tried to articulate. A single phrase—"tough diplomacy"—encapsulated Obama's approach. It was a formulation that promised words—hard-sounding words, perhaps, but "just words" after all. The trouble was that the consequences of failure, if "tough diplomacy" were found wanting, would not be merely rhetorical.

The Obama Cult

Meanwhile, the media-supported cult of personality around Obama would continue to flourish. Journalists who had covered the election, such as the ever-loyal Chris Matthews of MSNBC, opined that they now saw their role differently than they had seen it with Bush as president. Instead of holding the government to account, he would do his best to help the new administration: "I want to do everything I can to make this thing work, this new presidency work... This country needs a successful presidency."[73] Even Fox News head Roger Ailes was reported to have said that his journalists would go easy on the new president in the first days of his administration, to give him a chance to get the White House on its feet.[74]

Meanwhile, the Obama transition team continued its campaign-tested practice of resisting scrutiny by the media, using a loophole in federal campaign disclosure laws to ensure that its documents could remain under wraps.[75] The public might never know the true results, for example, of the internal investigation of the campaign's contacts and discussions with Illinois governor Rod Blagojevich. It seemed likely that the presidency would continue to operate in the same way, with limited access to journalists and little patience for questions from the media—an even more closed White House than the famously insular Bush administration. The Obama transition team boasted that it had held more press conferences than any of its predecessors, for example, but it was soon revealed that the president-elect routinely preselected which journalists would be allowed to ask questions the night before.[76] Obama studiously avoided Fox News for several press conferences, freezing out the conservative-leaning network entirely.[77] Even worse, when he finally did permit Fox to ask a question, the network's representative asked not about a matter of substance but about the sudden disappearance of commerce secretary-designate Bill Richardson's beard.[78] In time, more critical voices would re-emerge but for the first several weeks of Obama's presidency the deference would continue, with journalists tossing softball questions at Obama's first prime time press conference in February 2009.

Meanwhile, Democrats on Capitol Hill threatened to reduce the power of conservative talk radio and exert greater control over the media in general by reviving the "Fairness Doctrine." Such a policy would require broadcasting networks to provide equal time to opposing views. It sounded fair enough, except its entire purpose was to neutralize the one medium—talk radio—in which conservatives held the advantage. Effectively, it would use federal limits on freedom of speech to entrench the power of the new incumbent party. Though a resolution backing the Fairness Doctrine failed in the Senate in February 2009, Democrats seemed determined to apply its principles under future measures to be proposed under more innocuous-sounding names.

229

Whereas John McCain had pledged to end the era of the "permanent campaign" in Washington, Obama set about guaranteeing that it would continue. His campaign contacted voters and past supporters to donate vast sums of money—unrestricted by campaign finance laws—for the presidential inauguration, which cost roughly $160 million.[79] (And this in the midst of the "greatest economic crisis since the Great Depression," and against loud Democratic protests against Bush's comparatively modest $42 million inauguration in 2004.) The campaign's Internet operation was mobilized in support of the president-elect's transition team. Later, on the eve of the inauguration, Obama launched what became known as "Organizing for America," or "Obama 2.0."[80] He was not going to let his vast network lie dormant until the next election season. It would be used—as Obama aides admitted openly—to drive the new president's policy agenda. The first test of the system came in February 2009, when Obama called for 3,000 house meetings to push his stimulus plan.[81] Effectively, Obama intended to use grass-roots activists to promote his policies over possible objections from the public, from the Republicans and from his own party in Congress, using political operatives at the local level to drown out and defeat opposition and criticism.

America had never seen such a vast and independent political network before, least of all one tied directly to a single individual sitting in the White House with virtually unrestrained power. This was a political tool perhaps more appropriate to Hugo Chavez's Venezuela than to liberal democracy in America. It remained to be seen whether and how American society would react and adjust to the new political reality that such a network could impose. It was not hard to see how such tactics could be used to create a cloud of fear around political opponents—as well as about critics in the media, and even ordinary citizens complaining about poor service delivery or objecting to policy failures and broken promises. Indeed, in a troubling sign of Obama's willingness to use such tactics, he singled out conservative talk show host Rush Limbaugh for opprobrium in his first few days in the Oval Office—a highly unusual and alarming attack by a president on a media commentator.[82] That was followed by the release of a Department of Homeland Security report branding veterans, federalists, and opponents of abortion as potential sources of violent extremism.[83] It seemed the administration had a deep fear of opposition and dissent.

Two Dangerous Ideas

It seemed possible that Obama's continuing campaign could be used to promote two truly troubling ideas that he had brought with him to the White House. One was the conviction that the U.S. Constitution was meant to *do* something. It was not enough, according to this view, for a constitution to define the powers of the various branches of the government, to establish procedures for the functions of the state and to entrench the rights of citizens. Rather, according to this theory, the constitution must also serve a set of social goals, and becoming an instrument of the state in effecting lasting change.

That was not a view that Obama himself articulated as such, but it was a view implied by many of his policies, from universal state-provided health coverage to "spread[ing] the wealth around." It is also a prominent view in the left-wing legal academy that provided many of Obama's early mentors and staffed key posts in his administration. It was the view held by Obama's teachers at Harvard; it was the positive-rights dream that they shared. It was the vision that they had bequeathed to, and which they admired in, the new constitutions of the post-Cold War era, especially the South African constitution. The latter not only banned discrimination across an extremely wide range of social categories, but also provided the world's most ambitious set of socioeconomic rights. Other constitutions, like the Irish constitution, had included socioeconomic goals merely as "directive principles," not actual rights that each citizen could claim from the

231

state and which would be justiciable and enforceable in a court of law. But South Africa, India and a few other countries had opted to include these goals as fully-fledged rights, even though they could only be "progressively realized" over time.

In truth, these ambitious were rarely fulfilled, and more often than not their inclusion as constitutional rights seemed to guarantee that their goals would never be reached. Governments could take credit for having guaranteed the form of these socioeconomic rights while ignoring their substance. And once these issues were transformed into unshakeable state policy, political parties no longer felt the same need to compete with each other to offer the best policy prescriptions to reach the same goals. Socioeconomic rights effectively de-politicized socioeconomic goals, removing them from the sphere of democratic discourse and policy debate and tossing them to the mercies of the judiciary, which in turn was often reluctant to confront the will of the executive or the ruling party. The continued enthusiasm of the American academic left for these rights was one that could only be maintained through willful naïveté, and distance from the consequences of the recommendations they urged on foreign nations. It was a view un-tempered by empirical experience and its lessons, which were that constitutions that attempt to "do" something often do exactly the opposite of what they promise.

The problem had been anticipated a half-century before by philosophers such as Isaiah Berlin and Frederich A. Hayek, who warned that the state power necessary to provide "positive" rights or achieve broad socioeconomic goals would encroach on basic, fundamental democratic freedoms and human rights. The Soviet Constitution of 1936, for example, which had guaranteed a broad array of socioeconomic rights, had also coincided with the most brutal years of Stalin's repression. A constitution designed to make the government "do something" would entrench big-government policies, the more so since state power would be justified in the language of individual rights. And with bigger government would come new and increasing opportunities for corruption, as well as the steady erosion of "negative" rights—the classic freedoms of expression, assembly, arms and conscience, among others. States that tried to arrange socioeconomic outcomes in the name of "social justice" could only do so by breaking the most fundamental rule of the republic—equality before the law—and lead inexorably to the unfettered centralization of power. And by leading to a circumstance in which different people would be treated differently before the law, the idea of an "active" constitution would be far likelier to divide Americans, in time, than to unite them.

The second troubling idea that Obama's "permanent campaign" might promote was the seductive yet false notion that, to borrow his own terms, corruption was "in the eye of the beholder"—that some violations of ethical and democratic procedure were acceptable in the service of honorable ends. To be fair, one of his first acts as president was to freeze the salaries of senior staff, open White House files to public requests for information, and restrict the role of lobbyists in the executive. Yet on the very day he signed the executive orders enacting these policies, his choice for Secretary of the Treasury was trying to explain how he had failed to pay back taxes until being nominated—after a campaign in which Joe Biden had proclaimed paying higher taxes to be "patriotic."[84] And the very week he ordered lobbyists out of the White House, he created an army of activists to do essentially the same job of lobbying, while signing waivers for the many lobbyists he in fact chose to employ in his administration. There was a real danger that Obama's symbolic gestures at transparency would be contradicted by the actual operation of the government under his administration—just as his promises to clean up Washington had been contradicted by his behavior in the Senate. During the campaign, when Obama had to defend his request for nearly $1 billion in earmarks for his constituencies, he claimed that many of them went to worthy causes, and that the challenge was to eliminate "genuine" pork.[85]

But it was clear that to Obama and the circle of advisers that he surrounded himself with, some causes were more equal than others, especially those closely tied to political donors and power brokers. When it came to securing earmarks for his wealthy contributors, their business interests and their pet projects, Obama's purported concerns about procedural fairness, efficiency and oversight were rapidly jettisoned. Indeed, in the early weeks of his administration, he signed an additional spending bill loaded with billions of dollars in wasteful earmarks. To judge solely from his early performance, his was a style of governance that was dressed in the best rhetorical commitments to using taxpayer dollars to pursue the public interest, but which failed to deliver value for money in reality, and enabled a hidden system of influence-trading at odds with the spirit of democracy and the ethic of transparency.

Obama's opportunistic ideas about what did and did not constitute corruption were particularly dangerous given the sheer scale of the executive and economic powers he had inherited from George W. Bush, as well as the breadth and ambition of his own stated plans and promises. There would be numerous opportunities for him to dispense patronage to his supporters. Furthermore, Obama saw such practices as morally justifiable if they produced *some* benefit, however inefficiently or unfairly, to *some* needy constituency. That virtually guaranteed that unless he radically changed his own behavior, Obama's government would become less able to deliver, and less trusted by the public, even as its responsibilities and powers continued to increase. His words—his promises of hope and change—would become emptier over time.

The Meaning of Words

But words *do* matter. They are fundamental to our civilization, fundamental to our democracy, fundamental to the idea that our system of government rests on a social contract among the governed. American democracy emerged from within a tradition that took words extremely seriously. Its values were nurtured by colonists who had fled religious persecution in Europe and whose dissenting faith placed the highest value on the written words of the Bible, not on the authority of a church hierarchy. They, in turn, came from a kingdom that had, uniquely among all European empires, placed limits around the powers of its monarchs—limits described and maintained through the power of the written word, reaching back through time to the Magna Carta and the first constitutional impulses of our British forebears. The men who fought for American independence, and who wrote the American constitution, knew that among the many purposes, good and evil, that words could accomplish, the most important was to act as a restraint on power across the generations. If eternal vigilance is the price of liberty, words are the torch that allows democracy's sentinels to see the distant dangers.

Words like "hope" and "change" ought not lose their meaning because of the failings of Barack Obama or any other leader. But Obama's words can only be fulfilled if Americans begin to look beyond Obama himself. It is tempting to defer to the many great things Obama symbolizes, and to the new political realities that he has created—which, if his fundraising prowess and vast personal organization is anything to go by, may remain permanent fixtures of our political landscape for a long time to come. While Obama's opponents should welcome all that he does that is best for the country, there is no need to add to the genuflection he has already received and will continue to rely on from a docile media. It is the duty of the American people, and our public representatives in particular, to hold Obama accountable for his words. Only then will his words have any real value beyond the particular ambition they served to fulfill.

A new opposition has already begun to emerge—largely (though not exclusively) Republican in its composition, but less concerned about defending the party than fighting for its much-neglected principles. This new opposition has the task

235

of holding the Obama administration to account, measuring it against Obama's campaign promises as well as the expectations of the American people and the words and spirit of the Constitution. It continues to search for new leadership, as well as for a sense of vision, something the McCain campaign so desperately lacked. As a vision, "change" was effective for Obama, though it was always rather empty, and seemed to be wearing thin quite soon after the election, even among the people who voted and volunteered for Obama. There was not much else to hold the Obama coalition together, other than the charisma of the candidate himself, residual "Bush Derangement Syndrome," and the media's devotion to the man in whom they had invested the last shreds of their credibility. But vision is a powerful and necessary motivating force that a successful opposition cannot do without. True, American democracy is sorely in need of plain speaking. But "Straight Talk" is only a start. Words have a power to evoke emotions, and to create myths—and the new political opposition should not shy from them, from describing clearly the America it wants to build.

Most important, a strong opposition must stand up to, and dismantle, the anti-democratic weapons that the Obama camp had already begun to use in its campaign: the intimidating tactics of racial politics; the misleading but effective practice of "astroturfing"; the false voter registration and fundraising efforts; the singling out of conservative commentators; and, above all, the use of words to elevate a single individual beyond reason and reproach. The false consensus that Obama seeks to impose on American political discourse—with the help of a fawning national media—will actually prevent him from succeeding, because it will make it difficult for his own supporters to hold him accountable and for his opponents to prod him to improve his performance. Yet the strength of propaganda is never its ability to convince people of the truth of its arguments, but rather its power to make them consider all other alternatives ridiculous. That is why words have become more important than ever: they are the only means Americans have to break the tightening bonds of political conformity. The answer to Obama's style of charismatic politics is not to lose faith in words simply because of the flaws and failures of the speakers, but to treat words the same, whether they are uttered by Democrats or Republicans, blacks or whites, men or women. Likewise, we must weigh ideas according to the same measure, regardless of who they come from or how ably (or clumsily) they are expressed.

There is nothing so dangerous to democracy—and to the very idea of civilized society—as the idea that words do not matter. But words alone are not enough. Many words were spoken in the course of the election—some in bad faith and anger, on both sides. But many more words formed the basis of Obama's promise to America. And since voters had so little to go on besides the grandeur of those words—those magnificent speeches all around the world, in front of hundreds of thousands of cheering people who knew little about the man beyond the three syllables of his name—words were the very basis of Obama's victory. Yet throughout the election and its aftermath, Americans asked themselves: Had Obama meant all that he said? Had we understood him? Or had the voters handed authority to a new and dangerous kind of charismatic power?

Alexis de Tocqueville, the great nineteenth-century admirer of American democracy, warned in his classic *Democracy in America*: "Despotism, dangerous at all times, is therefore particularly to be feared in ages of democracy."[86] Tocqueville had in mind an all-powerful government, maintained in its absolutism by the simple fact that it had been popularly elected, and protected by the conformity of public opinion and the illusion of public participation. At the dawn of the Obama presidency, featuring at its heart a man standing on a pedestal of rhetoric, it seemed possible that in the very moment of celebrating its redemption, the nation had risked the safety of its democracy. And all for the sake of wishful thinking, all for the sake of words.

Ultimately, what the Obama era demands is that American citizens—not just those who voted against him, but *especially* those who voted *for* him—hold the president and other leaders responsible for their words. That is the only way to make sure that words really *do* matter, and to ensure that our democracy is one of laws and principles, not one of men alone, with their shifting ambitions and fickle desires.

Today, it seems that Obama could yet become a very successful president. I join those who hope that he does—though I contend that he is not likely to succeed unless he discards his radical, statist policies and his weak posture towards America's enemies. To borrow a turn of phrase from a close friend: my version of "hope" and "change" is that I hope *Obama* will change. Against the incessant argument that to oppose Obama and the Democrats is to oppose change itself, a new opposition must assert the fundamental values of equality before the law, and belief in the freedom of the individual as the greatest productive force in the history of human civilization. And it must find its own vision for the future—one grounded in ordinary aspirations and ordinary speech, but also that moves beyond empty promises, stale propaganda and tired nostalgia.

Above all, we must have courage. Courage is what allows democracy to function and flourish. It is the public virtue that best preserves the private freedoms we cherish. Courage creates room for a diversity of voices and animates the everyday with a sense of hope—real hope, not the messianic belief in one individual, but the conviction that we can, each of us, improve our lot and those of our fellow human beings. Amidst the failures of John McCain's presidential campaign, that spirit of courage remains his enduring legacy. His "Straight Talk Express" may never have reached its destination. He may have failed, and in a moment of truth he was tested and found wanting. Yet he fought on nonetheless, and gave the old American ideals the best chance they had against a new utopianism with great potential to unite and inspire but also great potential to destroy. An America of real courage and real hope is the kind of country we want to live in and believe in. That's the America we can build. That's the America we can know—and love. That's an America true to the words of its founders, and the dreams of the future.

Endnotes

Chapter 1 – The Power of Words

[1] Barack Obama, Speech in Milwaukee, Wisconsin, Feb. 16, 2008, ibid.

[2] Jeff Zeleny, "An Obama Refrain Bears Echoes of a Governor's Speeches," *New York Times*, Feb. 18, 2008, <http://www.nytimes.com/2008/02/18/us/politics/18video.html>.

[3] Howard Wolfson, quoted in Mike Allen, "Clinton aide accuses Obama of plagiarism," *Politico.com*, Feb. 18, 2008,
<http://www.politico.com/news/stories/0208/8570.html>.

[4] As a volunteer writer on the McCain campaign, the WWE speech was one of a handful of texts I wrote. This particular line, taken from wrestling legend Ric Flair, and the line about The Undertaker, are the only two in the WWE speech that I did *not* write—they were added in a later draft before the video was filmed.

[5] John McCain, "John McCain on WWE Monday Night RAW," Apr. 19, 2008, <http://www.youtube.com/watch?v=k8XkIeTz-NU>.

[6] Jerry Lawler, *Monday Night Raw*, USA Network television broadcast, Apr. 21, 2008, <http://www.youtube.com/watch?v=mWeZvuRZkIg>.

[7] John Bradshaw Layfield, *Your World With Neil Cavuto*, Fox News television broadcast, Apr. 22, 2008, <http://www.wwe.com/content/media/video/vms/none/2008/april22-28/6939642>

[8] John McCain, Remarks in Jacksonville, Florida, Sep. 15, 2008, quoted in Sam Stein, "McCain on 'Black Monday': Fundamentals of Our Economy are Still Strong," *HuffingtonPost.com*, Sep. 15, 2008, <http://www.huffingtonpost.com/2008/09/15/mccain-fundamentals-of-th_n_126445.html>.

[9] Barack Obama, Speech in Maquoketa, Iowa, December 13, 2007, quoted in Lynn Sweet, "Obama softens stump speech not to employ lobbyists," *Chicago Tribune*, Dec. 16, 2007, <http://www.suntimes.com/news/sweet/699806,CST-NWS-sweet16s1.article>.

[10] <http://www.newsday.com/news/politics/wire/sns-ap-obama-defense,0,2082617.story>

[11] Brian Ross and Rhonda Schwartz, "Emanuel Was Director of Freddie Mac During Scandal," *ABCNews.com*, Nov. 7, 2008, <http://abcnews.go.com/Blotter/story?id=6201900&page=1>.

[12] Campbell Brown, "Commentary: Obama already struggling with lobbyist promises," CNN television broadcast, Nov. 17, 2008, <http://www.cnn.com/2008/POLITICS/11/17/campbell.brown.lobbyists/index.html>.

[13] Justin Rood and Emma Schwartz, "Another Lobbyist Headed Into Obama Administration," *ABCNews.com*, Jan. 27, 2009,
<http://abcnews.go.com/Blotter/story?id=6735898&page=1>.

14 National Public Radio, "Can Obama Win the Black Vote?", *Talk of the Nation* broadcast, Feb. 14, 2007,
<http://www.npr.org/templates/story/story.php?storyId=7402914>.
15 Cornel West, remarks at Covenant With Black America conference, Hampton University, Hampton, Virginia, Feb. 10, 2007
<http://www.youtube.com/watch?v=HXj3_pjTTwg>.
16 Jesse Jackson, Fox News television broadcast, Jul. 6, 2008,
<http://www.youtube.com/watch?v=4aLGkFpsdHo>. Other news sources render the last word as "out," not "off."
17 Peggy Noonan, " 'At Least Bush Kept Us Safe'," *Wall Street Journal*, Dec. 5, 2008, <http://online.wsj.com/article/SB122843788060281477.html>.
18 Barbara Slavin, "Ahmadinejad congratulates Obama," *Washington Times*, Nov. 6, 2008, <http://www.washingtontimes.com/news/2008/nov/06/letter-ahmadinejad-congratulates-obama/>.
19 Bill Dupray, "Russia and China: Obama Won't Finish First Term," *The Patriot Room*, Jan. 27, 2009, <http://patriotroom.com/article/russia-and-china-obama-won-t-finish-first-term>.
20 "Iranian protestors burn Barack Obama pictures," *Times Online*, Jan. 13, 2009, <http://www.timesonline.co.uk/tol/news/world/middle_east/article5510665.ece>.
21 Martin Plissner, "Ready for Obama Already," *New York Times*, Feb. 7, 2007, <http://www.nytimes.com/2007/02/07/opinion/07plissner.html>.
22 Michell Obama, quoted in John Podhoretz, " 'It's Too Early. He Hasn't Done Anything Yet," *Contentions*, Oct. 31, 2008,
<http://www.commentarymagazine.com/blogs/index.php/jpodhoretz/40921>.
23 Barack Obama, Illinois Channel television broadcast, Nov. 8, 2004.
24 The Bradley effect was named for Tom Bradley, mayor of Los Angeles and Democratic candidate for governor of California in 1982. After leading the polls by double digits, Bradley, who would have been the state's first black governor, lost to his Republican rival. The "effect," and the given explanation for the loss, was that some white voters tended to lie to pollsters rather than admit openly that they were voting against a black candidate. However, this explanation has been contested, notably by Ken Khachigian, former strategist for Bradley's opponent George Deukmejian, who cited absentee ballots, among other factors, as the real reason for Bradley's loss. (Ken Khachigian, "Don't Blame the Bradley Effect," *Washington Post*, Nov. 2, 2008, <http://www.washingtonpost.com/wp-dyn/content/article/2008/10/30/AR2008103002396.html>.)
25 Christopher Cooper, Valerie Bauerlein and Corey Dade, "New Machine: In South, Democrats' Tactics May Change Political Game," *Wall Street Journal*, Jan. 23, 2008.
26 Brian Stelter, "The Facebooker Who Friended Obama," *New York Times*, Jul, 7, 2008, <http://www.nytimes.com/2008/07/07/technology/07hughes.html>.
27 Jon Friedman, "A look at McCain's '08 media strategy," *MarketWatch*, Oct. 19, 2005, <http://www.marketwatch.com/News/Story/Story.aspx?guid={6BAB8A05-5CFD-4E12-A6BA-0908901EDF0E}&siteid=google>.
28 Barack Obama, *The Audacity of Hope: Thoughts on Reclaiming the American Dream*, New York: Three Rivers Press, 2006. 11.

[29] Charles Krauhammer, "McCain—the most worthy nominee ever to be denied the prize," *Pittsburgh Post-Gazette*, Nov. 8, 2008, <http://www.post-gazette.com/pg/08313/926374-109.stm>.

[30] Richard Durbin, Speech at Democratic National Convention, Boston, Massachusetts, Jul. 27, 2004, <http://www.accessmylibrary.com/coms2/summary_0286-12784344_ITM>.

[31] Barack Obama, "The Audacity of Hope," Speech at the Democratic National Convention, Boston, Massachusetts, Jul. 27, 2004, <http://www.americanrhetoric.com/speeches/convention2004/barackobama2004dnc.htm>.

[32] William Saletan, "Blogging the Democratic Convention," *Slate.com*, Jul. 28, 2004, <http://www.slate.com/id/2104296/>.

[33] Ron Christie, "Obama's 95 Percent Tax Cut? 100 Percent Not True," *The Hill's Pundits Blog*, Oct. 22, 2008, <http://pundits.thehill.com/2008/10/22/obama%E2%80%99s-95-percent-tax-cut-100-percent-not-true/>.

[34] Fox News, "Raw verbates of Obama 2001 radio intvw and link to audio," Oct. 27, 2008. URL: <http://www.foxnews.com/urgent_queue/#50041ecb,2008-10-27>. *See also* Evie Stone, "McCain Jumps on Archival Obama Interview," National Public Radio blog, Oct. 27, 2008. URL: <http://www.npr.org/blogs/politics/2008/10/mccain_jumps_on_archival_obama.html>.

[35] Samuel J. Wurzelbacher, quoted in Jake Tapper, "Spread the Wealth?", *Political Punch*, Oct. 14, 2008, <http://blogs.abcnews.com/politicalpunch/2008/10/spread-the-weal.html>.

[36] Barack Obama, "American Recovery and Reinvestment," Speech at George Mason University, Jan. 8, 2009, <http://thepage.time.com/full-remarks-of-obamas-stimulus-speech/>.

[37] Lori Montgomery, "Obama Predicts Years of Deficits Over $1 Trillion," *Washington Post*, Jan. 7, 2009, <http://www.washingtonpost.com/wp-dyn/content/article/2009/01/06/AR2009010602849.html>.

[38] Chris Good, "Obama Joins Sens. Biden, Lugar on Bill to Triple Pakistan Aid," *The Hill's Blog Briefing Room*, Jul. 15, 2008, <http://briefingroom.thehill.com/2008/07/15/obama-joins-sens-biden-lugar-on-bill-to-triple-pakistan-aid/>.

[39] Amanda B. Carpenter, "Obama More Pro-Choice Than NARAL," *Human Events*, Dec. 26, 2006, <http://www.humanevents.com/article.php?id=18647>.

[40] Jill Stanek, "Obama Blocked Born Alive Infant Protection Act," *Citizenlink.com*, Apr. 2, 2008, <http://www.citizenlink.org/content/A000007034.cfm>.

[41] Carpenter, ibid.

[42] Brian Friel, Richard E. Cohen and Kirk Victor, "Obama: Most Liberal Senator in 2007," *National Journal*, Jan. 31, 2008, <http://nj.nationaljournal.com/voteratings/>.

[43] Shailagh Murray, "Years Later, Lewis Watches History Being Made," *Washington Post*, Aug. 22, 2002, <http://www.washingtonpost.com/wp-dyn/content/article/2008/08/27/AR2008082703978.html>.

[44] Mark R. Levin, "The Obama Temptation," *The Corner on National Review Online*, Oct. 25, 2008, <http://corner.nationalreview.com/post/?q=ZTI1NmUxYjA4ODczZjgxOWJhMzQ3ODI0MDRkOWFlMDQ=>.

[45] Barack Obama, Speech upon securing the Democratic nomination, St. Paul, MN, Jun. 3, 2008, <http://www.breitbart.com/article.php?id=D912VD200&show_article=1>.

[46] George Orwell, Apr. 17, 1949, *The Collected Essays, Journalism and Letters of George Orwell*, ed. Sonia Orwell and Ian Angus, Vol. 4, Boston: David R. Godine, 1968. 515.

[47] Patrick O'Connor, "Pelosi praises Dingell and Waxman," *Politico.com*, Nov. 20, 2008, <http://www.politico.com/blogs/thecrypt/1108/Pelosi_praises_Dingell_and_Waxman.html>.

[48] Klaus Marre, "Frank: Too much tax-cutting in Obama's plan," *The Hill.com*, Jan. 8, 2009, <http://thehill.com/leading-the-news/frank-too-much-tax-cutting-in-obamas-plan-2009-01-08.html>.

[49] Jeff Zeleny, "Obama's Down on the Farm," *New York Times*, Jul. 27, 2007, <http://thecaucus.blogs.nytimes.com/2007/07/27/obamas-down-on-the-farm/>.

[50] Mayhill Fowler, "Obama: No Surprise That Hard-Pressed Pennsylvanians Turn Bitter," *HuffingtonPost.com*, Apr. 11, 2008, <http://www.huffingtonpost.com/mayhill-fowler/obama-no-surprise-that-ha_b_96188.html>.

[51] Wendy Button, "So Long, Democrats," *The Daily Beast*, Oct. 28, 2008, <http://www.thedailybeast.com/blogs-and-stories/2008-10-28/so-long-obama/>.

[52] David Brooks, "The Insider's Crusade," *New York Times*, Nov. 21, 2008, <http://www.nytimes.com/2008/11/21/opinion/21brooks.html>.

[53] Greg Mankiw, "The Youth Vote and the GOP," *Greg Mankiw's Blog*, Nov. 5, 2008, <http://gregmankiw.blogspot.com/2008/11/youth-vote-and-gop.html>.

[54] Julianne Pepitone, "Consumer confidence index at all-time low," *CNNMoney.com*, Dec. 30, 2008, <http://money.cnn.com/2008/12/30/news/economy/consumer_confidence/index.htm?postversion=2008123010>.

[55] Fouad Ajami, "Obama and the Politics of Crowds," *Wall Street Journal*, Oct. 30, 2008, <http://online.wsj.com/article/SB122533157015082889.html>.

[56] Thanks to New Zealander Lewis Bollard for this insight.

[57] Bill Gross, "Getting ahead in a bailout nation," *BusinessSpectator.com*, Jan. 9, 2009, <http://www.businessspectator.com.au/bs.nsf/Article/Getting-ahead-in-a-bailout-nation-$pd20090109-N4QT3?OpenDocument&src=is&cat=financial%20markets-al>.

[58] Barack Obama, Speech at the American Israel Public Affairs Committee annual policy conference, Jun. 4, 2008, <http://www.npr.org/templates/story/story.php?storyId=91150432>.

[59] Hilary Leila Krieger, "Obama clarifies J'lem comment," *Jerusalem Post*, Jun. 6, 2008, <http://www.jpost.com/servlet/Satellite?cid=1212659672984&pagename=JPost%2FJPArticle%2FShowFull>.

Chapter 2 – The Illegitimate President

[1] Martina Stewart, "Leading Democrat: Bush 'the worst president we've ever had'," *CNNPolitics.com*, Jan. 4, 2009, <http://politicalticker.blogs.cnn.com/2009/01/04/leading-democrat-bush-the-worst-president-weve-ever-had/>.

[2] Ed Gillespie, "Myths & Facts About the Real Bush Record," *RealClearPolitics.com*, Dec. 22, 2008, <http://www.realclearpolitics.com/articles/2008/12/myths_and_facts_about_the_real.html>.

[3] Steve Hargreaves, "Obama rides economy to White House," *CNN.com*, Nov. 5, 2008, <http://money.cnn.com/2008/11/04/news/economy/election_polls/index.htm>.

[4] Kevin Sack, "Community health clinics increased during Bush years," *International Herald Tribune*, Dec. 26, 2008, <http://www.iht.com/articles/2008/12/26/americas/bush.php.>

[5] Michael A. Fletcher, "Bush Has Quietly Tripled Aid to Africa," *Washington Post*, Dec. 31, 2006, <http://www.washingtonpost.com/wp-dyn/content/article/2006/12/30/AR2006123000941.html>

[6] Ian Bremmer, "The axis of tyranny: Bush signals a revolution in foreign policy," *International Herald Tribune*, Jan. 29, 2005, <http://www.iht.com/articles/2005/01/29/edbremmer_ed3_.php>.

[7] Peggy Noonan, *What I saw at the revolution: A political life in the Reagan era*, New York: Random House, 1990. 280. Original emphasis.

[8] Stephen Slivinski, "The Grand Old Spending Party: How Republicans Became Big Spenders," *Policy Analysis*, No. 543 (May 2005), <www.cato.org/pubs/pas/pa543.pdf>.

[9] Jake Tapper, "Buchanan camp: Bush claims are 'nonsense'," *Salon.com*, Nov. 10, 2000, <http://dir.salon.com/story/politics/feature/2000/11/10/buchanan/>.

[10] Dan Keating and Dan Balz, "Florida Recounts Would Have Favored Bush," *Washington Post*, Nov. 12, 2001, <http://www.washingtonpost.com/wp-dyn/articles/A12623-2001Nov11.html>.

[11] Frank Davies, "Pelosi: '10-ton anvil lifted' when Bush departed," *Mercury-News.com*, Jan. 21, 2009, <http://www.mercurynews.com/news/ci_11518120?source=rss>.

[12] Christopher Hitchens, *Real Time with Bill Maher*, HBO television broadcast, Aug. 25, 2006, <http://www.youtube.com/watch?v=HECI4QK_mXA>.

[13] "Bush blocks abortion funding," *BBC News*, Jan. 23, 2001, <http://news.bbc.co.uk/2/hi/americas/1131329.stm>.

[14] "Republican senator loses to dead rival in Missouri," *CNN.com*, Nov. 8, 2000, <http://archives.cnn.com/2000/ALLPOLITICS/stories/11/07/senate.missouri/>.

[15] George W. Bush, First Presidential Debate, Boston, Massachusetts, Oct. 3, 2000, <http://www.debates.org/pages/trans2000a.html>.

[16] Barry Schweid, "After talks with angry Arabs, administration ready to ease sanctions on Iraq," *The BG News*, Feb. 27, 2001, <http://media.www.bgnews.com/

media/storage/paper883/news/2001/02/27/World/After.Talks.With.Angry
.Arabs.Administration.Ready.To.Ease.Sanctions.On.Iraq-1283213.shtml>.

[17] Michael Teplitsky, "Guest: U.S. should continue Afghan war through month of Ramadan," *Daily Northwestern*, Nov. 13, 2001,
<http://media.www.dailynorthwestern.com/media/storage/paper853/news/
2001/11/13/Forum/Guest.U.s.Should.Continue.Afghan.War.Through.Month.Of.
Ramadan-1908078.shtml>.

[18] Barack Obama, quoted in Robert Spencer, "Will Obama's 'Empathy' Prevent Another 9/11," *Human Events*, Sep. 17, 2008.
<http://www.humanevents.com/article.php?id=28573>.

[19] Barack Obama, quoted in David Brooks, "Obama Admires Bush," *New York Times*, May 16, 2008. URL: <http://www.nytimes.com/2008/05/16/opinion/
16brooks.html?partner=rssnyt&>.

[20] Barack Obama, quoted in Fareed Zakaria, Interview with Barack Obama, CNN television broadcast, Jul. 13, 2008.
<http://transcripts.cnn.com/TRANSCRIPTS/0807/13/fzgps.01.html>.

[21] Barack Obama, Remarks to the Chicago Council on Global Affairs, Nov. 22, 2005. URL: <http://www.thechicagocouncil.org/dynamic_page.php?id=102>.

[22] Barack Obama, Remarks at the Chicago Council on Global Affairs, Nov. 20, 2006. URL: <http://obama.senate.gov/speech/061120-a_way_forward_i/>.

[23] Jee Kim, ed., *Another World Is Possible: Conversations in a Time of Terror*, New Orleans: Subway & Elevated Press, 2001.

[24] S.C. Res. 1441, U.N. Doc. S/2002/1198 (Nov. 8, 2002). URL:
<http://www.un.org/News/dh/iraq/iraq-blue-e-110702-1198.pdf>.

[25] William Safire, "Essay; Kangaroo Courts," *New York Times*, Nov. 26, 2001,
<http://query.nytimes.com/gst/fullpage.html?res
=9802EFDE113AF935A15752C1A9679C8B63>.

[26] Dave Moniz and Tom Squitieri, "Rumsfeld offered to quit over Iraq abuse," *USA Today*, Feb. 3, 2005, <http://www.usatoday.com/news/washington/2005-
02-03-rumsfeld-cnn_x.htm>.

[27] George W. Bush, Speech at the National Endowment for Democracy,
Nov. 6, 2003.

[28] George W. Bush, quoted in Chris Suellentrop, "My Sharansky," *Slate.com*,
Jan. 26, 2005, <http://www.slate.com/id/2112699/>.

[29] Natan Sharansky, *The Case for Democracy: The Power of Freedom to Overcome Tyranny & Terror*, New York: PublicAffairs, 2004, 40-41.

[30] "Bush Focuses on Reviving Mideast Peace Process," Transcript of White House briefing, Oct. 2, 2001,
<http://transcripts.cnn.com/TRANSCRIPTS/0110/02/se.15.html>.

[31] James Bennet, "Sharon Invokes Munich in Warning U.S. on 'Appeasement'," *New York Times*, Oct. 5, 2001, <http://query.nytimes.com/gst/
fullpage.html?res=9C01E2D6163CF936A35753C1A9679C8B63>.

[32] Israel Ministry of Foreign Affairs, "Passover suicide bombing at Park Hotel in Netanya," Mar. 27, 2002, <http://www.mfa.gov.il/MFA/MFAArchive/2000
_2009/2002/3/Passover+suicide+bombing+at+Park+Hotel+in+Netanya.htm>.

[33] Edith M. Lederer, "UN Report Rejects Jenin Massacre Claim," *Associated Press*, Aug. 1, 2002, <http://www.why-war.com/news/2002/08/01/unreport.html>.

[34] David Usborne, "Bush: 'I regret saying the things I shouldn't have said'," *The Independent*, Nov. 13, 2008, <http://www.independent.co.uk/news/world/americas/bush-i-regret-saying-the-things-i-shouldnt-have-said-1015849.html>.

[35] George W. Bush, Speech to the Knesset, May 15, 2008.

[36] Daniel W. Reilly, "Biden: Bush's comments were 'bullshit'," *Politico.com*, May 15, 2008, <http://www.politico.com/blogs/thecrypt/0508/Biden_Bushs_comments_were_bullshit.html>.

[37] Aluf Benn, "Rice's visit / In the shadow of MLK," *Ha'aretz*, Jun. 16, 2007, <http://www.haaretz.com/hasen/objects/pages/PrintArticleEn.jhtml?itemNo=913369>.

[38] Dore Gold, "The false symmetry of UN Security Council Resolution 1860," *Jerusalem Post*, Jan. 11, 2009, <http://www.jpost.com/servlet/Satellite?cid=1231424927983&pagename=JPost%2FJPArticle%2FPrinter>.

[39] Terry Frieden, "Federal judge upholds Oregon assisted-suicide law," *CNN.com*, Apr. 17, 2002, <http://archives.cnn.com/2002/LAW/04/17/oregon.assisted.suicide/index.html>.

[40] Gail Russell Chaddock, "Despite earmark reforms, 'pork' spending rises," Apr. 3, 2008, <http://www.csmonitor.com/2008/0403/p02s01-uspo.html>.

[41] Ron Claiborne, "Stand-Up Guy: John McCain's Campaign Trail Comedy," *ABCNews.com*, Jan. 17, 2008, <http://abcnews.go.com/Politics/Vote2008/story?id=4148377&page=1>.

[42] John Kass, "Chickens dancing, roosting in 5th District," *Chicago Tribune*, Jan. 9, 2009, <http://www.chicagotribune.com/news/columnists/chi-kass-09-jan09,0,6818129.column>.

[43] " 'Can I quit now?' FEMA chief wrote as Katrina raged," *CNN.com*, Nov. 4, 2005, <http://www.cnn.com/2005/US/11/03/brown.fema.emails/>.

[44] U2 and Green Day, "The Saints Are Coming," YouTube music video, Oct. 27, 2006, <http://www.youtube.com/watch?v=seGhTWE98DU>.

[45] Joseph C. Wilson IV, "What I Didn't Find in Africa," *New York Times*, Jul. 6, 2003, <http://www.nytimes.com/2003/07/06/opinion/06WILS.html?ex=1372824000en=6c6aeb1ce960dec0ei=5007>.

[46] Public Law 107-56, 2001.

[47] "The Hubbell Standard," *Wall Street Journal*, Mar. 14, 2007, <http://www.opinionjournal.com/editorial/feature.html?id=110009784>.

[48] Bob Woodward, "Detainee Tortured, Says U.S. Official," *Washington Post*, Jan. 14, 2009, <http://www.washingtonpost.com/wp-dyn/content/article/2009/01/13/AR2009011303372.html>.

[49] Rahm Emanuel, quoted in "A 40-Year Wish List," *Wall Street Journal*, Jan. 28, 2009, <http://online.wsj.com/article/SB123310466514522309.html>.

[50] James Simpson, "Barack Obama and the Strategy of Manufactured Crisis," *American Thinker*, Sep. 28, 2008, <http://www.americanthinker.com/2008/09/barack_obama_and_the_strategy.html>.

[51] MBNYC, "George Bush, proud parent of the mortgage crisis," *DailyKos.com*, Sep. 23, 2008, <http://www.dailykos.com/story/2008/9/23/102817/214/793/607383>.

52 Steven A. Holmes, "Fannie Mae Eases Credit To Aid Mortgage Lending," *New York Times*, Sep. 30, 1999, <http://query.nytimes.com/gst/fullpage.html?res =9C0DE7DB153EF933A0575AC0A96F958260&sec=&spon=&pagewanted=1>
53 Scott A. Powell, "The Culprit Is All of Us," *Barron's*, Feb. 9, 2009, <http://online.barrons.com/article_email/SB123396551669058895-lMyQjAxMDI5MzAzNzkwNjc1Wj.html>.
54 Bureau of Economic Analysis, "Gross Domestic Product: Third Quarter 2008 (Final)," Dec. 23, 2008, <http://www.bea.gov/newsreleases/national/gdp/gdpnewsrelease.htm>.
55 Patrice Hill, "McCain adviser talks of 'mental recession'," *Washington Times*, Jul. 9, 2008, <http://www.washingtontimes.com/news/2008/jul/09/mccain-adviser-addresses-mental-recession/>.
56 David M. Herszenhorn, "Congressional Leaders Stunned by Warnings," *New York Times*, Sep. 19, 2008, <http://www.nytimes.com/2008/09/20/washington/19cnd-cong.html?ref=economy>.
57 Ryan Grim, "ACORN Issue Fueling Bailout Opposition," *CBS News*, Sep. 27, 2008, <http://www.cbsnews.com/stories/2008/09/27/politics/politico/thecrypt/main4483168.shtml>.
58 Mark Gongloff, "U.S. economic growth sizzles," *CNNMoney.com*, Oct. 30, 2003, <http://money.cnn.com/2003/10/30/news/economy/gdp/>.
59 Stuart M. Butler and Edwin Meese III, "The Bailout Package: Vital and Acceptable," *Heritage Foundation*, Sep. 29, 2008, <http://www.heritage.org/research/economy/wm2091.cfm>.

Chapter 3 – The Ambivalent Hero

1 Mark Murray, "NBC/WSJ poll: Obama holds significant lead," *MSNBC.com*, Nov. 3, 2008, <http://www.msnbc.msn.com/id/27488250/>.
2 Alex Cohen, "Congress Approval Rating Plummets Below Bush," *National Public Radio*, Jun. 30, 2008, <http://www.npr.org/templates/story/story.php?storyId=92034268>.
3 Michael Finnegan, "McCain's bid faltering in rough waters," *Los Angeles Times*, Jun. 30, 2007, <http://articles.latimes.com/2007/jun/30/nation/na-mccain30>.
4 Stuart Rothenburg, "McCain's '08 Dilemma: Can He Recapture the Magic He Once Had?", *Roll Call*, Jun. 25, 2007, <http://www.rollcall.com/issues/52_145/rothenberg/19096-1.html>.
5 Michael D. Shear, Dan Balz and Chris Cillizza, "Rivalries Split McCain's Team," *Washington Post*, Jul. 14, 2007, <http://www.washingtonpost.com/wp-dyn/content/article/2007/07/13/AR2007071302227.html>.
6 Jonathan Martin, "Win the Battle, Lose the Election?", *Politico*, Apr. 10, 2007, <http://www.politico.com/news/stories/0407/3473.html>.
7 CNN, "McCain, Edwards slip in New Hampshire poll," *CNN.com*, Jul, 18, 2007, <http://www.cnn.com/2007/POLITICS/07/18/nh.poll/>.
8 CNN, "Pentagon: Violence down in Iraq since 'surge'," *CNN.com*, Jun. 23, 2008, <http://www.cnn.com/2008/WORLD/meast/06/23/iraq.security/index.html>.

[9] John Kerry, quoted in Bill Schneider, "Bush campaign making strides," *CNN.com*, Mar. 19, 2004, <http://www.cnn.com/2004/ALLPOLITICS/03/19/bush.campaign/index.html>.

[10] Auren Hoffman, "It Takes Tech to Elect a President," *BusinessWeek*, Aug. 25, 2008, <http://www.businessweek.com/technology/content/aug2008/tc20080822_700775.htm>.

[11] Sam Youngman, "McCain camp warns of flawed exit polls," *TheHill.com*, Nov. 3, 2008, <http://thehill.com/campaign-2008/mccain-camp-warns-of-flawed-exit-polls-2008-11-03.html>.

[12] John Hellemann, "The New Politics: Barack Obama, Party of One," *New York*, Jan. 11, 2009, <http://nymag.com/news/features/all-new/53380/>.

[13] John McCain, Remarks at town hall meeting in Derry, New Hampshire, Jan. 3, 2008, <http://www.youtube.com/watch?v=vf7HYoh9YMM>. Emphasis added.

[14] www.barackobama.com, accessed Feb. 15, 2008. Emphasis added.

[15] Mark Murray, "McCain's Sunni-Shiite Faux Pas," *FirstRead*, Mar. 18, 2008, <http://firstread.msnbc.msn.com/archive/2008/03/18/780688.aspx>.

[16] Eli Lake, "McCain, Obama Clash Over Iran's Al Qaeda Role," *New York Sun*, Mar. 20, 2008, <http://www.nysun.com/national/mccain-obama-clash-over-irans-al-qaeda-role/73277/>.

[17] David Wright and Sunlen Miller, "Obama Gaffes on Iraq and Afghanistan," *ABCNews.com*, May 13, 2008,
<http://blogs.abcnews.com/politicalradar/2008/05/obama-gaffes-on.html>.

[18] John McCain, Interview with Peter Cook, Bloomberg television broadcast, Apr. 17, 2008, <http://www.realclearpolitics.com/articles/2008/04/john_mccain_on_bloomberg_tv.html>.

[19] Barack Obama, quoted in Aswini Anburajan, "Obama Goes After McCain on Economy," *FirstRead*, Apr. 19, 2008,
<http://firstread.msnbc.msn.com/archive/2008/04/19/920974.aspx>.

[20] Barack Obama, quoted in Susan Page, "Obama: beware 'you're on your own' society," *USA Today*, Mar. 27, 2008, <http://www.usatoday.com/news/politics/election2008/2008-03-26-obama_N.htm>.

[21] Barack Obama, quoted in Amy Chozick, "Clinton Touts Battle Scars," *Wall Street Journal*, Feb. 11, 2008,
<http://blogs.wsj.com/washwire/2008/02/11/clinton-touts-battle-scars/>.

[22] John McCain, Speech to Voters in Virginia Beach, VA, Feb 28, 2000, <http://transcripts.cnn.com/TRANSCRIPTS/0002/28/se.01.html>.

[23] Dan Balz, "McCain Reconnects With Liberty University," *Washington Post*, May 14, 2006, <http://www.washingtonpost.com/wp-dyn/content/article/2006/05/13/AR2006051300647_pf.html>.

[24] John McCain, Acceptance Speech at the Republican National Convention, St. Paul, MN, Sep. 4, 2008, <http://portal.gopconvention2008.com/speech/details.aspx?id=84>.

[25] Jim Rutenberg and Julie Bosman, "Dubious Claims in Obama's Ads Against McCain, Despite Vow of Truth," *New York Times*, Sep. 25, 2008, <http://www.nytimes.com/2008/09/26/us/politics/26ads.html?fta=y&pagewanted=all>.

26 Jake Tapper, "Attack gets personal," *Salon.com*, Mar. 3, 2000, <http://dir.salon.com/politics2000/feature/2000/03/03/mccain/index.html>.
27 Kyle-Anne Shiver, "Obama's Alinsky Jujitsu," *American Thinker*, Jan. 8 2008, <http://www.americanthinker.com/2008/01/obamas_alinsky_jujitsu.html>.
28 Barack Obama, *Dreams From My Father*, 93.
29 Barack Obama, Remarks in Lebanon, New Hampshire, Jan. 7, 2008.
30 Associated Press, "McCain Attends Services at Phoenix Church," *The Christian Post*, Jun. 23, 2008, <http://www.christianpost.com/church/Politics/2008/06/mccain-attends-services-at-phoenix-church-23/index.html>.
31 John McCain, quoted in Lucas Morel, "Faith and Philosophy Take Center Stage in Iowa," *Ashbrook Center*, Dec. 1999, <http://www.ashbrook.org/publicat/oped/morel/99/iowa.html>.
32 Neil Munro, "FEC Rules Leave Loopholes For Online Donation Data," *National Journal*, Oct. 24, 2008, <http://www.nationaljournal.com/njonline/no_20081024_9865.php>.
33 Aswini Anburajan, "Obama on his state senate records," *FirstRead*, Nov. 9, 2007, <http://firstread.msnbc.msn.com/archive/2007/11/09/457959.aspx>.
34 Lawrence K. Altman, "Release of McCain's Medical Records Provides Unusually Broad Psychological Profile," *New York Times*, Dec. 6, 1999, <http://query.nytimes.com/gst/fullpage.html?res=980DEFD7133EF935A35751C1A96F958260>.
35 Carol Marin, "Obama, Blago flip sides of Bizarro plotline," *Chicago Sun-Times*, Jan. 4, 2009, <http://www.suntimes.com/news/marin/1360142,CST-EDT-carol04.article>.
36 Ariel Sabar, "For Obama, bipartisan aims, party-line votes," *Christian Science Monitor*, Apr. 17, 2008, <http://www.csmonitor.com/2008/0417/p01s07-uspo.html>.
37 Martin Wisckol, "McCain discusses bill for illegal immigrants," *Orange County Register*, Jul. 14, 2008, <http://www.ocregister.com/articles/mccain-speech-border-2093607-group-immigration>.
38 Barack Obama, *The Audacity of Hope*, 127.
39 Elisabeth Bumiller, "McCain Criticizes Katrina Response as 'Disgraceful'," *New York Times*, Apr. 25, 2008, <http://www.nytimes.com/2008/04/25/us/politics/24cnd-mccain.html?_r=1&hp&oref=slogin>.
40 Elisabeth Bumiller and John M. Broder, "McCain regrets vote against King holiday," *International Herald-Tribune*, Apr. 4, 2008, <http://www.iht.com/articles/2008/04/04/america/04mccain-king.php>.
41 Andrew Malcolm, "Obama's small donor base image is a myth, new study reveals," *Los Angeles Times*, Nov. 25, 2008, <http://latimesblogs.latimes.com/washington/2008/11/obama-money.html>.
42 Fredreka Schouten, "Obama opts out of public funds," *USA Today*, Jun. 20, 2008, <http://www.usatoday.com/news/politics/election2008/2008-06-19-obama-campaign-finance_N.htm>.
43 MoveOn.org, "My Friends," advertisement, Sep. 16, <http://www.youtube.com/watch?v=CPuoAWaVStE>.
44 Markos Moulitsas, "Obama's birth certificate," *DailyKos.com*, Jun. 12, 2008, <http://www.dailykos.com/story/2008/6/12/11012/6168/320/534616>.

[45] Jim Popkin, "Obama's missing 'thesis'," *FirstRead*, Jul. 24, 2008, <http://firstread.msnbc.msn.com/archive/2008/07/24/1219722.aspx>.

[46] Barack Obama, Debate at Saddleback Church, Orange County, California, Aug. 17, 2008, <http://www.clipsandcomment.com/2008/08/17/full-transcript-saddleback-presidential-forum-sen-barack-obama-john-mccain-moderated-by-rick-warren/>.

[47] John McCain, Debate at Saddleback Church, Orange County, California, Aug. 17, 2008, <http://www.clipsandcomment.com/2008/08/17/full-transcript-saddleback-presidential-forum-sen-barack-obama-john-mccain-moderated-by-rick-warren/>.

[48] John McCain, Speech at Greater Columbus Convention Center, Columbus, Ohio, May 15, 2008, <http://www.nytimes.com/2008/05/15/us/politics/15text-mccain.html>.

[49] Mike Allen and Jonathan Martin, "Exclusive: No single-term pledge for McCain," *Politico.com*, Aug. 21, 2008, <http://www.politico.com/news/stories/0808/12681.html>.

[50] There was not much I could see myself, from my desk in a forgotten corner of the media department—nor would I be inclined to report anything I could have seen, had I been able to. And the grand story of McCain's campaign has yet to be told, by abler witnesses than me. But some problems were obvious to all, even from the outside.

[51] Nielsen Wire, "McCain Tops Obama's Record-Breaking Ratings," Sep. 5, 2008, <http://blog.nielsen.com/nielsenwire/media_entertainment/mccain-tops-obamas-record-breaking-ratings/>.

[52] John McCain, Remarks at Sturgis Motorcycle Rally, Aug. 5, 2008, <http://www.youtube.com/watch?v=sK-LEyyf7d4>.

[53] The speech was later blasted on left-wing blogs for a comment McCain made later on in which he suggested that his wife participate in the rally's beauty pageant, featuring scantily-clad women. (*See* John Marshall, "Take My Wife, Please!", *Talking Points Memo*, Aug. 5, 2008, <http://www.talkingpointsmemo.com/archives/207172.php>.) The complaints say more about the left's lack of humor than McCain's lack of tact.

[54] Never eager to admit he had been wrong about anything, Obama continued to insist he had not meant to invite unconditional talks with Mahmoud Ahmadinejad, the Holocaust-denying president of Iran, but with the supreme religious leader of the country, Ayatollah Ali Khamenei. Even after taking office, Obama attempted to continue this fiction by writing Khamenei, not Ahmadinejad, a letter attempting to resolve the two countries' differences.

[55] Stephen Harper, quoted in CBC News, "McCain hails NAFTA and Canada's role in Afghanistan," *CBC News*, Feb. 29, 2008, <http://www.cbc.ca/world/usvotes/story/2008/02/29/mcain-nafta.html>.

[56] Michael Luo, "Memo Gives Canada's Account of Obama Campaign's Meeting on Nafta," *New York Times*, Mar. 4, 2008, <http://www.nytimes.com/2008/03/04/us/politics/04nafta.html>.

[57] Associated Press, "McCain calls for a summer 'gas-tax holiday'," *MSNBC.com*, Apr. 15, 2008, <http://www.msnbc.msn.com/id/24120727/>.

58 Foon Rhee, "Obama slams gas tax holiday as a gimmick," *Political Intelligence*, Apr. 29, 2008, <http://www.boston.com/news/politics/politicalintelligence/2008/04/obama_slams_gas.html>.

59 Scott Horsley, "Obama Says Illinois' Gas Tax Holiday Didn't Work," *National Public Radio*, May 9, 2008, <http://www.npr.org/templates/story/story.php?storyId=90309571>.

60 Barack Obama, Acceptance Speech at the Democratic National Convention, Denver, Colorado, Aug. 28, 2008, <http://www.nytimes.com/2008/08/28/us/politics/28text-obama.html>.

61 Michael D. Shear and Perry Bacon, Jr., "Anger is Crowd's Overarching Emotion at McCain Rally," *Washington Post*, Oct. 10, 2008, <http://www.washingtonpost.com/wp-dyn/content/article/2008/10/09/AR2008100903169_pf.html>.

62 Karl Rove, quoted in "Rove: Some McCain ads don't pass '100 percent truth' test," *CNN.com*, Sep. 14, 2008, <http://politicalticker.blogs.cnn.com/2008/09/14/rove-some-mccain-ads-dont-pass-100-percent-truth-test/>.

63 Barack Obama, quoted in Christi Parsons, "Questions about pastor fair game, Obama says," *The Seattle Times*, Apr. 28, 2008, <http://seattletimes.nwsource.com/html/politics/2004377847_camp28.html>.

64 Reuters, "McCain says N.C. Republicans out of touch over ad," *Reuters.com*, Apr. 25, 2008, <http://www.reuters.com/article/marketsNews/idUSN2535509420080425>.

65 "Stephanopoulos: Obama Considered Joining the Military," *ABCNews.com*, Sep. 7, 2008, <http://blogs.abcnews.com/politicalradar/2008/09/obama-to-step-6.html>.

66 Barack Obama, "Obama: McCain is 'losing his bearings'," *CNN.com*, May 8, 2009, <http://politicalticker.blogs.cnn.com/2008/05/08/obama-mccain-is-losing-his-bearings/>.

67 Craig Ferguson, quoted on *The View*, ABC television broadcast, Apr. 21, 2008.

68 John McCain, Remarks at Murrells Inlet, South Carolina, Apr. 19, 2007, <http://www.npr.org/templates/story/story.php?storyId=9688222>.

69 "McCain to Obama: I Have 'Guts' to Bring Up Ayers," *ABCNews.com*, Oct. 14, 2008, <http://blogs.abcnews.com/politicalradar/2008/10/mccain-obama-pr.html>.

70 Joanna Walters, "Obama fights for every vote to close on Clinton," *Guardian*, Apr. 20, 2008, <http://www.guardian.co.uk/world/2008/apr/20/uselections2008.hillaryclinton>.

71 Jim Rutenberg et al., "For McCain, Self-Confidence on Ethics Poses Its Own Risk," *New York Times*, Feb. 21, 2008, <http://www.nytimes.com/2008/02/21/us/politics/21mccain.html?_r=2&bl&ex=1203656400&en=d0734db651c10475&ei=5087%0A&oref=slogin>.

72 Hendrik Hertzberg, "Comment: They've Got Personality," *New Yorker*, Nov. 6, 2000, 37.

Chapter 4 – The Obama Insurgency

[1] Jose Antonio Vargas, "Ron Paul Beats Own Fundraising Record," *Boston Globe*, Dec. 17, 2007, <http://blog.washingtonpost.com/44/2007/12/17/ron_paul_beats_own_fundraising.html>.

[2] Fredreka Schouten, "Obama, Paul net most military workers' campaign donations," *USA Today*, Sep. 16, 2007, <http://www.usatoday.com/news/politics/election2008/2007-09-13-military-donors_N.htm>.

[3] J. Patrick Coolican, "Ron Paul campaign dominates convention," *Las Vegas Sun*, Apr. 27, 2008, <http://www.lasvegassun.com/news/2008/apr/27/ron-paul-campaign-dominates-convention/>.

[4] Jamie Kirchik, "Angry White Man," *The New Republic*, Jan. 8, 2008, <http://www.tnr.com/politics/story.html?id=e2f15397-a3c7-4720-ac15-4532a7da84ca>.

[5] Brian Todd, "Ron Paul '90s newsletters rant against blacks, gays," *CNN.com*, Jan. 11, 2008, <http://www.cnn.com/2008/POLITICS/01/10/paul.newsletters/index.html>.

[6] Ann Coulter, "Obama's Dimestore 'Mein Kampf'," *Human Events*, Apr. 2, 2008, <http://www.humanevents.com/article.php?id=25831>.

[7] Douglas Waller, "How John Kerry Won Iowa," *Time*, Jan. 20, 2004, <http://www.time.com/time/election2004/article/0,18471,579103,00.html>.

[8] Christopher Wills, "Fact Check: Obama's 'present' votes," *Boston.com*, Jan. 24, 2008, <http://www.boston.com/news/nation/articles/2008/01/24/fact_check_obamas_present_votes/>.

[9] Jodi Kantor, "Teaching Law, Testing Ideas, Obama Stood Slightly Apart," *New York Times*, Jul. 30, 2008, <http://www.nytimes.com/2008/07/30/us/politics/30law.html>.

[10] Drew Griffin and Kathleen Johnston, "Obama played hardball in first Chicago campaign," CNN television broadcast, May 30, 2008, <http://www.cnn.com/2008/POLITICS/05/29/obamas.first.campaign/index.html>.

[11] Todd Spivak, "Barack Obama and Me," *Houston Press*, Feb. 28, 2008, <http://www.houston-press.com/2008-02-28/news/barack-obama-screamed-at-me/full>.

[12] David Axelrod, "A Well-Oiled Machine: A system that works?", *Chicago Tribune*, Aug. 21, 2005.

[13] Economist.com, "The Obamamercial," *Economist.com*, Oct. 29, 2008, <http://www.economist.com/blogs/democracyinamerica/2008/10/the_obamamercial.cfm>.

[14] Shailagh Murray and Jonathan Weisman, "Both Clinton and Obama Embellish Their Roles," *Washington Post*, Mar. 24, 2008, <http://www.washingtonpost.com/wp-dyn/content/article/2008/03/23/AR2008032301706_pf.html>.

[15] Abdon M. Pallasch, "Strong, silent type," *Chicago Sun-Times*, Dec. 17, 2007, <http://www.suntimes.com/news/politics/obama/700499,CST-NWS-Obama-law17.article>.

16 Binyamin Appelbaum, "Grim proving ground for Obama's housing policy," *The Boston Globe*, Jun. 27, 2008, <http://www.boston.com/news/nation/articles/2008/06/27/grim_proving_ground_for_obamas_housing_policy/>.

17 Chris Fusco and Dave McKinney, "Obama grant being probed," *Chicago Sun-Times*, Sep. 25, 2008, <http://www.suntimes.com/news/watchdogs/1184049, CST-NWS-watchdog25.article>.

18 David Wright and Sunlen Miller, "Obama Dropped Flag Pin in War Statement," *ABCNews.com*, Oct. 4, 2007, <http://abcnews.go.com/Politics/Story?id=3690000&page=1>.

19 Howard G. Goldberg, "Wine industry excited by Obama," *Decanter.com*, Jan. 15, 2009, <http://www.decanter.com/news/275116.html>.

20 Mickey Kaus, "Don't Fear the Burberry," *Slate.com*, May 13, 2008, <http://www.slate.com/id/2190574/>.

21 Fowler, *HuffingtonPost.com*, Apr. 12, 2008, ibid.

22 David Greenberg, "Too Good for Politics," *Slate.com*, Nov. 16, 2007, <http://www.slate.com/id/2178075/>.

23 Marissa Brostoff, "Chicago Temple Takes New Security in Stride," *Forward*, Nov. 26, 2008, <http://www.forward.com/articles/14637/>.

24 Kenneth T. Walsh, "Obama 'Typical White Person' Comment Delights Clinton Aides," *U.S. News & World Report*, Mar. 21, 2008, <http://www.usnews.com/blogs/news-desk/2008/03/21/obama-typical-white-person-comment-delights-clinton-aides.html>.

25 Mark Murray, "Obama: Buchenwald, not Auschwitz," *FirstRead*, May 28, 2008, <http://firstread.msnbc.msn.com/archive/2008/05/28/1070102.aspx>.

26 Nick Pisa, "Barack Obama's 'lost' brother found in Kenya," *Telegraph.co.uk*, Aug. 21, 2008, <http://www.telegraph.co.uk/news/worldnews/northamerica/usa/barackobama/2590614/Barack-Obamas-lost-brother-found-in-Kenya.html>.

27 David Cohen, "Barack Obama's broken promise to African village," *Evening Standard*, Jul. 25, 2008, <http://www.thisislondon.co.uk/standard/article-23520981-details/Barack+Obama%27s+broken+promise+to+African+village/article.do>.

28 James Bone, Rob Crilly and Ben MacIntyre, "Found in a rundown Boston estate: Barack Obama's aunt Zeituni Onyango," *TimesOnline*, Oct. 30, 2008, <http://www.timesonline.co.uk/tol/news/world/us_and_americas/us_elections/article5042571.ece>.

29 Jon Coplon, "White House DJ Battle," *Blender.com*, Jul. 30, 2008, <http://www.blender.com/WhiteHouseDJBattle/articles/39518.aspx>.

30 Tammerlin Drummond, "What was Barack Obama like in 1990?", *Toronto Star*, Jan. 18, 2009, <http://www.thestar.com/news/uselection/article/572960>.

31 Monifa Thomas, "Caroline Kennedy sees Obama carrying on JFK legacy," *Chicago Sun-Times*, Jan. 27, 2008, <http://www.suntimes.com/news/politics/obama/761962,CST-NWS-caroline27.article>.

32 Barack Obama, quoted in Robert Maginnis, "Obama Promises to Dismantle Our Armed Forces," *Human Events*, Apr. 20, 2008, <http://www.humanevents.com/article.php?id=25942>.

[33] Amy Chozick, "Obama Touts Single-Payer System for Health Care," *Wall Street Journal*, Aug. 19, 2008, <http://blogs.wsj.com/washwire/2008/08/19/obama-touts-single-payer-system/>.

[34] Barack Obama, Interview with the *San Francisco Chronicle*, Jan. 17, 2008, <http://cdn.sfgate.com/blogs/sounds/sfgate/chroncast/2008/01/17/20080117-obama-interview.mp3>.

[35] Associated Press, "Obama plane has 'President' label on seat," *Chicago Sun-Times*, Jul. 22, 2008, <http://www.suntimes.com/news/politics/obama/1068218,obplane072208.article>.

[36] *See, e.g.* Charles Johnson, "Searching Obama's Site for 'Jewish Lobby'," *Little Green Footballs*, Jun. 8, 2008, <http://littlegreenfootballs.com/article/30242_Searching_Obamas_Site_for_Jewish_Lobby>; Charles Johnson, "Obama Campaign Throws Antisemitic Blog Down Memory Hole," *Little Green Footballs*, Jun. 8, 2008, <http://littlegreenfootballs.com/article/30243_Obama_Campaign_Throws_Antisemitic_Blog_Down_the_Memory_Hole/comments/>.

[37] Shelby Steele, "Obama's post-racial promise," *Los Angeles Times*, Nov. 5, 2008, <http://www.latimes.com/news/opinion/commentary/la-oe-steele5-2008nov05,0,6553798.story>.

[38] Reuters, "Obama says Republicans will use race to stoke fear," *Reuters.com*, Jun. 20, 2008, <http://www.reuters.com/article/politicsNews/idUSN2040982720080620>.

[39] Sean Wilentz, "Race Man," *The New Republic*, Feb. 27, 2008, <http://www.tnr.com/politics/story.html?id=aa0cd21b-0ff2-4329-88a1-69c6c268b304>

[40] Cinque Henderson, "Maybe We Can't," *The New Republic*, May 28, 2008, <http://www.tnr.com/politics/story.html?id=331c77bb-9591-422c-aa2b-11a741c6ebb9&p=2>.

[41] Michelle Malkin, "B.S. alert: Hillary's 'Iron My Shirt' hecklers, *Michelle Malkin.com*, Jan. 7, 2008, <http://michellemalkin.com/2008/01/07/bs-alert-hillarys-iron-my-shirt-hecklers/>.

[42] Geoff Earle, "Bill Clinton's Bigmout of the South," *New York Post*, Jan. 28, 2008 ,<http://www.nypost.com/seven/01282008/news/nationalnews/hes_bigmouth___of_the_south_811092.htm>.

[43] FOXNews.com, "Bill Clinton Bristles Anew Over Questions About 'Race Card'," *FOXNews.com*, Apr. 22, 2008, <http://www.foxnews.com/politics/elections/2008/04/22/bill-clinton-blisters-over-racism-portrayal-in-radio-interview/>.

[44] Father Michael Pfleger, quoted in Mike Flannery, Jay Levine and Joanie Lum, "Pfleger Mocks Clinton Losses, Then Apologizes," CBS2 Chicago television news broadcast, May 30, 2008, <http://cbs2chicago.com/politics/fleger.obama.clinton.2.736268.html>.

[45] William Jefferson Clinton, quoted in Jake Tapper, "Bill Clinton Assails Vanity Fair's Purdum After Tough Story," *Political Punch*, Jun. 2, 1008, <http://blogs.abcnews.com/politicalpunch/2008/06/bill-clinton-as.html>.

[46] Erik Rush, "Obamination," *RenewAmerica*, Feb. 21, 2007, <http://www.renewamerica.us/columns/rush/070221>.

[47] Jeremiah Wright, quoted in "Wright: 'U.S. of KKKA' knew about Pearl Harbor," *WorldNetDaily*, Mar. 15, 2008, <http://www.worldnetdaily.com/index.php?fa=PAGE.view&pageId=59044>.

[48] Jeremiah Wright, quoted in Brian Ross and Rehab El-Buri, "Obama's Pastor: God Damn America, U.S. to Blame for 9/11," *ABCNews.com*, Mar. 13, 2008, <http://abcnews.go.com/blotter/story?id=4443788>.

[49] Jeff Goldblatt, "Obama's Ex-Church Has Won $15M in Federal Grant Money," *FOXNews.com*, Jun. 2, 2008, <http://www.foxnews.com/politics/elections/2008/06/02/obamas-ex-church-has-won-15m-in-federal-grant-money/>.

[50] Jeff Goldblatt, "Obama's Former Pastor Getting $1.6M Home in Retirement," *FOXNews.com*, Mar. 27, 2008, <http://www.foxnews.com/politics/elections/2008/03/27/obamas-former-pastor-builds-a-multimillion-dollar-retirement-home/>.

[51] Lynn Sweet, "Sweet blog extra: Barack and Michelle Obama earned $991,296 in 2006," *Chicago Sun-Times*, Apr. 16, 2007, <http://blogs.suntimes.com/sweet/2007/04/sweet_blog_extra_barack_and_mi.html>.

[52] Chris Matthews, quoted in Media Research Center, "MSNBC's Chris Matthews Wins 'Quote of the Year'," Press Release, Dec. 22, 2008, <http://www.mediaresearch.org/press/2008/press20081222.asp>.

[53] Chris Matthews, "Hardball with Chris Matthews," MSNBC television broadcast, Mar, 18, 2008, <http://www.msnbc.msn.com/id/23707778/>.

[54] Mitt Romney, "Faith in America," Speech in College Station, Texas, Dec. 6, 2007, <http://www.thebostonchannel.com/politics/14789305/detail.html>.

[55] Barack Obama, "A More Perfect Union," Speech in Philadelphia, Pennsylvania, Mar. 18, 2008, <http://blogs.wsj.com/washwire/2008/03/18/text-of-obamas-speech-a-more-perfect-union/>.

[56] Charles Krauthammer, "The Speech: A Brilliant Fraud," *RealClearPolitics.com*, Mar. 21, 2008, <http://www.realclearpolitics.com/articles/2008/03/questions_for_obama_1.html>.

[57] Jeremiah Wright, Remarks at the National Press Club, Washington, D.C., Apr. 28, 2008, <http://www.foxnews.com/politics/elections/2008/04/28/transcript-rev-wright-at-the-national-press-club/>.

[58] Clark Hoyt, "The Preacher's New Pulpit," *New York Times*, May 4, 2008, <http://www.nytimes.com/2008/05/04/opinion/04pubed.html?partner=rssuserl and&emc=rss&pagewanted=all>.

[59] Cathleen Falsani, "Obama: I have a deep faith," *Chicago Sun-Times*, Apr. 5, 2004, <http://www.suntimes.com/news/falsani/726619,obamafalsani040504.article>.

[60] Hillary Clinton, quoted in Agence France-Presse, "Clinton vows to shatter glass ceiling," Oct. 15, 2007, <http://afp.google.com/article/ALeqM5jpNzLN25XyRcDHMQVWdN9cTmzu2Q>.

[61] Hillary Clinton, remarks at Martin Luther King, Jr. Day rally, Columbia, South Carolina, Jan. 21, 2008, <http://www.youtube.com/watch?v=ND-Yq7j8-oM>.

[62] Alessandra Stanley, "20th Debate: Reality Show or Spinoff?", *New York Times*, Feb. 27, 2008, <http://www.nytimes.com/2008/02/27/us/politics/27watch.html>.

[63] Hillary Clinton, quoted in Alex Koppelman, "Hillary Clinton, sniper fire and Sinbad," *War Room*, Mar. 17, 2008, <http://www.salon.com/politics/war_room/2008/03/17/clinton_speech/>.

[64] David Gardner, "Clinton under fire: Video contradicts Hillary's claim she ran from sniper shots in Bosnia," *Daily Mail*, Mar. 26, 2008, <http://www.dailymail.co.uk/news/article-544633/Clinton-Video-contradicts-Hillarys-claim-ran-sniper-shots-Bosnia.html>.

[65] Samantha Power, quoted in Gerri Peev, " 'Hillary Clinton's a monster': Obama aide blurts out attack in Scotsman interview," *The Scotsman*, Mar. 7, 2008, <http://thescotsman.scotsman.com/latestnews/Inside-US-poll-battle-as.3854371.jp>. In the same interview, Power referred to Clinton as a "monster"; she resigned from the campaign but returned afterwards as Obama's national security adviser, a position in which she was forced to work with—or compete with—Clinton on foreign policy issues.

[66] Seattle Times news services, "How did pollsters blow it in Clinton-Obama race?", *Seattle Times*, Jan. 10, <http://seattletimes.nwsource.com/html/politics/2004116840_poll10.html>.

[67] Sean Wilentz, "Why Hillary Clinton should be winning," *Salon.com*, Apr. 7, 2008, <http://www.salon.com/opinion/feature/2008/04/07/hillary/>.

[68] Gary Hart, quoted in Jake Tapper, "Gary Hart: How Super Delegates Did Me In in '84," *ABCNews.com*, Feb. 13, 2008, <http://blogs.abcnews.com/politicalpunch/2008/02/gary-hart-how-s.html>.

[69] Michael Saul, "2008 candidates are super generous when it comes to superdelegates," *New York Daily News*, Feb. 15, 2008, <http://www.nydailynews.com/news/politics/2008/02/15/2008-02-15_2008_candidates_are_super_generous_when_.html>.

[70] Lanny Davis, "Obama's Minister Problem," *Wall Street Journal*, Apr. 9, 2008, <http://online.wsj.com/public/article_print/SB120770107738700007.html>.

[71] "L.A. Times Article on Obama-Wright Controversy Downplays the Most Damning Details," *Patterico's Pontifications*, Mar. 15, 2008, <http://patterico.com/2008/03/15/la-times-article-on-obama-wright-controversy-downplays-the-most-damning-details/>.

[72] Andrew C. McCarthy, "The *L.A. Times* Suppresses Obama's Khalidi Bash Tape," *National Review Online*, Oct. 27, 2008, <http://article.nationalreview.com/?q=ZDFkMGE2MmM1M2Q5MmY0ZmExMzUxMWRhZGJmMTAyOGY=>.

[73] Associated Press, "Party seats Florida, Michigan delegations," *MSNBC.com*, Jun. 1, 2008, <http://www.msnbc.msn.com/id/24905193/>.

[74] Harold Ickes, "Late Edition with Wolf Blitzer," CNN television broadcast, Jun. 1, 2008.

[75] Barack Obama, Interview with Eye on Books, 1995, <http://eyeonbooks.com/ibp_obama.php>.

[76] Barack Obama, Speech in St. Paul, Minnesota, Jun. 3, 2008, <http://www.nytimes.com/2008/06/03/us/politics/03text-obama.html?pagewanted=all>

[77] Bill Carter, Richard Pérez-Peña and Jeff Zeleny, "Want Obama in a Punch Line? First, Find a Joke," *New York Times*, Jul. 15, 2008,

<http://query.nytimes.com/gst/fullpage.html?res=9806EFD91F3AF936A25754 C0A96E9C8B63>.

Chapter 5 – The Fall

1 Paul Alexander, *Man of the People: The Life of John McCain*, Hoboken: John Wiley & Sons, 2003, 84-86.

2 Stanley Kurtz, "Obama and Ayers Pushed Radicalism on Schools," *Wall Street Journal*, Sep. 23, 2008, <http://online.wsj.com/article/SB122212856075765367.html>.

3 Mark Smylie, Stacy Wenzel, Elaine Allensworth, Carol Fendt, Sara Ray Stoelinga (credited as Sara Hallman), Stuart Luppescu, and Jenny Nagaoka, "The Chicago Annenberg Challenge: Successes, Failures, and Lessons for the Future," Aug. 2003, <http://ccsr.uchicago.edu/content/publications.php?pub_id=60>.

4 Yuval Levin, "A Theme for McCain's Pudding," *Weekly Standard*, May 26, 2008, <http://www.weeklystandard.com/Content/Public/Articles/000/000/015/118u vhoa.asp>.

5 John McCain, Speech in New Orleans, Louisiana, Jun. 3, 2008, <http://www.cnn.com/2008/POLITICS/06/03/mccain.speech.transcript/>

6 Geir Moulson, "Merkel uneasy over Obama Brandenburg Gate address," *USA Today*, Jul. 9, 2008, <http://www.usatoday.com/news/politics/2008-07-09-1595782577_x.htm>.

7 Angela Merkel, quoted in Moulson, ibid.

8 Carla Marinucci, "Berlin crowd cheers Obama," *San Francisco Chronicle*, Jul. 25, 2008, <http://www.sfgate.com/cgi-bin/article.cgi?f=/c/a/2008/07/24/MN7311UUL2.DTL>.

9 Barack Obama, Speech at Victory Column in Berlin, Germany, Jul. 24, 2008, <http://edition.cnn.com/2008/POLITICS/07/24/obama.words/>.

10 Elizabeth Holmes, "McCain Ad: Celebrity (Obama) vs. Hero (McCain)," | *Wall Street Journal*, Jul. 30, 2008, <http://blogs.wsj.com/washwire/2008/07/30/mccain-ad-celebrity-obama-vs-hero-mccain/>.

11 Bob Herbert, "Morning Joe," MSNBC television broadcast, Aug. 4, 2008, <http://newsbusters.org/blogs/mark-finkelstein/2008/08/04/obamania-has-herbert-hallucinating>.

12 Barack Obama, quoted in Jonathan Martin, "McCain campaign chief: Obama 'played the race card'," *Politico.com*, Jul. 31, 2008, <http://www.politico.com/blogs/jonathanmartin/0708/McCain_campaign_chief_Obama_playing_race _card.html>.

13 Rasmussen Reports, "Only 22% Say McCain Ad Racist, But Over Half (53%) See Obama Dollar-bill Comment That Way," Aug. 3, 2008, <http://www.rasmussenreports.com/public_content/politics/elec- tion_20082/2008_presidential_election/only_22_say_mccain_ad_racist_but_over _half_53_see_obama_dollar_bill_comment_that_way>

14 Patrick Donahue and Julianna Goldman, "Obama Cancels Trip to Visit Wounded U.S. Soldiers Update4)," *Bloomberg.com*, Jul. 25, 2008,

<http://www.bloomberg.com/apps/news?pid=20601100&sid
=a1S5Gl1jyzbw&refer=germany>.

[15] John McCain, "Statement by John McCain on Russia's Aggression in Georgia," Aug. 8, 2008, <http://www.votesmart.org/speech_detail.php?sc_id=399834
&keyword=&phrase=&contain=>.

[16] Barack Obama, "Statement from Barack Obama on the Grave Situation in Georgia," Aug. 8, 2008, <http://www.barackobama.com/2008/08/08/statement
_from_barack_obama_on.php>.

[17] Jake Tapper, "President McCain Sends Secretary of State Lieberman and Defense Secretary Graham to Tbilisi," *Political Punch*, Aug. 15, 2008, <http://blogs.abcnews.com/politicalpunch/2008/08/president-mccai.html>.

[18] Peter Hamby, "Obama moves closer to McCain on Russia stance," *CNN.com*, Aug. 11, 2008, <http://politicalticker.blogs.cnn.com/2008/08/11/obama-moves-closer-to-mccain-on-russia-stance/>.

[19] Matthew Lee Anderson, "The New Evangelical Scandal," *The City*, Jan. 15, 2009, <http://www.civitate.org/2009/01/the-new-evangelical-scandal/>.

[20] Ibid.

[21] Barack Obama, quoted in Ben Smith, " 'Stop these abortions'," *Politico.com*, Mar. 29, 2008, <http://www.politico.com/blogs/bensmith/0308/Stop_these_abortions_.html>.

[22] Ben Smith, "Obama backed same-sex marriage in 1996," *Politico.com*, Jan. 13, 2008, <http://www.politico.com/blogs/bensmith/0109/Obama_backed
_samesex_marriage_in_1996.html>.

[23] Michael Saul, "Obama: I'll end don't-ask, don't-tell," *New York Daily News*, Apr. 11, 2008, <http://www.nydailynews.com/news/politics/2008/04/11/2008-04-11_obama_ill_end_dontask_donttell-1.html>.

[24] Barack Obama, Remarks at Saddleback Forum, Aug. 17, 2008, <http://transcripts.cnn.com/TRANSCRIPTS/0808/17/se.01.html>.

[25] John McCain, Remarks at Saddleback Forum, ibid.

[26] Maeve Reston, Seema Mehta, "Barack Obama, John McCain discuss faith, issues at Saddleback Church forum," *Los Angeles Times*, Aug. 17, 2008, <http://www.latimes.com/news/la-na-saddleback17-2008aug17,0,1227797.story?track=ntothtml>

[27] Katharine Q. Seelye, "Despite Assurances, McCain Wasn't in a 'Cone of Silence'," *New York Times*, Aug. 17, 2008, <http://www.nytimes.com/2008/08/18/us/politics/18mccain.html>.

[28] Stuart Silverstein and Johanna Neuman, "Joe Biden is Obama's running mate," *Los Angeles Times*, Aug. 23, 2008, <http://www.latimes.com/news/
printedition/front/la-na-biden23-2008aug23,0,7564344.story>.

[29] Glenn Kessler, "Biden Played Less Than Key Role in Bosnia Legislation," *Washington Post*, Oct. 7, 2008, <http://www.washingtonpost.com/wp-dyn/content/article/2008/10/06/AR2008100602681_pf.html>.

[30] Scott MacLeod, "Biden on the Middle East: Experienced, Yes. But Smart?", *Time.com*, Aug. 27, 2008, <http://mideast.blogs.time.com/2008/08/27/
biden_on_the_middle_east_exper/>.

[31] Ryan Lizza, "Biden's Brief," *New Yorker*, Oct. 20, 2008, <http://www.newyorker.com/reporting/2008/10/20/081020fa_fact_lizza>.

32 Joe Biden, quoted in Xuan Thai and Ted Barrett, "Biden's description of Obama draws scrutiny," *CNN.com* Feb. 9, 2007, <http://www.cnn.com/2007/POLITICS/01/31/biden.obama/>.

33 June Kronholz, "Want Tickets to Obama's Acceptance Speech? Forget Ticketmaster," *Wall Street Journal*, Jul. 30, 2008, <http://blogs.wsj.com/washwire/2008/07/30/want-tickets-to-obamas-acceptance-speech-forget-ticketmaster/>.

34 Kaylene Johnson, *Sarah: How a Hockey Mom Turned the Political Establishment Upside Down*, Kenmore, Washington: Epicenter Press, 2008, 80.

35 Kyle Hopkins, "Same-sex benefits ban gets Palin veto," *Anchorage Daily News*, Dec. 29, 2006, <http://dwb.adn.com/news/government/legislature/story/8525563p-8419318c.html>.

36 David Plouffe, quoted in Sam Stein, "Plouffe Off-Record Campaign Comments Come Out," *HuffingtonPost.com*, Feb. 13, 2009, <http://www.huffingtonpost.com/2009/02/13/plouffe-palin-was-our-bes_n_166683.html>.

37 Bill Burton, quoted in John Harwood, "McCain Shakes Up Race By Picking Sarah Palin for VP," *CNBC.com*, Aug. 29, 2008, <http://www.cnbc.com/id/26454655>.

38 Sarah Palin, Speech at the Republican National Convention, St. Paul, Minnesota, Sep. 3, 2008, <http://elections.nytimes.com/2008/president/conventions/videos/transcripts/20080903_PALIN_SPEECH.html>.

39 *Boston Herald*, Sep. 4, 2008, 1.

40 Jill Serjeant, "John McCain speech draws record TV ratings," *Reuters.com*, Sep. 5, 2008, <http://www.reuters.com/article/wtMostRead/idUSN0439266820080905>.

41 Abby Callard and David Plotz, "Your Dreams (and Nightmares) About Sarah Palin," *Slate.com*, Sep. 12, 2008, <http://www.slate.com/id/2200015/>.

42 Thomas Friedman, "From the Gut," *New York Times*, Sep. 9, 2008, <http://www.nytimes.com/2008/09/10/opinion/10friedman.html?em>.

43 Associated Press, "McCain, Obama agree: Don't use Palin's pregnant daughter as political fodder," *Chicago Sun-Times*, Sep. 1, 2008, <http://www.suntimes.com/news/elections/rnc/1138831,CST-NWS-react01web.article>.

44 Martina Stewart, "New ad targets Palin, highlights McCain's age and health," *CNN.com*, Oct. 2, 2008, <http://politicalticker.blogs.cnn.com/2008/10/01/new-ad-targets-palin-highlights-mccain-age-and-health/>.

45 MoveOn.org, "This ad works: Help us get the truth out about John McCain," Advertisement, <https://pol.moveon.org/donate/alexad.html>.

46 Sarah Lai Stirland, "Biden: Obama Ad Mocking McCain's Computer Illiteracy 'Terrible'," *Wired Blog Network*, Sep. 22, 2008, <http://blog.wired.com/27bstroke6/2008/09/biden-obama-ad.html>.

47 Mike Dorning, "Obama: Lipstick, pigs and hockey moms," *The Swamp*, Sep. 9, 2008, <http://www.swamppolitics.com/news/politics/blog/2008/09/barack_obama_sarah_palin_lipst.html>.

48 Ben Smith, "Obama camp: 'Disgusting lies', 'Not worthy'," *Politico.com*, Sep. 13, 2008, <http://www.politico.com/blogs/bensmith/0908/Obama_camp_Disgusting_lies_not_worthy.html?showall>.

[49] Jake Tapper, "Cindy McCain: Obama Has 'Waged the Dirtiest Campaign in American History'," *Political Punch*, Oct. 7, 2008, <http://blogs.abcnews.com/politicalpunch/2008/10/cindy-mccain-ob.html>.

[50] Joe Klein, "John McCain and the Lying Game," *Time*, Sep. 17, 2008, <http://www.time.com/time/politics/article/0,8599,1842030,00.html>.

[51] Byron York, "On Sex-Ed Ad, McCain Is Right," *National Review Online*, Sep. 16, 2008, <http://article.nationalreview.com/print/?q=NzI3ZDUzOTE0ZThlMTU3MTY0MDI4ZTY0MTZhY2I2MGY=>.

[52] David Mark and Avi Zenilman, "Historians say McCain camp not sleaziest," *Politico.com*, Sep. 16, 2008, <http://www.politico.com/news/stories/0908/13490.html>.

[53] Rasmussen Reports, "Just 23% Say Presidential Campaign More Negative Than Most," Press Release, Sep. 17, 2008, <http://www.rasmussenreports.com/public_content/politics/election_20082/2008_presidential_election/just_23_say_presidential_campaign_more_negative_than_most>.

[54] Rasmussen Reports, "69% Say Reporters Try To Help The Candidate They Want To Win," Press release, Sep. 10, 2008, <http://www.rasmussenreports.com/public_content/politics/election_20082/2008_presidential_election/69_say_reporters_try_to_help_the_candidate_they_want_to_win>.

[55] Steve Cohen, quoted in Ben Smith, " 'Jesus was a community organizer'," *Politico.com*, Sep. 10, 2008, <http://www.politico.com/blogs/bensmith/0908/Cohen_Jesus_was_a_community_organizer.html?showall>.

[56] Mary Ann Akers, "Jewish Rep. Cohen Battles Antisemitism and Racism in Re-Election," *Washington Post*, Feb. 13, 2007, <http://voices.washingtonpost.com/sleuth/2008/02/jewish_rep_cohen_battles_antis.html>.

[57] Andrew M. Seder, "Secret Service says 'Kill him' allegation unfounded," *Times Leader*, Mar. 3, 2009, <http://www.timesleader.com/news/breakingnews/Secret_Service_says_Kill_him_allegation_unfounded_.html>.

[58] William Daroff et al, "An Open Letter to the Jewish Community," quoted in Ben Smith, "Jewish leaders fight back on Obama smears," *Politico.com*, Jan. 15, 2008, <http://www.politico.com/blogs/bensmith/0108/Beating_back_the_smears.html>.

[59] Rusty Shackleford, "Hope, Change, & Lies: Orchestrated "Grassroots" Smear Campaigns & the People that Run Them [Updated]," *The Jawa Report*, Sep. 22, 2008, <http://mypetjawa.mu.nu/archives/194057.php>.

[60] Charles Gibson, Interview with Sarah Palin, Full Transcript, Sep. 11, 2008, <http://www.marklevinshow.com/gibson-interview/>.

[61] Charles Krauthammer, "Charlie Gibson's Gaffe," *Washington Post*, Sep. 13, 2008, <http://www.washingtonpost.com/wp-dyn/content/article/2008/09/12/AR2008091202457.html>.

[62] Charles Gibson, Interview with Barack Obama, ABC television broadcast, Jun. 4, 2008, <http://abcnews.go.com/WN/story?id=5000184&page=1>.

[63] Katie Couric, Interview with Sarah Palin, CBS television broadcast, Sep. 24, 2008, <http://www.cqpolitics.com/wmspage.cfm?docID=news-000002962978>.

64 Maureen Ryan, "Did Tina Fey out-Palin Palin on 'Saturday Night Live'?", *Chicago Tribune*, Sep. 14, 2008, <http://featuresblogs.chicagotribune.com/ entertainment_tv/2008/09/saturday-night.html>.

65 Jack Kelly, "Not so smart after all," *Pittsburgh Post-Gazette*, Nov. 23, 2008, <http://www.post-gazette.com/pg/08328/929775-373.stm>.

66 Bill Maher, "The View," ABC television broadcast, Sep. 30, 2008,

67 Jeanne Cummings, "RNC shells out $150k for Palin fashion," *Politico.com*, Oct. 22, 2008, <http://www.politico.com/news/stories/1008/14805.html>.

68 Heidi N. Moore, "Bank of America-Merrill Lynch: A $50 Billion Deal From Hell," *Wall Street Journal*, Jan. 22, 2009, <http://blogs.wsj.com/deals/2009/01/ 22/bank-of-america-merrill-lynch-a-50-billion-deal-from-hell/>.

69 Justin Fox, "The Economy Really Is Fundamentally Strong," *Time*, Oct. 16, 2008, <http://www.time.com/time/business/article/0,8599,1850909,00.html>.

70 Stephen Moore, " 'Reform. Reform. Reform.'," *Wall Street Journal*, Nov. 26, 2006, <http://www.opinionjournal.com/editorial/feature.html?id=110007600>.

71 John McCain, quoted in Eugene Robinson, "McCain Flunks Economics," *RealClearPolitics.com*, Sep. 19, 2008, <http://www.realclearpolitics.com/articles/ 2008/09/mccain_show_his_economic_inexp.html>.

72 John McCain, quoted in Michael Cooper, "McCain on U.S. economy: from 'strong' to 'total crisis' in 36 hours," *International Herald-Tribune*, Sep. 17, 2008, <http://www.iht.com/articles/2008/09/17/america/mccain.php>.

73 Barack Obama, quoted in National Public Radio, "Candidates' Statements on the AIG Bailout," *Vox Politics*, Feb. 2, 2009, <http://www.npr.org/blogs/politics /2008/09/candidates_statements_on_aig_b.html>.

74 William Kristol, "A Fine Mess," *New York Times*, Sep. 21, 2008, <http://www.nytimes.com/2008/09/22/opinion/22kristol.html?hp>.

75 Liz Halloran, "McCain Suspends Campaign, Shocks Republicans," *U.S. News & World Report*, Sep. 24, 2008, <http://www.usnews.com/articles/news/campaign- 2008/2008/09/24/mccain-suspends-campaign-shocks-republicans.html>.

76 Elisabeth Bumiller and Michael Cooper, "Obama Rebuffs McCain on Debate Delay," *New York Times*, Sep. 24, 2008, <http://www.nytimes.com/2008/09/25/us/politics/25mccain.html>.

77 SurveyUSA, "Results of SurveyUSA News Poll #14454," Sep. 24, 2008, <http://www.surveyusa.com/client/PollReportUC.aspx?g=54d651a7-a62b -4420-bb32-9dd6b2df8c02>.

78 Klaus Marre, "Republicans fault Pelosi speech for bailout's failure," *The Hill*, Sep. 29, 2008, <http://thehill.com/leading-the-news/republicans-fault-pelosi-for- bailouts-failure-2008-09-29.html>.

79 George W. Bush, Remarks at the Manhattan Institute, New York, New York, Nov. 13, 2008, <http://www.clipsandcomment.com/2008/11/15/full-text- president-george-w-bush-speech-on-the-financial-markets-and-world-economy- manhattan-institute-november-13/>.

80 Martin Feldstein, "The Problem Is Still Falling House Prices," *Wall Street Journal*, Oct. 4, 2008, <http://online.wsj.com/article/SB122307486906203821.html?mod =googlenews_wsj>.

[81] CNN, "U.S. markets bounce as bailout revived," *CNN.com*, Sep. 30, 2008, <http://www.cnn.com/2008/BUSINESS/09/30/us.bailout.deal.markets/index.html>.

[82] Mark Glassman, "Stocks Fall as Bailout Passes," *SmartMoney.com*, Oct. 4, 2008, <http://www.smartmoney.com/breaking-news/?story=20081003090641>.

[83] Mary Anastasia O'Grady, "Obama Is Wrong About Columbia," *Wall Street Journal*, Oct. 20, 2008, <http://online.wsj.com/article/SB122445952046648609.html>.

[84] David Bauder, "Vice Presidential Debate Ratings: Early Numbers 42% Higher Than First Presidential Debate," *HuffingtonPost.com*, Oct. 3, 2008, <http://www.huffingtonpost.com/2008/10/03/vice-presidential-debate_n_131671.html>.

[85] Associated Press, "PBS' Ifill dismisses questions of partisanship," *MSNBC.com*, Oct. 1, 2008, <http://www.msnbc.msn.com/id/26978194/?GT1=43001>.

[86] Sarah Palin, Vice-Presidential Debate, Oct. 2, 2008, <http://www.cnn.com/2008/POLITICS/10/02/debate.transcript/>.

[87] Alexander Marquardt, "Obama: Republicans must think you're stupid," *CNN.com*, Sep. 6, 2008, <http://politicalticker.blogs.cnn.com/2008/09/06/obama-republicans-must-think-you%E2%80%99re-stupid/>.

[88] Barack Obama, Remarks in Oregon, Ohio, Oct. 12, 2008, <http://blogs.abcnews.com/politicalpunch/2008/10/spread-the-weal.html>.

[89] Barack Obama, Remarks in Londonderry, New Hampshire, Oct. 16, 2008.

[90] Bob Dart and Julia Malone, "Republicans Invite Tourists to Fill House Chamber Over Energy Bill," *Cox News Service*, Aug. 4, 2008, <http://www.coxwashington.com/hp/content/reporters/stories/2008/07/8/5/2008/08/04/GOP_PROTEST05_COX.html>.

[91] Brian Stelter, "Solid Ratings for Obama-mercial," *The Caucus*, Oct. 30, 2008, <http://thecaucus.blogs.nytimes.com/2008/10/30/solid-ratings-for-obama-mercial/?apage=2>.

[92] John McCain, Speech at the Biltmore Hotel, Phoenix, Arizona, Nov. 4, 2008.

[93] Barack Obama, Speech at Grant Park, Chicago, Illinois, Nov. 4, 2008, <http://news.bbc.co.uk/2/hi/americas/us_elections_2008/7710038.stm>.

Chapter 6 – Obama's America

[1] George W. Bush, quoted in CNN.com, "You are either with us or against us," *CNN.com*, Nov. 6, 2001, <http://archives.cnn.com/2001/US/11/06/gen.attack.on.terror/>.

[2] George W. Bush, quoted in Liz Marlantes, "More John Wayne rhetoric infuses politics," *Christian Science Monitor*, Jul. 18, 2003, <http://www.csmonitor.com/2003/0718/p02s02-usfp.html>.

[3] George W. Bush, Speech at the National Endowment for Democracy, Washington, D.C., Nov. 6, 2003, <http://www.ned.org/events/anniversary/20thAniv-Bush.html>.

4 George W. Bush, Speech to the Knesset, May 15, 2008, <http://newsbusters.org/blogs/noel-sheppard/2008/05/15/text-video-president-bushs-speech-israeli-knesset>.

5 John S. McCain, "Face The Nation," CBS television broadcast, Feb. 8, 2009, <http://www.youtube.com/watch?v=DM893CFgCnw>.

6 Thomas Friedman, "We Found the W.M.D.", *New York Times*, Nov. 22, 2008, <http://www.nytimes.com/2008/11/23/opinion/23friedman.html>.

7 "The Obameter: Tracking Obama's Campaign Promises," *PolitiFact.com/St. Petersburg Times*, <http://www.politifact.com/truth-o-meter/promises/>.

8 William A. Jacobson, "It's Time to Speak Out Against The 'Mormon Boycott'," *American Thinker*, Dec. 4, 2008, <http://www.americanthinker.com/2008/12/its_time_to_speak_out_against.html>.

9 Associated Press, "Black and Latino voters backed California marriage ban," *New York Daily News*, Nov. 5, 2008, <http://www.nydailynews.com/latino/2008/11/05/2008-11-05_black_and_latino_voters_backed_californi.html>.

10 Farai Chideya, "Black, Gay Communities Collide Over Gay Marriage," NPR radio broadcast, Nov. 13, 2008, <http://www.npr.org/templates/story/story.php?storyId=96963827>.

11 Michael Rothfeld, "Schwarzenegger: Proposition 8 fight isn't over," *Boston Globe*, Nov. 10, 2008, <http://www.boston.com/news/nation/articles/2008/11/10/schwarzenegger_proposition_8_fight_isnt_over/>.

12 Domenico Montanaro, "Chambliss: Palin's 'A Rock Star'," *FirstRead.com*, Dec. 2, 2008, <http://firstread.msnbc.msn.com/archive/2008/12/02/1695590.aspx>.

13 Icarus, "Does Barack Obama Want To Keep Saxby Chambliss In The Senate," *RedState.com*, Nov. 19, 2008, <http://www.redstate.com/icarus/2008/11/19/does-barack-obama-want-to-keep-saxby-chamblis/>.

14 Andy Barr, "Obama little help to Dems post-election," *Politico.com*, Dec. 7, 2008, <http://www.politico.com/news/stories/1208/16291.html>.

15 Philip Elliott, "Obama Campaign Mulls What To Do With $30M Surplus," *HuffingtonPost.com*, Dec. 5, 2008, <http://www.huffingtonpost.com/2008/12/05/obama-campaign-mulls-what_n_148904.html?page=6>.

16 Peggy Joseph, Remarks at Obama rally, Sunrise, Florida, Nov. 1, 2008, <http://www.youtube.com/watch?v=381gFG4Crr8>.

17 Zogby International, "Zogby America National Poll of Barack Obama Voters," Nov. 2008, <http://www.zogby.com/news/wf-dfs.pdf>.

18 Peter Wehner and Paul Ryan, "Beware of the Big-Government Tipping Point," *Wall Street Journal*, Jan. 16, 2009, <http://online.wsj.com/article/SB123207075026188601.html>.

19 Jennifer Agiesta and Jon Cohen, "As Election Day Nears, Poll Shows Obama Leads McCain," *Washington Post*, Oct. 25, 2008, <http://www.washingtonpost.com/wp-dyn/content/article/2008/10/25/AR2008102501427.html>.

20 Jackie Calmes, "Peter R. Orszag," *New York Times*, Nov. 18, 2008, <http://www.nytimes.com/2008/11/19/us/politics/18web-orszag.html?_r=1>,

21 Max Boot, "Obama's Picks," *Contentions*, Nov. 25, 2008, <http://www.commentarymagazine.com/blogs/index.php/boot/44551>.

[22] Jonathan Martin, "James Jones for Obama's Veep?", *Politico.com*, Jun. 10, 2008, <http://www.politico.com/blogs/jonathanmartin/0608/James_Jones_for _Obamas_Veep.html>.

[23] Evan Perez, "Rendition Case Under Bush Gets Obama Backing," *Wall Street Journal*, Feb. 10, 2009, <http://online.wsj.com/article/SB123422915277565975 .html?mod=googlenews_wsj>.

[24] Aluf Benn, "Obama's atomic umbrella: U.S. nuclear strike if Iran nukes Israel," *Ha'aretz*, Nov. 12, 2008,
<http://www.haaretz.com/hasen/spages/1045687.html>.

[25] James Oliphant, "Hilda Solis deflects Republican questions over union issues," *Los Angeles Times*, Jan. 10, 2009, <http://www.latimes.com/news/nationworld/ nation/la-na-solis10-2009jan10,0,4404834.story>.

[26] Daniel Scarpinato, "Napolitano endorses Obama," *Arizona Daily Star*, Jan. 12, 2008, <http://www.azstarnet.com/sn/related/220273>.

[27] Cary Budoff Brown, "School buds: 20 Harvard classmates advising Obama," *Politio.com*, Dec. 5, 2008,
<http://www.politico.com/news/stories/1208/16224.html>.

[28] Matthew Pinsker, "Lincoln and the myth of 'Team of Rivals'," *Los Angeles Times*, Nov. 18, 2008, <http://www.latimes.com/news/opinion/commentary/ la-oe-pinsker18-2008nov18,0,1360359.story>.

[29] Cass Sunstein, "The Empiricist Strikes Back," *The New Republic*, Sep. 10, 2008, <http://www.tnr.com/politics/story.html?id=864f5c8e-e036-473f-8d36-cd09e5ad54f9>.

[30] Stephen Dinan, "Obama's climate czar has socialist ties," *Washington Times*, Jan. 12, 2009, <http://www.washingtontimes.com/news/2009/jan/12/obama-climate-czar-has-socialist-ties/>.

[31] Lynn Sweet, "Fitzgerald press conference on Blagojevich. Transcript," *Chicago Sun-Times*, Dec. 9, 2008, <http://blogs.suntimes.com/sweet/2008/12/ fitzgerald_press_conference_on.html>.

[32] Kenneth P. Vogel and Carrie Budoff Browm, "Obama's five rules of scandal response," *Politico.com*, Dec. 24, 2008,
<http://www.politico.com/news/stories/1208/16836.html>.

[33] Associated Press, "Prosecutors Seek to Delay Sentencing of Tony Rezko," *FoxNews.com*, Oct. 7, 2008,
<http://www.foxnews.com/story/0,2933,433624,00.html>.

[34] John Fund, "Obama Was Mute on Illinois Corruption," *Wall Street Journal*, Dec. 15, 2008, <http://online.wsj.com/article/SB122895356506696347.html>.

[35] John Dickerson, "What Didn't He Know, and When Didn't He Know It?", *Slate.com*, Dec. 9, 2008, <http://www.slate.com/id/2206428/>.

[36] Peter Baker, "Obama Follows a Tradition of Testifying for Prosecutors," *New York Times*, Dec. 25, 2008,
<http://www.nytimes.com/2008/12/26/us/politics/26testify.html>.

[37] John Dickerson, "No Change for Sale," *Slate.com*, Dec. 9, 2008,
<http://www.slate.com/id/2206349/>.

[38] Justin Rood, "Funds Tie Obama to Richardson Probe Figure," *ABCNews.com*, Jan. 6, 2009,
<http://abcnews.go.com/Blotter/Politics/story?id=6586275&page=1>.

[39] Associated Press, "Obama's lawyer clears him in Blagojevich scandal," *Rocky Mountain News*, Dec. 23, 2008, <http://www.rockymountainnews.com/news/2008/dec/23/biden-report-clear-obama-aides-governor-probe/>.

[40] "World waits as real Obama prepares to reveal himself," *Irish Times*, Dec. 29, 2008, <http://www.irishtimes.com/newspaper/world/2008/1229/1229728601353.html>.

[41] Kyle Drennen, "ABC's GMA Looks at Obama's Hawaiian Christmas Vacation," *Newsbusters.org*, Dec. 22, 2008, <http://newsbusters.org/blogs/kyle-drennen/2008/12/22/abc-s-gma-looks-obama-s-hawaiian-christmas-vacation>.

[42] Dan Eggen, "Bush Says He's Not a Golfer in Wartime," *Washington Post*, May 14, 2008, <http://www.washingtonpost.com/wp-dyn/content/article/2008/05/13/AR2008051302783.html>.

[43] Eli Saslow, "As Duties Weigh Obama Down, His Faith in Fitness Only Increases," *Washington Post*, Dec. 25, 2008, <http://www.washingtonpost.com/wp-dyn/content/article/2008/12/24/AR2008122402590.html>.

[44] Reuters, "Obama says he won't be smoking in White House," Dec. 7, 2008, <http://www.reuters.com/article/politicsNews/idUSTRE4B61GF20081207>.

[45] Barack Obama, Remarks at press conference, Feb. 9, 2009, <http://www.cbsnews.com/stories/2009/02/10/politics/100days/main4789627.shtml>.

[46] Barack Obama, Remarks in Elkhart, Indiana, Feb. 9, 2009, <http://www.cnn.com/2009/POLITICS/02/09/obama.indiana.trip/index.html>.

[47] Reuters, "Factbox: How does Obama's stimulus plan rank against the New Deal?", *National Post*, Feb. 9, 2009, <http://network.nationalpost.com/np/blogs/posted/archive/2009/02/09/factbox-how-does-obama-s-stimulus-plan-rank-against-the-new-deal.aspx>.

[48] Paul Krugman, "The Obama Gap," *New York Times*, Jan. 8, 2009, <http://www.nytimes.com/2009/01/09/opinion/09krugman.html?_r=2>.

[49] Associated Press, "Bush pushes computerized medical records," *MSNBC.com*, Jan. 27, 2005, <http://www.msnbc.msn.com/id/6876192/>.

[50] Brian Faler, "Much of Stimulus Won't Be Spent Before 2011, CBO Says (Update1)," *Bloomberg.com*, Jan. 20, <http://www.bloomberg.com/apps/news?pid=20601087&sid=aJAoR5GECKWo>.

[51] Josiah Ryan, "Obama Suggested FDR's 'New Deal' Was Too Small, House Republicans Say," *CSNNews.com*, Jan. 29, 2009, <http://www.cnsnews.com/public/content/article.aspx?RsrcID=42697>.

[52] Matthew Benjamin, "Obama to Boost Stimulus With Funds for Roads, Energy," *Bloomberg.com*, Nov. 25, 2009, <http://www.bloomberg.com/apps/news?pid=20601110&refer=&sid=a9u3x70pCs_4>.

[53] "A 40-Year Wish List," *Wall Street Journal*, Jan. 28, 2009, <http://online.wsj.com/article/SB123310466514522309.html>.

[54] Eric Bolling, "Is Obama Really Bad at Math?", *The Fox Forum*, Jan. 12, 2009, <http://foxforum.blogs.foxnews.com/2009/01/12/bolling_obama/>.

[55] David Brooks, "Cleaner and Faster," *New York Times*, Jan. 29, 2009, <http://www.nytimes.com/2009/01/30/opinion/30brooks.html>.

[56] Christina D. Romer and David H. Romer, "The Macroeconomic Effects of Tax Changes: Estimates Based on a New Measure of Fiscal Shocks," University of California, Berkeley, Mar. 2007, <http://www.econ.berkeley.edu/%7Ecromer/RomerDraft307.pdf>.

[57] Christina Romer and Jared Bernstein, "The Job Impact of the American Recovery and Reinvestment Plan," Jan. 10, 2009, <http://otrans.3cdn.net/45593e8ecbd339d074_l3m6bt1te.pdf>.

[58] Doug Bandow, "The Geithner Confirmation Exception," *American Spectator*, Jan. 18, 2009, <http://spectator.org/blog/2009/01/18/the-geithner-confirmation-exce>.

[59] Sally C. Pipes, "Obama Will Ration Your Health Care," *Wall Street Journal*, Dec. 30, 2008, <http://online.wsj.com/article/SB123060332638041525.html>.

[60] Richard Harris, "The Mystery of Global Warming's Missing Heat," *National Public Radio*, Mar. 19, 2008, <http://www.npr.org/templates/story/story.php?storyId=88520025>.

[61] Rich Lowry, "Last Gasp for Limited Government?", *National Review*, Feb. 10, 2009, <http://article.nationalreview.com/?q=ZDk5NzExYWQxYjZhMjJlMzY0MzlmYWM5NzY3OGJmMGU=>.

[62] Barack Obama, quoted in Aaron Blake, "Clinton camp goes after Obama's Reagan comments," *TheHill.com*, Jan. 18, 2008, <http://thehill.com/campaign-2008/clinton-camp-goes-after-obamas-reagan-comments-2008-01-18.html>.

[63] Paul Kengor, "Dreams from Frank Marshall Davis," Oct. 30, 2008, <http://www.americanthinker.com/2008/10/dreams_from_frank_marshall_dav.html>.

[64] Jonathan Martin and Carol E. Lee, "Obama to GOP: 'I won'," *Politico.com*, Jan. 23, 2009, <http://www.politico.com/news/stories/0109/17862.html>.

[65] Barack Obama, Speech in Milwaukee, Wisconsin, Feb. 16, 2008, <http://www.youtube.com/watch?v=7ffwY74XbS4>.

[66] Barack H. Obama, "We Can't Afford to Wait," Speech in Elkhart, Indiana, Feb. 9, 2009, <http://www.realclearpolitics.com/articles/2009/02/we_cant_afford_to_wait.html>.

[67] Rich Lowry, "At Least He's Calm," *National Review Online*, Mar. 10, 2009, <http://article.nationalreview.com/?q=NGM3MTAyNjZjNzVjNTJlMTMzOTdmYTk5ODBlY2Q5NzE=>.

[68] Rasmussen Reports, "Daily Presidential Tracking Poll," Mar. 16, 2009, <http://www.rasmussenreports.com/public_content/politics/obama_administration/daily_presidential_tracking_poll>.

[69] Barack Obama, quoted in Carrie Dann, "Obama on Judges, Supreme Court," *FirstRead*, Jul. 17, 2007, <http://firstread.msnbc.msn.com/archive/2007/07/17/274143.aspx>.

[70] Barack Obama, Remarks in Pendleton, Oregon, May 18, 2008, <http://www.youtube.com/watch?v=ew5qP2oPdtQ>.

[71] Caroline Glick, "Our World: Your abortions or your lives!", *Jerusalem Post*, Sep. 23, 2008, <http://www.jpost.com/servlet/Satellite?apage=2&cid=1222017359617&pagename=JPost%2FJPArticle%2FShowFull>.

[72] Tom Gross, "First exit poll of actual American votes from Israel shows big McCain win," *National Review Online*, Oct. 30, 2008,

<http://media.nationalreview.com/post/
?q=ZjAwMzA2ZGY5ZTVmNTAwNTBkMTc3Y2YxZDRmMTk0nDc=>.
[73] Chris Matthews, "Morning Joe," MSNB television broadcast, Nov. 6, 2008.
<http://newsbusters.org/blogs/mark-finkelstein/2008/11/06/odd-job-
matthews-says-his-role-make-obama-presidency-success>.
[74] Roger Ailes, quoted in Rush & Molloy, "Side Dish: The Boss keeps 'em laughing," *New York Daily News*, Nov. 7, 2008, <http://www.nydailynews.com/
other/2008/11/07/2008-11-07_side_dish_the_boss_keeps_em_laughing.html>.
[75] Kenneth P. Vogel, "Blago records may stay under wraps," *Politico.com*, Dec. 22,
2008, <http://www.politico.com/news/stories/1208/16779.html>.
[76] Carol Marin, "Obama, Blago flip sides of Bizarro plotline," *Chicago Sun-Times*,
Jan. 4, 2009, <http://www.suntimes.com/news/marin/1360142,CST-EDT-
carol04.article>.
[77] "0-4 for Fox News," *FishbowlDC*, Nov. 26, 2008,
<http://www.mediabistro.com/fishbowlDC/west_wing_reportage/04_for_fox_
news_101879.asp>.
[78] Jake Tapper, "Obama Expresses Sorrow with Loss of Richardson Beard," *Political Punch*, Dec. 3, 2008,
<http://blogs.abcnews.com/politicalpunch/2008/12/obama-expresses.html>.
[79] Michael Saul, "Obama's inauguration is most expensive ever at $160 million,"
New York Daily News, Jan. 14, 2009,
<http://www.nydailynews.com/news/politics/2009/01/13/2009-01-
13_obamas_inauguration_is_most_expensive_ev.html>.
[80] Marc Ambinder, "Obama For America Becomes Organizing For America,"
Atlantic, Jan. 17, 2009, <http://marcambinder.theatlantic.com/archives/
2009/01/obama_for_american_becomes_org.php>.
[81] Mary Katharing Ham, "Activists Left Hoping for Change at Obama's Stimulus
Parties," *Weekly Standard*, Feb. 9, 2009, <http://www.weeklystandard.com/
weblogs/TWSFP/2009/02/hoping_for_change_at_obamas_st.asp>.
[82] Tim Shipman, "Barack Obama picks a fight with Rush Limbaugh as bipartisan
spirit crumbles," *Telegraph.co.uk*, Jan. 26, 2009, <http://www.telegraph.co.uk/
news/worldnews/northamerica/usa/barackobama/4331839/Barack-Obama-
picks-a-fight-with-Rush-Limbaugh-as-bipartisan-spirit-crumbles.html>
[83] U.S. Department of Homeland Security, *Rightwing Extremism: Current Economic
and Political Climate Fueling Resurgence in Radicalization and Recruitment*, Apr. 7, 2009,
<http://www.fas.org/irp/eprint/rightwing.pdf>
[84] Associated Press, "Biden calls paying higher taxes a patriotic act," *MSNBC.com*,
Sep. 18, 2008, <http://www.msnbc.msn.com/id/26771716/>.
[85] Barack Obama, Remarks to U.S. Conference of Mayors, Miami, Florida, Jun. 21,
2008, <http://www.barackobama.com/2008/06/21/remarks_of_senator
_barack_obam_80.php>.
[86] Alexis de Tocqueville, *Democracy in America*, Trans. George Lawrence, Ed. J. P.
Mayer, New York: HarperPerennial, 1969. 510.

Index

2000 presidential election, 15, 25, 35, 41, 69, 77, 85

2004 presidential election, 38

2006 mid-term elections, 36, 214

2008 Democratic National Convention, 27, 97, 149, 164, 166

2008 Democratic primary, 85

2008 Republican National Convention, 97, 170, 206

ABC News, 132, 148

Abortion, 20, 39, 55, 70, 78, 161, 167, 171

Abramoff, Jack, 58

Abu Ghraib, 47–49

ACORN, 65, 116

Afghanistan, 26, 33, 41, 43, 163

Ailes, Roger Eugene, 228

Ajami, Fouad A., 27

Alito, Samuel Anthony Jr., 224

Al-Qaeda, 32, 41, 46, 69

American Insurance Group, 64, 179

American Israel Public Affairs Committee (AIPAC), 29, 226

American Recovery and Reinvestment Act, 218

Annapolis process, 53

Anti-war movement, 45, 118

Arafat, Yasser, 50

Ashcroft, John David, 36, 40, 55

Axelrod, David, 175, 216

Ayers, William Charles, 103, 104, 136, 148, 152–153, 186, 217

Bailout, 19, 61, 64–66, 179–183, 185, 189, 203, 220

Bear Stearns, 64

Berlin, Isaiah, 232

Bernanke, Ben Shalom, 64

Biden, Joseph Robinette, Jr, 1, 19, 52, 130, 142, 164–165, 168, 171–172, 177, 187, 208, 233

Birth certificate conspiracy theory, 89

Black Panthers, 194

BlackBerry, 172

Blagojevich, Milorad R. ("Rod"), 136, 215–217, 229

Blair, Anthony Charles Lynton ("Tony"), 34, 41

Booker, Corey, 8

Boot, Max, 212

Bosnia, 142, 165

"Bradley effect", 9

Brooks, David, 24

Brown, Michael DeWayne, 35, 56

Browner, Carol A., 214

Bryan, William Jennings, 122
Bulworth, 202
Burma (Myanmar), 43
Bush Derangement Syndrome, 38, 236
"Bush Doctrine", 175
Bush v. Gore, 37
Bush, George W., 8, 11, 15–16, 19–20, 23–26, 28–29, 31–64, 66–69, 72, 74, 76–78, 82, 84–85, 88, 93, 101, 103, 105, 107, 113, 117, 139, 148, 152–154, 160, 169, 175–176, 179–183, 185, 189–191, 193–194, 200–201, 203–204, 207, 210–213, 215, 218–219, 220, 223–224, 226, 228–230, 234, 236
  speeches, 43, 48, 51, 182, 200
Campaign finance reform, 14, 82, 84, 88, 202
Cao, Anh ("Joseph"), 206
Card Check ("Employee Free Choice Act"), 213
Carter, James Earl ("Jimmy"), 35, 61, 67, 145, 160
CBS News, 39, 193
Chads, 37
Chambliss, Clarence Saxby, 206
Chavez, Hugo, 230
Cheney, Richard Bruce ("Dick"), 36, 60

Chicago, 56, 79, 113–114, 116–117, 120, 131, 137, 144, 146, 152, 195, 215–217, 225, 241
Chicago Annenberg Challenge, 152
China, 7, 44, 159
Climate change, 78, 84, 95, 221
Clinton, Hillary Rodham, 1–3, 6, 8, 10–11, 15, 19, 21–23, 32, 36, 39–40, 54, 61–62, 67, 70, 73, 93, 99–100, 106–107, 115, 117, 120, 123, 128–131, 136, 138–149, 151–152, 162, 165, 168, 173, 203, 210–214, 222, 227–228, 241
Clinton, William Jefferson ("Bill"), 11, 23, 32, 36, 53, 59, 117, 120, 128, 129–131, 147, 152, 165, 203, 211, 214, 222
Colbert, Stephen Tyrone, 25
Columbia, 90, 186, 211
Community Reinvestment Act, 61
"compassionate conservatism", 36, 54, 66, 74, 201
Congressional Budget Office, 219
Couric, Katherine Anne ("Katie"), 175–176
Craig, Larry Edwin, 57
crowdsourcing, 24
Cuba, 19, 46, 223

Daley, Richard Michael, 56,
114, 215
Daschle, Thomas Andrew,
214, 221
Davis, Frank Marshall, 146,
147, 217, 222
Davis, Lanny J., 146
Dayton, Soren, 94
de Tocqueville, Alexis, 237
Dean, Howard Brush III,
12, 112–113, 125
Democratic Party, 11–12,
14–26, 31, 35, 37, 39, 55–
56, 58–59, 62–63, 65,
67–68, 72–74, 77–79, 82,
84, 86, 96, 98–99, 104,
113, 122–123, 126, 129,
138–141, 145–149, 151,
160–161, 166–168, 172,
174, 181–184, 187–188,
190–192, 195, 203, 205–
206, 210–211, 213–214,
216, 219, 221–222, 224,
229, 237–238
Department of Education,
209
Dowd, Maureen, 133
Drudge, Matthew Nathan,
192
Dukakis, Michael Stanley,
93
Durbin, Richard Joseph
("Dick"), 16, 115
Edwards, Johnny Reid
("John"), 67, 139–140
Election Day, 10, 24, 37, 72,
73, 89, 104, 177, 191,
193–194, 208

Emanuel, Rahm, 5, 61, 189,
212, 214, 216, 241
Evangelical movement, 20,
57, 122, 160–161
Facebook, 11
Fairness Doctrine, 229
Falwell, Jerry Lamon Sr., 78
Fannie Mae *see also* Freddie
Mac, 61–62, 103, 189
Fatah, 52–53
Federal Reserve, 20
Federal Reserve ("Fed"),
20, 62–64, 178
Feingold, Russell Dana
("Russ"), 15, 84
Feldstein, Martin Stuart,
183
Ferguson, Craig, 105
Fey, Elizabeth Stamantina
("Tina"), 177, 208
Financial crisis of
September 2008, 26, 31–
32, 54, 61–62, 64–65,
105, 177–179, 183–185,
188, 190, 195, 203
Fitzgerald, Patrick J., 215
Florida, 25, 37, 40, 58, 70,
123, 144, 148, 162, 178,
191, 195, 241
Foley, Mark Adam, 58
Foreign policy, 2, 8, 16, 26,
40–41, 49, 50, 75, 79, 98,
101, 142, 151–152, 156,
160, 163, 165, 169, 179,
185, 207, 209, 212, 226–
228
Fox News, 228–229, 241

Frank, Barnett ("Barney"), 23
Freddie Mac *see also* Fannie Mae, 5, 61–62, 103, 189, 241
Free trade, 73, 99, 101, 122, 140, 186, 211
Friedman, Thomas L., 49, 171, 204
Fuel prices, 64, 100, 178, 192, 221
"fundamentals of our economy are strong", 3, 178
Gay marriage, 78, 161, 205
Gay rights, 57, 161, 205
Gaza, 50, 52–53, 227
Gaza War, 53, 227
Geithner, Timothy Franz, 214, 220–221
Geneva Convention, 46, 60
Georgia conflict, 21, 25, 91, 159–160, 179, 206
Gibson, Charles deWolf ("Charlie"), 175–176
Gingrich, Newton Leroy ("Newt"), 25, 154
Giuliani, Rudolph William Louis ("Rudy"), 69–70
Goldwater, Barry Morris, 54, 75, 87, 101, 144
Gonzales, Alberto R., 36
Goolsbee, Austan Dean, 99
Gramm, William Philip ("Phil"), 63
Great Depression, 218, 230
Greenspan, Alan, 62

Guantánamo Bay detention facility, 33, 46, 49, 209, 223
Haggard, Ted Arthur, 57
Hamas, 42, 51–53
Harper, Stephen Joseph, 99
Hart, Gary, 145
Harvard Law School, 79, 129, 213, 226
Harvard Law Review, 6, 116, 120, 138, 152, 213
Harvard University Harvard College, 208
Hawaii, 119, 160, 162, 166, 218
Hayek, Friedrich August, 232
Herbert, Robert ("Bob"), 158
Heritage Foundation, 66, 183
Hitchens, Christopher Eric, 39
Hizbollah, 42, 52
Holder, Eric Himpton, 212
Huckabee, Michael Dale ("Mike"), 69–70, 95
Hughes, Chris, 11
Hurricane Gustav, 206
Hurricane Katrina, 26, 35, 56–57, 87, 206
Ickes, Harold McEwen, 149
Illinois, 8, 16, 20, 82–83, 100, 113–115, 117, 121, 123, 136, 197, 215–216, 229

Immigration, 6, 14–15, 28, 34, 39, 84, 95, 115, 157, 206

Inauguration, 7, 204, 210, 223, 230

Internal Revenue Service (IRS), 221

International Monetary Fund (IMF), 221

Internet, 9, 11–12, 24, 58, 70, 88, 108–110, 113, 124, 131, 172, 174–175, 230

Iowa, 11, 69–70, 112, 127, 165, 241

Iran, 7, 19, 27, 50, 53, 105, 209, 212, 226–227

Iraq, 2, 12, 15–17, 19, 23, 26, 31, 33, 38–39, 41–45, 47–49, 51, 57–58, 67–69, 72, 74–75, 98, 101, 105, 109–110, 112, 117, 128, 139, 141–142, 156, 163, 165, 185, 200–201, 209, 212, 218

"surge", 15, 69, 98, 156, 185

Irish constitution, 231

Islam, 41–42, 45, 49–50, 118, 157, 163, 174, 200

Israel, 29, 41, 49–53, 60, 110, 136, 156, 200, 209, 212, 226–227

J P Morgan, 64

Jews, 37, 119, 174, 209, 226–227

Jindal, Piyush ("Bobby"), 206

"Joe the Plumber" (Samuel Joseph Wurzelbacher), 18, 24, 190–191

Johnson, Charles Foster, 193

Johnson, Lyndon Baines, 201

Jones, Emil Jr., 114

Jones, James Logan Jr., 212

Joseph, Peggy, 208

Karine A affair, 50

Kennedy, Edward Moore ("Ted"), 84–85

Kennedy, John Fitzgerald, 87, 121, 157, 166, 186

Kerry, John Forbes, 35, 65, 68, 72, 77, 112, 139, 140, 151, 161

Keynesianism, 19, 218

Klein, Joe, 146–147, 173

Kosovo, 43

Krauthammer, Charles, 13, 38, 134, 175

Kristol, William, 181

Krugman, Paul Robin, 218

Lamont, Edward Miner Jr. ("Ned"), 12, 112–113, 125

Layfield, John Bradshaw, 3, 241

Lebanon, 52

Lehman Brothers, 64, 178

Levin, Mark Reed, 21, 28

Levin, Yuval, 153

Lewinsky, Monica Samille, 193

Lewis, John Robert, 21, 58, 146, 215

Libby, I. Lewis ("Scooter"), 58, 215

Lieberman, Joseph Isadore ("Joe"), 12, 84, 112–113, 115

Lincoln, Abraham, 31, 51, 121, 133, 197, 201, 213

"lipstick on a pig", 173

Lobbyists, 5, 89, 223, 233, 241

Lowry, Richard A., 222

Lynn, William J. III, 5

Madoff, Bernard Lawrence ("Bernie"), 63

Maher, William Jr. ("Bill"), 177

Mahoney, Timothy Edward ("Tim"), 58

Matthews, Christopher, 133, 228

McCain, John Sidney III "Maverick", 13, 67, 74, 78, 84, 95, 117, 181
   "Straight Talk" style, 2–4, 202–203
   books, 14
   Keating Five, 82
   prisoner-of-war, 13
   speeches, 2, 87, 97, 107, 155, 160, 170, 196, 241

Medicare, 33, 220

Merrill Lynch, 64, 178

Messianism, 81, 122, 126, 138, 150, 238

Michelle Obama, 8

Michigan, 144, 148

microtargeting, 25, 72, 124

Miers, Harriet Ellan, 35

Millenarianism, 29, 36, 122, 160, 202

Moderation, 13, 15, 21, 26, 68, 71–73, 90, 96, 104, 112–113, 125, 139, 177, 188, 212–214, 221

Mondale, Walter Frederick, 145

Moseley-Braun, Carol, 125

MoveOn.org, 89, 172

MSNBC, 133, 141–142, 228

Myanmar see Burma, 43

"Name That Party", 58

Napolitano, Janet Ann, 213

"netroots", 77, 90

New Democrats, 21, 73, 74, 113, 139, 151, 210–211

New Hampshire, 69, 74, 123–124, 129, 143, 149, 189, 191, 194–195

New York Times, 24, 47, 49, 58–59, 106, 133, 136, 141, 147, 158, 164, 171, 173, 181, 204, 216, 218, 241

Nixon, Richard Milhouse, 186, 222

Nolan, David Fraser, 71

Noonan, Peggy, 35

North Atlantic Treaty Organization (NATO), 41, 159

North Korea, 19

Obama, Barack Hussein
   "community organizer", 79, 119, 170, 174
   "czar", 214

"hope and change", 210, 220

"Just Words", 1, 4, 30, 199, 201–202, 207, 223, 226–228

broken promises, 88

Dreams from My Father, 90, 111

false claims about McCain, 74, 76–77, 98, 105, 214

National Journal rating, 20

speeches, 3, 5, 23, 29, 42, 99, 102, 114, 116, 120, 123–124, 131, 133, 150, 157, 191, 196, 226, 232

technology, 11, 13, 109, 124, 191

The Audacity of Hope, 12, 20, 83, 85, 133

Offshore oil drilling, 99–100, 158, 192

Olbermann, Keith Theodore, 39

Operation Defensive Shield, 51

Originalism, 224, 226

Orwell, George, 23

Osama bin Laden, 2, 19, 41, 163

Palestine Liberation Organization, 147

Palestinians, 29, 50–53, 147, 226

Palin, Bristol, 168, 172

Palin, Sarah Louise, 24, 77, 96, 166–172, 174–177,

187–188, 191, 203, 206, 208, 227

speeches, 170

victimized by smears, 175

Palin, Todd, 167

Palin, Trig, 167, 171–172

Palmer, Alice, 114

Panetta, Leon Edward, 212–214

Patrick, Deval, 1

Paul, Ronald Ernest ("Ron"), 12, 70, 95, 109, 111, 113, 125, 154, 193

Paulson, Henry Merritt Jr. ("Hank"), 64–66, 179

Pelosi, Nancy Patricia D'Alesandro, 23, 38, 67, 103, 182, 192, 220

"permanent campaign", 230, 233

Perot, Henry Ross, 85

Perry, Anthony Joseph ("Joe"), 194

Peters, Winston Raymond, 27

Petraeus, David Howell, 69, 163

Pfleger, Michael Louis, 131, 136

Plame, Valerie Elise, 58, 215

Plouffe, David, 168

Polls, 3, 8, 68–70, 72, 81, 100, 109, 138, 143, 156, 164, 166, 169, 174, 181–182, 185–186, 188–189, 194–195, 208, 227

Posner, Richard Allen, 225

Powell, Colin Luther, 8, 22, 125, 194

Presidential debates, 66, 104, 181, 185, 187

Proposition 8, 205

Public financing, 86, 88, 168

PUMA - Party Unity My Ass, 21, 149

Putin, Vladimir Vladimirovich, 159, 176

racism, 9, 126–129, 134–136, 141, 158

Raines, Franklin Delano ("Frank"), 189

Rasmussen Reports, 158

Rather, Daniel Irvin Jr. ("Dan"), 39, 193

Reagan, Ronald Wilson, 14, 31, 145, 211, 222

Recession, 19, 32, 63, 178, 219, 220

Reid, Harry Mason, 31, 67, 103, 220

Republican National Committee (RNC), 95, 156, 177

Republican Party, 14–17, 19–25, 36–37, 54–55, 57–58, 63, 65–70, 73–74, 77, 82, 85–86, 89, 96, 98, 103, 106–107, 113, 124, 128, 139, 144–145, 153–154, 164, 168, 181–182, 188, 191–193, 195, 202, 205–207, 209–210, 213, 215, 222–223, 230, 237

Republican primary, 70

Rezko, Antonin ("Tony"), 116, 136, 153, 216–217

Rice, Condoleezza, 8

Richardson, William Blaine III ("Bill"), 217, 229

Roberts, John Glover Jr. (Chief Justice), 224

Roe v. Wade, 78

Romer, Christina, 220

Romney, Willard Mitt, 68, 69–70, 95, 133, 179

Roosevelt, Franklin Delano, 47, 121

Roosevelt, Theodore, 81, 154

Rove, Karl Christian, 72, 103

Rumsfeld, Donald Henry, 36, 48

Russia, 7, 44, 159–160, 176–177, 179, 208, 226

Ryan, Paul D. Jr., 208

Saakashvili, Mikheil, 160

Saddam Hussein al-Tikriti, 15, 38, 41, 43–45, 48, 140

Saddleback Forum, 90, 92, 162

Safire, William L., 47

Sanders, Bernard ("Bernie"), 20

Sarbanes-Oxley Act, 62

Saudi Arabia, 45

Scalia, Antonin Gregory, 224, 226

Schmidt, Steve, 107

Schwarzenegger, Arnold Alois, 205

Sexism, 141–142
Sharansky, Natan, 49
Sharon, Ariel, 50
Sharpton, Alfred Charles
  ("Al"), 125
Social Security, 220
Socialism, 20, 66, 191, 209,
  222
Solis, Hilda L., 213
Somalia, 40
South Africa, 7, 118, 231
Soviet Constitution of 1936,
  232
Soviet Union (Union of
  Soviet Socialist
  Republics), 90, 101, 119,
  150, 159, 226, 232
Soviet Union, Union of
  Soviet Socialist
  Republics, 49
Special appropriations
  ("earmarks" or "pork"),
  35, 55, 65, 82, 114, 116,
  153, 185, 219, 233–234
Speechwriting, 14, 24, 35,
  120
Stalin, Joseph, 232
Steele, Shelby, 126
Stephanopoulos, George
  Robert, 147
Stevenson, Adlai Ewing,
  117
Stewart, Jonathan ("Jon"),
  150
Sub-prime mortgage crisis
  see also Financial crisis of
  September 2008, 5, 26,
  61–63, 178, 189

Sudan, 34, 43, 162
Sullivan, Andrew Michael,
  172
Summers, Lawrence Henry,
  211, 220
Sununu, John Edward, 195
Superdelegates, 145–146
Supreme Court, 18, 36–37,
  46, 205, 224
"swift-boating", 77
Syria, 44, 53
Taliban, 33, 41, 43
Tax cuts, 32, 35, 40, 73,
  115, 209, 220–221
TelePrompTer, 107, 123,
  227
Terrorism, 2, 15, 19, 26, 32,
  34–35, 40, 42, 46–47,
  49–53, 59–60, 75, 101,
  153, 179, 200–201, 210,
  212, 223
  September 11, 2001, 19,
    26, 32, 34, 40–43, 47,
    50, 54, 59, 62, 69, 117,
    132, 135, 200, 203
Thompson, Fred Dalton,
  69, 70
Torture, 4, 13, 15, 46, 48,
  60, 80, 84
"tough diplomacy", 19, 210,
  228
Town hall meetings, 87, 106
"Tuzla dash", 142–143
Twitter, 94, 192
U.S. Constitution, 15, 84,
  134, 140, 226, 231
United Nations, 38, 43–44,
  51, 53, 160, 165, 227

"unlawful combatants", 33, 46

USA PATRIOT Act, 59

vice-presidential debate, 187

Victory Column, 157–158

Vietnam, 3, 13–14, 40, 79, 80, 83, 93, 112, 152, 202, 206

Volcker, Paul Adolph, 21

Wall Street Journal, 179, 208, 219

Warren, Richard Duane ("Rick"), 90, 162

Wehner, Peter, 208

West Bank, 51

West, Cornel, 6

Will.I.Am, 124

Winfrey, Oprah J., 126

Winner & Associates, 175

Wright, Jeremiah Alvesta Jr., 9, 81, 94, 103, 112, 128, 131–136, 138, 144, 146–148, 153, 161, 217, 226

www.ReadTheStimulus.org, 219

"Yes We Can", 124

York, Byron, 173

YouTube, 11, 94, 118, 124

Yugoslavia, 43

Ziegler, John, 208

Zimbabwe, 34, 43

Zogby International, 208